VAMPIRES IN ITALIAN CINEMA, 1956–1975

VAMPIRES IN ITALIAN CINEMA, 1956–1975

Michael Guarneri

EDINBURGH
University Press

Edinburgh University Press is one of the leading university presses in the UK. We publish academic books and journals in our selected subject areas across the humanities and social sciences, combining cutting-edge scholarship with high editorial and production values to produce academic works of lasting importance. For more information visit our website: edinburghuniversitypress.com

© Michael Guarneri, 2020, 2022

Edinburgh University Press Ltd
The Tun – Holyrood Road
12(2f) Jackson's Entry
Edinburgh EH8 8PJ

First published in hardback by Edinburgh University Press 2020

Typeset in 10/12.5 pt Sabon
by IDSUK (DataConnection) Ltd

A CIP record for this book is available from the British Library

ISBN 978 1 4744 5811 5 (hardback)
ISBN 978 1 4744 5812 2 (paperback)
ISBN 978 1 4744 5813 9 (webready PDF)
ISBN 978 1 4744 5814 6 (epub)

The right of Michael Guarneri to be identified as the author of this work has been asserted in accordance with the Copyright, Designs and Patents Act 1988, and the Copyright and Related Rights Regulations 2003 (SI No. 2498).

CONTENTS

Figures and tables	vi
Acknowledgements	viii
Introduction	1

PART I THE INDUSTRIAL CONTEXT

1.	The Italian film industry (1945–1985)	23
2.	Italian vampire cinema (1956–1975)	41

PART II VAMPIRE SEX AND VAMPIRE GENDER

3.	Female vampires	77
4.	Male vampires	107

PART III SANGUINE ECONOMY, BLOODY POLITIC

5.	Vampires of the late 1950s and early 1960s	127
6.	Post-1968 vampires	149

Appendix A: Three Italian vampire films that were never made	173
Appendix B: Files from the Italian Show Business Bureau fonds at the Archivio Centrale dello Stato in Rome	177
Bibliography	179
Index	209

FIGURES AND TABLES

Figures

Cover A rare colour image from the set of *La maschera del demonio* (photo by Osvaldo Civirani available at Archivio Centrale dello Stato – Archivio fotografico Civirani (film) – 098 Maschera del demonio La – 098–0516)

1.1 Mario Bava emerging from a grave on the set of *La maschera del demonio* (photo by Osvaldo Civirani available at Archivio Centrale dello Stato – Archivio fotografico Civirani (film) – 098 Maschera del demonio La – 098–0483) 37
2.1 'The greatest, most sensational film of all times': advertisement for the Italian release of the Hammer *Dracula* 43
3.1 Charnel eroticism: Barbara Steele on the set of *La maschera del demonio* (photo by Osvaldo Civirani available at Archivio Centrale dello Stato – Archivio fotografico Civirani (film) – 098 Maschera del demonio La – 098–0004) 79
4.1 Arturo Dominici as makeshift Dracula Javutich on the set of *La maschera del demonio* (photo by Osvaldo Civirani available at Archivio Centrale dello Stato – Archivio fotografico Civirani (film) – 098 Maschera del demonio La – 098–0232) 111

Tables

0.1	The Italian vampire cinema corpus to be studied	8–11
2.1	Censorship and box-office data for 1956–1965 Italian vampire films	55–57
2.2	Censorship and box-office data for 1969–1975 Italian vampire films	64–65

ACKNOWLEDGEMENTS

I wish to thank my family, my colleagues and my friends.

Special thanks to Daniela Mor, Alvaro Guarneri, Russ Hunter, Peter Hutchings, Stefano Baschiera, Jamie Sexton, Steve Jones, Johnny Walker, Jin Wang, John Hemy, Corrado Farina, Ernesto Gastaldi, Fabio Frizzi, Paolo Noto, Francesco Di Chiara, Michele Canosa, Carmela Pontecorvo, Barbara Corsi, Dario Stefanoni, Andreas Ehrenreich, Nikolas Weiss, Stefano Lalla, Tommaso Moscati and Sergio Bissoli.

Parts of Introduction and of Chapter 1 rework my open-access journal article, 'The Gothic Bet: Riccardo Freda's *I vampiri* (1957) and the Birth of Italian Horror Cinema from an Industrial Perspective'.

If not otherwise stated, foreign-language quotations (including film dialogues) have been translated into English by me.

This book is dedicated to the memory of Isolina Aletti, Peter Hutchings and Marco Balzarini.

INTRODUCTION

NEW BLOOD FOR THOUGHT

For more than 200 years now, the vampire has been one of the most popular characters in fiction across media all over the world. The term 'vampire' became a buzzword throughout Western Europe thanks to police inquiries, medical reports and religious treatises compiled in the wake of the epidemics that scourged Eastern and Southeast Europe between the late seventeenth and the early eighteenth century (Dimic 1984; Wilson 1985; Groom 2018: 23–40, 56–94), but it was not until the publication of John Polidori's short story *The Vampyre* in 1819 that the bogeyman became a cash cow. The key to commercial success was simple: with a felicitous intuition undoubtedly inspired by his working experience as Lord Byron's travelling physician, Polidori turned the Slavic folklore's 'plump and ruddy' (Barber 2010: 4), 'repulsive, smelly, poor' (Douglas 1967: 36) peasant revenant preying on fellow villagers and livestock into a thin, pale, rich, elegant, urbane, sexually attractive aristocrat – a template that would be more or less faithfully followed by all the most popular male and female vampires to come, from Sheridan Le Fanu's 1871 novella *Carmilla* and Bram Stoker's 1897 novel *Dracula* to Anne Rice's *The Vampire Chronicles* book saga (1976–present) and Stephenie Meyer's *Twilight* book saga (2005–8); from the very many British and French theatre adaptations of Polidori's seminal tale to Hamilton Deane's and John L. Balderston's 1920s theatre adaptations of the Stoker novel; and from the Universal *Dracula* (Tod Browning, 1931) and the Hammer *Dracula* (Terence Fisher, 1958) to *Bram Stoker's Dracula* (Francis

Ford Coppola, 1992), *Interview with the Vampire* (Neil Jordan, 1994), TV series *Buffy the Vampire Slayer* (1997–2003) and the *Twilight* film saga (2008–12).

As they branched out from folklore to literature, theatre, cinema and TV, vampires became popular in the academia too. Eastern European tales about the dead sucking the blood of the living started attracting scholarly attention at the beginning of the eighteenth century, when 'learned essays on questions relating to superstition were by no means uncommon', and vampire legends presented a special appeal to both the high ranks of the Catholic church (Augustin Calmet, Giuseppe Antonio Davanzati and Prospero Lambertini, among others) and those enlightened 'philosophers [. . .] who were pledged to the idea of progress [and] enjoyed amassing evidence about what they called the "primitive" and "dark" areas' (Frayling 1991: 23). It was only in the early twentieth century that the focus of scholarly discourse shifted from whether or not vampires really exist to the broader socio-cultural significance of vampire lore and fiction. To account for such socio-cultural significance, three theoretical tools have been mainly used: psychoanalysis; Marxism; and feminism.

Starting from the idea that the literal content of any form of expression is a coded manifestation of the troubling sexual secrets buried in the unconscious mind, psychoanalytic studies see vampire attacks as the uncanny return of the repressed sexual wishes of infancy and childhood. Here, the vampire is a universal symbol, and symptom, of human anxieties related to interfamilial sexual strife, expressing (1) a dread of the father figure and (2) a horror of the maternal body. The former is described in the Oedipal readings of vampire lore and fiction based on Freud ([1913] 1950 and [1919] 2003) such as Jones (1931: 98–130), Richardson (1959), Bierman (1972 and 1998), MacGillivray (1972), Astle (1980) and Twitchell (1981, 1985: 105–59). The latter is described in the pre-Oedipal readings of vampire fiction centred on the *vagina dentata* scenario first outlined by Bonaparte ([1934] 1971), and later reprised and reworked by other scholars (Bentley [1972] 1988; Dadoun [1970] 1989; Creed 1993: 59–72, 105–21; 2005: 68–95; Berenstein 1995; Roth [1977] 1997; Mulvey-Roberts 1998).

On the other hand, Marxist studies take their cue from Marx's ([1867] 1954: 224–85) indictment of the nineteenth-century European bourgeoisie as vampiric and focus on the political and socio-economic implications of bloodsucking rather than on the psychosexual sphere. Here, the vampire is a scapegoat in invasion narratives concerned with the dialectics of class and nationalism-tinged imperialistic struggle – a monstrous, polluting Other who uses sex appeal, cunning and brute force to subjugate the members of a given community, be it a class within the nation-state's social body or a whole nation-state (Kracauer [1947] 1971: 77–9, 108–9; Roth 1979 and [1984] 2004; Hatlen [1980] 1988; Zanger 1991; Gelder 1994: 1–41, 65–107; Halberstam 1995: 86–105; Arata [1990] 1997; Valdez Moses 1997; Valente 2002; Hutchings 2003: 34–78; Moretti

[1983] 2005; Phillips 2005: 11–33; Gibson 2006: 15–95; Abbott 2007: 61–72; Kaes 2009: 87–129; Ulin 2015; Mulvey-Roberts 2016: 129–78; Hudson 2017: 21–114, 163–91).

Finally, feminist studies of vampire fiction combine a transhistorical approach based on the psychoanalytic notion of sexual repression with a historicist approach imbued with Marxist insights into socio-political oppression to account for the struggle for gender definition and domination within the framework of the Western bourgeoisie's patriarchal order. Here, vampire narratives seem to maintain an ambiguous relationship with the patriarchal status quo, enforcing masculine domination over females through misogyny and gynocide while occasionally offering glimpses of strong, rebellious, self-sufficient, aggressive femininity (Demetrakopoulos 1977; Wood [1970] 1979b and [1983] 1996; Veeder 1980; Senf 1982 and 1988; Johnson 1984; Waller 1985: 50–4, 85–134; Cranny-Francis 1988; Griffin [1980] 1988; Brennan 1992; Boone 1993; Auerbach 1995: 38–47, 124–9; Benshoff 1997: 77–81; Craft [1984] 1997; Eltis 2002; Wilcox and Lavery 2002; Zimmerman [1981] 2004; Williamson 2005: 5–28, 51–96; Levine and Parks 2007; Pirie 2008: 66–78, 95–112; Housel and Wisnewski 2009; Parke and Wilson 2011).

The above brief, and by no means exhaustive, survey of vampire studies shows that Anglophone scholars have mainly dealt with Anglo-American fiction. As for vampire cinema specifically, the lion's share of academic attention has gone to box-office hits like the 1931 *Dracula*, the 1958 *Dracula* and Hammer's subsequent vampire films, *Twilight* (Catherine Hardwicke, 2008) and its sequels. The exception that confirms the rule is *Nosferatu, eine Symphonie des Grauens / Nosferatu: A Symphony of Horror* (F. W. Murnau, 1922), which managed to avoid scholarly oblivion by virtue of its being considered the first surviving vampire film, and thanks to its association with the then aesthetically ground-breaking and hugely influential, and now critically acclaimed, German Expressionist cinema of the early 1920s. The gap in vampire cinema studies is therefore easy to identify: Murnau's *Nosferatu* aside, there is a lack of scholarly consideration for non-American and non-British national declinations of the vampire figure.

Since the worldwide box-office success of the Hammer *Dracula* in the late 1950s triggered a vampire cinema production frenzy all over the globe, with an estimated total of around 400 vampire movies made in England, US, Mexico, Italy, France, Spain, West Germany, Middle East, Hong Kong, Japan, South and Southeast Asia between the early 1960s and the late 1970s alone (Ursini and Silver 1975; Pirie 1977; Murphy 1979) – most of which were originally released in theatres and/or broadcast on TV in English-speaking countries, and currently enjoy a wide availability on DVD and online – the vast neglect towards world-cinema vampires on the part of Anglophone researchers is somewhat puzzling. Yet, as demonstrated by recent investigations of vampire movies from Sweden, Spain, Mexico, Russia, Turkey, Philippines, Singapore,

3

Malaysia, Pakistan, Bollywood, Nollywood, Tanzania, Hong Kong, South Korea and Japan (see the dedicated chapters in Schneider 2003; Browning and Picart 2009; Gelder 2012; Khair and Höglund 2012; Weinstock 2012; Hunt et al. 2014; Abbott 2016; Hudson 2017; Edwards and Höglund 2018), the cinematic vampires' Anglocentrism is being repeatedly put into question lately, and bloodsuckers from all over the world are increasingly becoming a matter of scholarly interest. It is to this small, but ever-growing, body of literature revealing, indicting and making up for the academic neglect towards world-cinema vampires that the present monograph seeks to contribute by zooming in on the vampire-themed products of the Italian film industry.

Answering Cohen's (1996) and Hutchings's (2004: 38–9) calls for culturally specific monsterologies, *Vampires in Italian Cinema, 1956–1975* takes as its subject a corpus of thirty-three vampire movies made, distributed and exhibited during the peak years of film production in Italy, and certified to be of Italian nationality by state institutions such as the Direzione Generale dello Spettacolo (henceforth referred to as the Italian Show Business Bureau) and the Commissioni per la Revisione Cinematografica (henceforth referred to as the Italian Film Censorship Office). Positioning itself at the intersection of Italian film history, horror studies and cultural studies, the monograph asks: why, and how, is the protean, transnational and transmedial figure of the vampire appropriated by Italian cinema practitioners between 1956 and 1975? Or, more concisely, what do the vampires of post-war Italian cinema mean? The aim is to show that – in spite of Italian vampire cinema's imported and derivative nature, and its great reliance on profits coming from distribution on the international market – Italian cinematic vampires reflect their national zeitgeist from the economic miracle of the late 1950s to the mid-1970s austerity, twenty years of large political and socio-economic change in which gender politics were also in relative flux.

As the first, systematic, historically grounded exploration of Italian vampires across several, more or less popular film genres, *Vampires in Italian Cinema, 1956–1975* not only makes a decisive contribution to vampire studies, but also advances Italian cinema scholarship by providing a fresh perspective on, and new information to, the study of post-war Italian cinema – a field in which, as it has been recently lamented (O'Rawe 2008; O'Leary and O'Rawe 2011), academic attention has focused almost completely on the *cinema d'autore* of directors like Roberto Rossellini, Vittorio De Sica, Luchino Visconti, Federico Fellini, Michelangelo Antonioni and Pier Paolo Pasolini. The result of an original research into film production data, film censorship files, screenplays, trade papers, film magazines and vampire-themed paraliterature, the monograph in fact leaves the well-trod track of award-winning art films to shed light on some of the so-called 'lower forms' of cinematic culture, looking for the economic backbone and cultural instrumentality[1] of post-war Italian cinema in the run-of-the-mill genre movies rushed through a cheap production and into domestic and international distribution to parasitically (vampirically?) exploit a given commercially successful film. In so doing, *Vampires in Italian Cinema, 1956–1975* integrates and expands the English-language body of literature born in the recent period of burgeoning interest in Italian horror (Baschiera and Hunter 2016; Fisher and Walker 2017) and other so-far neglected genres produced in post-war Italy like melodrama, adventure, western and comedy (Lagny 1992; Wagstaff 1992; Frayling 1998; Günsberg 2005; Fournier-Lanzoni 2008; Bini 2011b; Brizio-Skov 2011; Burke 2011; Fisher 2011; Bayman 2013 and 2014; O'Brien 2013 and 2014; Fullwood 2015).

The corpus

Putting together the corpus of Italian vampire films to be studied has first of all required an engagement with the notion of national cinema, because distinguishing Italian movies from non-Italian ones is not as intuitive and clear-cut an operation as distinguishing vampire narratives from non-vampire ones. In fact, as we shall see in Chapters 1 and 2, the post-war Italian film industry relied heavily on international capital, artistic personnel and distribution channels, effectively complicating any claim to the national purity of its output. Over the past forty years, there have been several attempts in the academia to answer the question of what national cinema is, thereby establishing under which conditions a film can be said to come from, or belong to, a given nation-state (Rosen 1984; Higson 1989 and 2000; Crofts 1993; Sorlin 1996: 1–15; Bergfelder 2000; Eleftheriotis 2001: 1–67; Willemen 2006; Wagstaff 2013). Unfortunately, these interventions have been unable to produce a satisfactory, universally accepted definition of national cinema, to the point that 'transnational' has become more and more popular a category in film studies. Therefore, in the building of its corpus, the present monograph has adopted a pragmatic, industry-based approach as far as film nationality is concerned, considering as Italian those movies that were (1) made in Italy or across the globe with the financial backing of at least one Italian company, (2) distributed in Italy, and (3) certified to be of Italian nationality by the Italian Show Business Bureau and the Italian Film Censorship Office.

As for the vampire theme, the building of the corpus has started by cross-referencing vampire cinema filmographies (Ursini and Silver 1975; Pirie 1977; Murphy 1979; Flynn 1992; Browning and Picart 2010) with lists of Italian fantastic films made between the 1950s and the 2010s (Lippi and Codelli 1976; Colombo and Tentori 1990; Avondola et al. 1997; Gomarasca et al. 2002; Castoldi 2005a and 2005b; Fassone and Nocturno editorial team 2009; Della Casa and Giusti 2013 and 2014; Curti 2015, 2017b and 2019). Further research has been conducted on the website of the Italian Film Censorship

Office (www.italiataglia.it) by searching the keyword 'vampir*' in the online database containing information about all the movies reviewed for rating purposes from 1913 to 2000. This way, four currently lost, vampire-themed films produced by Italian companies in the 1910s have been found: *La torre dei vampiri* (Gino Zaccaria, 1913), *La vampira indiana* (Roberto Roberti, 1913), *Il vampiro* (Vittorio Rossi Pianelli, 1914) and *La carezza del vampiro* (Romolo Bacchini, 1918). At the same time, the scrutiny of Italian silent cinema filmographies (Martinelli 1991a, 1991b, 1992a, 1992b, 1992c, 1992d, 1995a, 1995b, 1996a, 1996b and 1996c; Bernardini and Martinelli 1993a, 1993b, 1993c, 1993d, 1994a, 1994b, 1995a, 1995b, 1996a and 1996b) has shown that, prior to 1913, no references to vampires were made in the titles and synopses of Italian films. A list of about sixty vampire-themed Italian movies has then been put together and the entries divided into two groups: a silent phase going from 1913 *La torre dei vampiri* to 1918 *La carezza del vampiro*, and a sound phase spanning from *I vampiri / Lust of the Vampire* (Riccardo Freda, 1957) to *Dracula 3D* (Dario Argento, 2012). From this initial list, more than twenty films have been excluded for a variety of thematic and industrial reasons.

The main thematic reason has to do with the definition of vampire movie. This monograph considers as vampire movies only those works that feature as main characters human or supernatural beings living on human blood, which excludes from the corpus all the films featuring (1) small, cameo-like vampire parts, (2) revenants or parasites feeding on people's psychic energies, memories, feelings or bodily fluids other than blood, (3) gold-digging vamps, and (4) human characters impersonating vampires for pranks or scams but never actually performing bloodsucking or blood transfusions. The four entries from the silent phase have therefore been discarded from the corpus,[2] and so were sound films like *Caltiki il mostro immortale / Caltiki, the Immortal Monster* (Riccardo Freda as Robert Hamton, 1959), *Seddok, l'erede di Satana / Atom Age Vampire* (Anton Giulio Majano, 1960), *Sexy proibitissimo / The Most Prohibited Sex* (Mario Amendola as Marcello Martinelli), *Malenka, la nipote del vampiro / Fangs of the Living Dead* (Amando de Ossorio, 1969),[3] *Necropolis* (Franco Brocani, 1970), *L'amante del demonio / The Devil's Lover* (Paolo Lombardo, 1971), *Riuscirà l'avvocato Franco Benenato a sconfiggere il suo acerrimo nemico il pretore Ciccio De Ingras?* (Mino Guerrini, 1971), *Il gatto di Brooklyn aspirante detective* (Oscar Brazzi, 1972), *Salomé* (Carmelo Bene, 1972), *La morte negli occhi del gatto / Seven Dead in the Cat's Eye* (Antonio Margheriti as Anthony M. Dawson, 1973), *Leonor / Mistress of the Devil* (Juan Luis Buñuel, 1975) and *40 gradi all'ombra del lenzuolo / Sex with a Smile* (Sergio Martino, 1976).

As for industrial reasons, the main criteria are two. Expanding on the aforementioned pragmatic, industry-based approach to the question of national cinema, the first criterion is a focus on feature films made with the financial backing of at least one Italian company and exhibited in the industrial circuit of Italian cinema theatres. This excludes not only short movies like *Il figlio di Dracula* (Corrado Farina, 1960) and *Il vampiro della strada* (Luciano Paganini, 1963), the TV mini-series *Nella città vampira* (Giorgio Bandini, 1978), and the TV- or straight-to-video movies *Anemia* (Alberto Abruzzese, Achille Pisanti, 1986), *A cena col vampiro / Dinner with a Vampire* (Lamberto Bava, 1989) and *Sete da vampira* (Roger A. Fratter, 1998), but also *L'ultimo uomo della Terra / The Last Man on Earth* (Ubaldo Ragona, 1964) and *Los monstruos del terror / Assignment Terror* (Tulio Demicheli, 1970). In fact, in spite of having been classified as an Italian feature film by the Italian Show Business Bureau, *L'ultimo uomo della Terra* actually was a US runaway production fully financed by American companies and directed by American Sidney Salkow, with the Italian producers and Ragona acting as dummies in order for foreign investors to access Italian fiscal benefits (Moras 2005). Demicheli's feature film, on the other hand, was a co-production between Spanish, West German and Italian companies according to the opening credits, but it was never rated by the Italian Film Censorship Office and therefore never distributed in Italy.

The second criterion is a focus on the so-called 'golden age' of post-war Italian cinema, that is to say the period of intensive film production that – favoured by Christian Democrat legislation, American investments and European co-productions as detailed in Chapter 1 – went from the early 1950s to the 1977 productive crisis that greatly diminished the yearly output of Italian-made movies for all the late 1970s, the 1980s and the 1990s. This criterion explains the exclusion of the four post-1975 vampire features made in Italy or across Europe with the financial backing of at least one Italian company and exhibited in the industrial circuit of Italian cinema theatres: *Fracchia contro Dracula* (Neri Parenti, 1985), *Nosferatu a Venezia / Vampire in Venice* (Augusto Caminito, 1989), *Zora la vampira* (Antonio and Marco Manetti as Manetti Bros., 2000) and Argento's *Dracula 3D*.

The corpus of thirty-three films resulting from the overlap of the above thematic and industrial reasons is presented in Table 0.1, and includes horrors, thrillers, comedies, adventures and erotica, or a combination thereof.

Although the corpus comprises genres other than horror, production and release dates suggest a periodisation of Italian vampire cinema that perfectly matches the history of the Italian horror film that scholars have been constructing for the past four decades. The starting point is *I vampiri*, which, by bundling up the Erzsébet Báthory legend and the Frankenstein myth, is generally considered the first Italian horror movie (Mora 1978: 290; Troiano 1985 and 1989; Newman 1986a; Hunt [1992] 2000; Di Chiara 2009: 39; Bini 2011a; Della Casa and Giusti 2014: 92–4; Pezzotta 2014; Curti 2015: 21–30). After Freda's prototype – immediately dubbed by contemporary Italian critics 'the first "black

Table 0.1 The Italian vampire cinema corpus to be studied.

Italian title / Most popular English title on IMDB, if existing	Director as credited in Italian prints (director's nationality)	Nationality of the film	Year in which production began	Year of Italian Film Censorship Office's review	Genre
I vampiri / Lust of the Vampire	Riccardo Freda (Italian)	Italian	1956	1957	Horror, thriller
Tempi duri per i vampiri / Uncle was a Vampire	Stefano Vanzina as Steno (Italian)	Italian	1959	1959	Horror, comedy
L'amante del vampiro / The Vampire and the Ballerina	Renato Polselli (Italian)	Italian	1959	1960	Horror
Il sangue e la rosa / Blood and Roses	Roger Vadim (French)	Italian, French	1959	1960	Horror
Il mulino delle donne di pietra / Mill of the Stone Women	Giorgio Ferroni (Italian)	Italian, French	1959	1960	Horror, thriller
La maschera del demonio / Black Sunday	Mario Bava (Italian)	Italian	1960	1960	Horror
L'ultima preda del vampiro / The Playgirls and the Vampire	Piero Regnoli (Italian)	Italian	1960	1960	Horror
Maciste contro il vampiro / Goliath and the Vampires	Giacomo Gentilomo (Italian)	Italian	1961	1961	Adventure
Ercole al centro della Terra / Hercules in the Haunted World	Mario Bava (Italian)	Italian	1961	1961	Adventure
La strage dei vampiri / Slaughter of the Vampires	Giuseppe Tagliavia as Roberto Mauri (Italian)	Italian	1961	1962	Horror

Italian title / Most popular English title on IMDB, if existing	Director as credited in Italian prints (director's nationality)	Nationality of the film	Year in which production began	Year of Italian Film Censorship Office's review	Genre
Il mostro dell'Opera	Renato Polselli (Italian)	Italian	1961	1964	Horror
L'orribile segreto del Dr. Hichcock / The Terror of Dr. Hichcock	Riccardo Freda as Robert Hampton (Italian)	Italian	1962	1962	Horror, thriller
I tre volti della paura / Black Sabbath	Mario Bava (Italian)	Italian, French	1962	1963	Horror, thriller
Ercole contro Moloch / Conquest of Mycene	Giorgio Ferroni (Italian)	Italian, French	1963	1963	Adventure
Danza macabra / Castle of Blood	Antonio Margheriti as Anthony M. Dawson (Italian)	Italian, French	1963	1963	Horror
Roma contro Roma / War of the Zombies	Giuseppe Vari (Italian)	Italian	1963	1964	Adventure
La cripta e l'incubo / Crypt of the Vampire	Camillo Mastrocinque as Thomas Miller (Italian)	Italian, Spanish	1963	1964	Horror
Maciste e la regina di Samar / Hercules against the Moon Men	Giacomo Gentilomo (Italian)	Italian, French	1964	1964	Adventure
Amanti d'oltretomba / Nightmare Castle	Mario Caiano as Allan Grünewald (Italian)	Italian	1965	1965	Horror

(*Continued*)

Italian title / Most popular English title on IMDB, if existing	Director as credited in Italian prints (director's nationality)	Nationality of the film	Year in which production began	Year of Italian Film Censorship Office's review	Genre
La vendetta di Lady Morgan	Massimo Pupillo as Max Hunter (Italian)	Italian	1965	1965	Horror
Il Conte Dracula / Count Dracula	Jesús Franco as Jesse Franco (Spanish)	Italian, Spanish, West-German	1969	1973	Horror
La notte dei dannati / Night of the Damned	Filippo Walter Ratti as Peter Rush (Italian)	Italian	1970	1971	Horror, erotic
… Hanno cambiato faccia	Corrado Farina (Italian)	Italian	1970	1971	Horror
La corta notte delle bambole di vetro / Short Night of Glass Dolls	Aldo Lado (Italian)	Italian, Yugoslavian, West-German	1971	1971	Thriller
Nella stretta morsa del ragno / Web of the Spider	Antonio Margheriti as Anthony M. Dawson (Italian)	Italian, French, West-German	1971	1971	Horror
La notte dei diavoli / Night of the Devils	Giorgio Ferroni (Italian)	Italian, Spanish	1971	1972	Horror
Riti, magie nere e segrete orge nel Trecento … / The Reincarnation of Isabel	Renato Polselli as Ralph Brown (Italian)	Italian	1971	1972	Horror, erotic

Italian title / Most popular English title on IMDB, if existing	Director as credited in Italian prints (director's nationality)	Nationality of the film	Year in which production began	Year of Italian Film Censorship Office's review	Genre
Il prato macchiato di rosso	Riccardo Ghione (Italian)	Italian	1972	1972	Thriller
Le vergini cavalcano la morte / The Legend of Blood Castle	Jorge Grau (Spanish)	Italian, Spanish	1972	1973	Horror, thriller
L'uomo che uccideva a sangue freddo / Shock Treatment	Alain Jessua (French)	Italian, French	1972	1973	Thriller
Il plenilunio delle vergini / The Devil's Wedding Night	Luigi Batzella as Paolo Solvay (Italian)	Italian	1972	1973	Horror, erotic
Dracula cerca sangue di vergine . . . e morì di sete!!! / Blood for Dracula	Antonio Margheriti as Anthony M. Dawson (Italian), acting as a front man for Paul Morrissey (American)	Italian, French	1973	1974	Horror, comedy, erotic
Il cav. Costante Nicosia demoniaco, ovvero: Dracula in Brianza / Dracula in the Provinces	Lucio Fulci (Italian)	Italian	1975	1975	Horror, comedy

film" of Italian sound cinema' (Anonymous 1957c), 'the first [. . .] Edgar-Allan-Poe-style *film di orrore*' (Marinucci 1957) – a sustained production of Italian vampire films started in 1959, triggered by the worldwide box-office success of the Hammer *Dracula*, and lasted until the exhaustion of the Italian Gothic horror cycle in the mid-1960s. The production of Italian vampire films resumed on a smaller scale in the early 1970s, through Italian Gothic horror's 'late and bastardised excrescences, [. . .] isolated splinters' (Curti 2011: 300) trying to cash in on either the classics of the previous two decades or new hits like *Night of the Living Dead* (George Romero, 1968), *Rosemary's Baby* (Roman Polanski, 1968), *L'uccello dalle piume di cristallo / The Bird with the Crystal Plumage* (Dario Argento, 1970) and *The Exorcist* (William Friedkin, 1973).

Given that the notion of horror as a film genre was formalised by the Anglo-American press and censorship bodies in the early 1930s, after the inception of Universal's and Paramount's horror cycles (Peirse 2013: 5–9), the question is: why the first Italian horror film – and a vampire one at that – appeared only in 1956–1957? Detailed information about the national, international and transnational industrial context of Italian vampire cinema will be provided in Chapters 1 and 2. However, in order to introduce some key elements of Italian cultural specificity, it is useful here to outline a brief history of literary and cinematic horror fiction in Italy prior to the late 1950s, with particular attention to vampire-themed works.

A scant heritage of horror

Although a favourite setting for British and American Gothic novels and uncanny short stories since the second half of the eighteenth century,[4] the Italian peninsula never fostered an autochthonous horror tradition worthy of the name. From the early nineteenth until well into the twentieth century, the most prominent Italian intellectuals championed rationalism, classicism and realist literary genres as the true expressions of the Italian character, repeatedly criticising Anglo-American Gothic fiction and English and German Romanticism for their focus on the disproportionate, the undefined, the macabre, the oneiric and the supernatural (Tardiola 1991: 12–13; Lattarulo 1995; Curti 2011: 17–21; Camilletti 2014): in spite of the abundance of ghosts and witches in Italian folklore (Spagnol and Santi 1966 and 1967; Batini 1968), notable figures such as Giacomo Leopardi, Alessandro Manzoni and Benedetto Croce maintained that Italy is no country for the 'Nordic cavalcade of spectres, dying virgins, angelic demons, [. . .] creaking skeletons, and sighs and cries and laughters of crazy people, and the deliria of the feverish' (Croce, quoted in Curti 2011: 18). These pronouncements against the inclusion of fantastic stories into the Italian literary canon probably explain the absence of a conspicuous heritage of horror in the *bel paese*.

As for Italian vampire literature in particular, leaving aside the cursory references to bloodsucking creatures in Leopardi's 1824 philosophical dialogue *Dialogo di Federico Ruysch e delle sue mummie*, in Francesco Domenico Guerrazzi's 1854 historical novel *Beatrice Cenci*, in Francesco Mastriani's 1868 satirical novel against human greed *I vampiri. Romanzo umoristico*, in Gabriele D'Annunzio's 1894 erotic-philosophical novel *Il trionfo della morte*, in Edoardo Calandra's 1909 novella *Juliette*, and in the avant-garde works by the Scapigliati and the Futurists (Cammarota 1984: 65–9; Pautasso 1998), only a handful of texts have been written prior to the late 1950s. The first in chronological order seems to be *Il vampiro*, an 1801, currently lost opera seria by A. De Gasparini (Tardiola 1991: 83). This was followed by two comic takes on the vampire lore – Giuseppe Palomba's 1812 opera buffa *Vampiri*, 'partly based' on an eighteenth-century 'dissertation on vampirism by the Archbishop of Trani', and Angelo Brofferio's 1827 comedy *Il vampiro*, a parody of Polidori's *The Vampyre* and its various French and English stage transpositions, centred around 'a fake undead terroris[ing] the inhabitants of a castle in Westfalia' (Giovannini 1997: 238–9).

The first full-fledged Italian vampire novel is Franco Mistrali's 1869 *Il vampiro. Storia vera*. The title ('The vampire. True story') manifests the unease of the Italian writer in approaching the critically discredited genre of the fantastic, and so does the plot. Set in 1862 in Monte Carlo, just outside Italy's newly established nation-state borders, the story adopts the first-person perspective of a detective who explains away the seemingly supernatural case of a 'blood-drinking, sepulchral spectre [that] leaves the cemetery at night, wrapped in its shroud, looking for sleeping victims' (Mistrali 1869: 42) by exposing the Secret Society of Vampires, a group of Eastern-European political conspirators who dabble in poisoning and blood transfusions. After Mistrali's detective novel – which was neither a bestseller nor a critical success – in Italian literature vampire figures would play a leading role only in a dozen short stories, namely man-versus-giant-bat jungle adventures such as Emilio Salgari's 1912 *Il vampiro della foresta*, and uncanny tales dealing with supernatural beings or objects that drain human lifeblood (Francesco Ernesto Morando's 1885 *Vampiro innocente*, Giuseppe Tonsi's 1902 *Il vampiro*, Luigi Capuana's 1907 *Un vampiro*, Daniele Oberto Marrama's 1907 *Il dottor Nero*, Enrico Boni's 1908 *Vampiro*, Vittorio Martella's 1917 *Il vampiro*, Giuseppe de Feo's 1921 *Il vampiro* and Cifra's 1940 *Il vampiro*).

Italian editions of foreign vampire literature classics such as Le Fanu's *Carmilla* and Stoker's *Dracula* were similarly scarce in the nineteenth and early twentieth centuries. The former was translated in Italian only in horror anthologies of the early 1960s (Camilletti 2018: 42), while the first Italian edition of the latter – printed by Milanese publishing house Sonzogno in 1922 under the title *Dracula. L'uomo della notte* ('Dracula. The man of the night') as part of a mystery-novels-for-the-whole-family series – was a heavily abridged version of Stoker's own abridged text of 1901.[5] The Italian translation of the full 1897 text of *Dracula* was first printed in Milan in September 1945, and again in 1952, by publisher Fratelli Bocca Editori, a specialist in the occult. It is not known if the hiatus between the 1922 and the 1945 edition was due to the Fascist regime's opposing horror fiction. What is certain is that the only book-length piece of vampire fiction published in Italy during the Fascist *ventennio* was Mary Tibaldi Chiesa's *Gli enigmi del vampiro*, an Italian translation/reworking of Somadeva Bhatta's eleventh-century collection of Indian novellas narrated by a *vetala*, the Hindu equivalent of a vampire.

Printed by Milanese publishing house Mondadori in 1936, *Gli enigmi del vampiro* ('The riddles of the vampire') opens with a preface by a prestigious Orientalist scholar of the time confirming the Italian rationalist prejudice against the fantastic:

> We [Italians] do not believe in vampires and sprites any more; nowadays these are but fantasies good for children and old ladies [. . .]; our philosophy taught us that unsolvable riddles are just wrongly posed questions, whose words are devoid of any meaning and connection to concrete reality. (Pizzagalli 1936: 15)

The same nationalism-tinged scepticism, based on the *auctoritas* of Leopardi, Manzoni and Croce, returns over and over in Italian film criticism too, every time an Italian director would try to unsettle the audience by pushing the boundaries of verisimilitude. For instance, in a 1913 review of *Il suicida n. 359* (Roberto Roberti, 1913) – an adaptation of Robert Louis Stevenson's 1878 short-story collection *The Suicide Club* – a film critic wrote: 'I think that Italian companies should not make this kind of frightening, implausible films. Certain acts of collective madness might often happen in the Nordic mists of the Thames, but certainly not on the lovely, sunny shores of river Po' (quoted in Bernardini and Martinelli 1993b: 271). Reviewing *La terrificante visione* (Ugo De Simone, 1915) upon its premiere, another critic noted that Italian fantastic films lacked 'the talent in the strange, the genius in the unlikely, the vivacity and courage in the illogic' to be found in their foreign counterparts that had launched the fantastic trend in the first place (quoted in Martinelli 1992b: 243). The long-standing bias is encapsulated in a 1940 review of *Bride of Frankenstein* (James Whale, 1935) written by Pietro Bianchi: 'We good Mediterraneans have no sympathy for horrors. We leave spirits, monsters and ghosts to Nordic people' (quoted in Venturini 2014: 5).

More than a decade after Bianchi's categorical refusal, the horror genre was still perceived as alien to Italian culture, to the point that the first Italian-language article surveying the history of the horror film was written by a Spanish scholar, who located the fathers of horror cinema in France, Scandinavia, Germany and the US (Rotellar 1952). Consequently, upon writing the screenplay of *I vampiri* in 1956, Freda opted for setting his Frankensteinian-vampiric tale abroad, Mistrali-style, while his producers decided mid-shoot to remove the most fantastic and gruesome scenes and insert a detection subplot which was deemed to be more appealing to Italian audiences than pure horror (see Freda, quoted in Cozzi 2007: 324–5), most probably because of the huge commercial success of Anglo-American whodunit and crime novels published in Italian translation ever since 1929 in Mondadori's *I libri gialli* series.[6] Moreover, as recounted by Freda (quoted in Lourcelles and Mizrahi 1963: 28), by the late 1950s the prejudice against fantastic films made in Italy was widespread even among Italian audiences, which led the director to adopt an Anglophone pseudonym for his 1959 sci-fi/horror hybrid *Caltiki il mostro immortale*:

> I had the idea [of using an Anglophone pseudonym] while I was in the foyer of a cinema in Italy. I noticed that, after glancing at the film poster for *I vampiri*, lots of people said: 'Riccardo Freda? [...] It is an Italian film, so it must not be very good. If it came from the US, it would be worth seeing!'

As a matter of fact, Italy had always been a strong importation market for foreign fantastic cinema. Although occasionally hindered by the Italian Film Censorship Office, films of 'the Nordic school' (Rotellar 1952: 296) like *Der Student von Prag / The Student of Prague* (Henrik Galeen, Stellan Rye, 1913), *Homunculus* (Otto Rippert, 1916), *Das Cabinet des Dr. Caligari / The Cabinet of Dr. Caligari* (Robert Wiene, 1920), *Der Golem, wie er in die Welt kam / The Golem* (Carl Boese, Paul Wegener, 1920), *Körkarlen / The Phantom Carriage* (Victor Sjöström, 1921), *Das Wachsfigurenkabinett / Waxworks* (Paul Leni, 1924), *Orlacs Hände / The Hands of Orlac* (Robert Wiene, 1924), *Der Student von Prag / The Student of Prague* (Henrik Galeen, 1926) and *Faust: Eine deutsche Volkssage / Faust* (F. W. Murnau, 1926) circulated in Italy between the 1910s and the late 1920s, and so did between the mid-1920s and the late 1950s Hollywood pictures such as *Dr. Jekyll and Mr. Hyde* (John S. Robertson, 1920), *The Phantom of the Opera* (Rupert Julian, 1925), *Frankenstein* (James Whale, 1931) and its sequels, *Dr. Jekyll and Mr. Hyde* (Rouben Mamoulian, 1931), *The Mummy* (Karl Freund, 1932), *The Invisible Man* (James Whale, 1933), *Mystery of the Wax Museum* (Michael Curtiz, 1933), *Dr. Jekyll and Mr. Hyde* (Victor Fleming, 1941), *The Phantom of the Opera* (Arthur Lubin, 1943), *The Thing from Another World* (Christian Nyby, 1951) and *House of Wax* (André De Toth, 1953). Vampire cinema was not trendy, though, as Murnau's *Nosferatu*, Browning's *Dracula*, *Vampyr, ou l'étrange aventure de David Gray / Vampyr* (Carl Theodor Dreyer, 1932),

Mark of the Vampire (Tod Browning, 1935), *Dracula's Daughter* (Lambert Hillyer, 1936) and *Son of Dracula* (Robert Siodmak, 1943) seem to have never been imported.[7] Prior to the late 1950s, the only vampire-themed movies officially imported and released in Italy were monster mash-ups *House of Dracula* (Erle C. Kenton, 1945) and *Abbott and Costello Meet Frankenstein* (Charles T. Barton, 1948), and detective stories *London after Midnight* (Tod Browning, 1927) and *The Return of Doctor X* (Vincent Sherman, 1939) – the latter one bearing a few similarities with Freda's *I vampiri* (the Frankensteinian reanimation of corpses, scientific vampires that feed via blood transfusions and reporters playing detectives).

While there have been attempts (Venturini 2014: 5–19, 29–41; Curti 2015: 11–15; Hunter 2016 and 2017) to trace a horror sensibility in pre-1957 Italian films adapting the very few ventures of Italian writers into the fantastic,[8] reworking texts from German and Anglo-American literature,[9] or simply displaying macabre imagery or supernatural elements,[10] scholars agree on seeing *I vampiri* as the first, full-fledged, Italian-made horror. Besides the rationalist mindset of the Italian intelligentsia, the scant heritage of cinematic horrors before *I vampiri* is generally explained through three structural causes. First, in response to moralising campaigns launched by magistrates and high-ranking clergymen, a state-run Italian Film Censorship Office was created in 1913, in order to ban from Italian screens anything obscene, anti-patriotic and anti-religious, including 'truce, repugnant or cruel scenes [. . .]; shocking murders and suicides and, in general, perverse actions or events that might perturb the spirits, teach or spur people to commit crimes and do evil' (Royal Legislative Decree 532 of 31 May 1914, quoted in Argentieri 1974: 20–1). Second, we have both the moralising influence of the Vatican on the state-run board of film censors within the frame of the alliance between the Holy See and powerful Italian politic parties of Roman Catholic ideology, and the diligent, incessant activity of the Vatican's own censors to influence film producers by controlling the market of Catholic cinemas, which were open only to films possessing moral standards established by the Pope (Argentieri 1974: 74–8, 87–92; Valli 1999: 5–41; Treveri Gennari 2009: 38–57, 72–7, 112–13; Subini 2015). In fact, starting with its foundation in 1935, the Vatican film censorship office Centro Cattolico Cinematografico took upon itself the task of assessing the morality of all Italian and foreign films to be released in Italy, and published its judgements on bulletins, newspapers and magazines to prevent supposedly unchristian works from being exhibited in the very many Italian theatres owned by the Catholic church itself (the so-called 'parish cinemas') or owned/run by devout Catholics. Third, during both the Fascist *ventennio* and the 1948–1963 absolute rule of Christian Democracy, the governing right-wing parties closely monitored the content of the films ever since the screenwriting phase via special state bureaus, pressuring industry people to focus on light entertainment (Argentieri 1974: 23–127; Quaglietti

1980: 74–94; Forgacs 1990: 55–82, 103–29; Bonsaver 2014), while the majority of Italian left-wing intellectuals tended to despise genre cinema of all kinds until well into the 1970s (Forgacs 1990: 152–67; Gundle 2000: 23–7, 43–54, 118–24; O'Rawe 2008; Bisoni 2009: 39–124; Noto 2011: 11–40; O'Leary and O'Rawe 2011; Burato 2018), and to devalue fantastic cinema in particular (Fofi 1963; Spinazzola 1963, 1965a and 1965b; Fink 1966; Giacci 1973; Lippi and Codelli 1976: 11–13; Ghigi 1977; Mora 1978: 289–90), as an escapist flight from the analysis of present-day social reality.

Chapter outlines

The monograph is structured around three parts composed of two chapters each. Entirely dedicated to industrial analysis, Part I outlines the national, international and transnational industrial context of 1956–1975 Italian vampire cinema. Chapter 1 provides an overview of the history of the post-war Italian film industry from crisis to crisis, that is to say from the ground zero of 1945 (when the whole Italian film business had to be politically and economically reorganised, together with the rest of the war-torn country) to the ground zero of 1985 (the year in which, for the first time in almost three decades, Italian film production fell below the rate of 100 films made per year, as the culmination of a crisis that started in the mid-1970s). Chapter 1 opens with an in-depth production history of Freda's *I vampiri*, followed by an account of the 1958–1964 boom in the production of historical-mythological adventures of the sword-and-sandal kind (also known as 'peplum cinema'). Both cases (an isolated commercial failure the former, a short-lived box-office goldmine the latter) are emblematic of the functioning of the Italian film industry between the early 1950s and the mid-1980s – a state-subsidised system mostly based on a constellation of medium, small and minuscule business ventures piggy-backing on popular genres/trends in the local and/or global film market. Once the concept of *filone*-filmmaking is introduced as the serialised manufacturing of low-cost imitations of a given commercially successful movie, Chapter 2 details the success of the Hammer *Dracula* in late-1950s and early-1960s Italy, and explains why, where, by whom and with which commercial results a series of vampire films were made by Italian companies from 1959 to 1975. While revealing the imported and derivative nature of Italian vampire cinema, the industrial analysis conducted in Part I shows how local factors such as distribution-fed production, time- and cost-saving shooting practices, state censorship and state aids made the Italian vampire rip-offs into variations on the theme mixing foreign models with distinctively national traits rather than into slavish plagiarisms.

After the industrial context of 1956–1975 Italian vampire cinema has been laid out, Part II and Part III move to the field of cultural studies proper, employing the theoretical tools of psychoanalysis, Marxism and feminism to analyse the thirty-three vampire movies contained in the corpus, and to link these film texts to their national socio-historical context of production and consumption. Part II zooms in on the cultural instrumentality of the vampire metaphor in Italy by studying Italian-made vampire movies as struggles for gender definition and domination that reflect the zeitgeist of post-war Italy, when a perceived decline in masculine authority due to the vicissitudes of the Second World War, the hardships of reconstruction and the post-1958 neocapitalist consumerism went hand in hand with women's ever-increasing challenges to traditional gender roles. Chapter 3 argues that the female vampires of Italian horror are not simplistically villainous, power-hungry sexual predators that misogynistic-reactionary narratives put to death as a punishment for attempting to subvert the patriarchal status quo. They also are empathy-inducing characters caught between rebellion and hyper-identification with traditional values: victims returning from the grave to seek revenge against their male oppressors, and tragic lovers dreaming of a monogamous heterosexual relationship that looks strangely similar to marriage. Chapter 4, on the other hand, ventures into the so-far-uncharted territory of the Italian male vampires that populate horror parodies, straightforward horrors and horror-tinged adventures. It investigates how, within a masculinity-in-crisis framework, Italian makeshift Draculas act as champions of traditional virility, irresistible Latin lovers and tyrannical *patres familias* seeking to reassure Italian men of their gender leadership.

Concerned with the political and socio-economic implications of Italian vampire cinema, Part III identifies Italian vampires with enemies within (a specific group of people in the nation-state's social body) and enemies without (scheming foreigners). Chapter 5 focuses on the vampire movies made in the 1959–1965 period, which coincided with the 1958–1963 economic miracle that turned vastly backward, prevalently agricultural Italy into a modern, industrial country. Taking horror parody *Tempi duri per i vampiri* as its main case study, the chapter describes a parable of class struggle pointing to the need of renegotiating ancestral class identities in order to survive the dramatic socio-economic changes brought about by the so-called 'boom'. At the same time, a careful analysis of horror-tinged adventures reveals them to be a re-enactment of the Nazi occupation of Italy in the last years of Second World War and, possibly, an allusion to the neofascist resurgence of the early 1960s. Chapter 6, on the other hand, focuses on six Italian vampire films of various genres made between 1970 and 1975. Directly referencing Marx and Marxist thinkers, . . . *Hanno cambiato faccia, La corta notte delle bambole di vetro, Il prato macchiato di rosso, L'uomo che uccideva a sangue freddo, Dracula cerca sangue di vergine . . . e morì di sete!!!* and *Il cav. Costante Nicosia demoniaco, ovvero: Dracula in Brianza* liken the contemporary ruling political caste and capitalist class to greedy, self-serving vampires that are undefeatable due to their power of adaptation, thereby providing an apocalyptic view on the post-'boom' period, from the late-1960s wave of anti-authoritarian protests in Italian universities and factories to the mid-1970s plans for an alliance between Christian Democrats and Communists. Methodology-wise, Chapter 6 is the only chapter of the monograph in which the tools of auteur theory – and especially the idea that a film is the emanation of the screenwriter-director's personal beliefs as shaped by his or her political, socio-economic and cultural background – are consistently employed. In fact, as we shall see in detail at the end of Chapter 2 and throughout Chapters 1 and 5, Italian genre cinema practitioners largely conceived of filmmaking as a means for financial gain rather than as an outlet for social commentary, and were therefore reluctant, if not opposed, to discuss authorial intentions and message, at least until the socio-political upheavals of the second half of the 1960s.

Notes

1. The expression 'cultural instrumentality' designs the cultural work films perform as 'reflections of social trends and attitudes of the time, mirroring the preoccupations of the historical moment in which the films were made'; as 'society's representations of itself in and for itself'; as texts able to 'do [things] to and for their spectators', evoking pleasures and triggering fantasies; as 'actively involved in a whole network of intertexts, of cultural meanings and social discourses' (Kuhn 1990: 10).
2. *La torre dei vampiri* is set in 1790s France and deals with the 'executioner of Paris' who, 'after the fall of monarchy', takes refuge in the countryside and resorts to murder and false accusations to steal beautiful peasant Fornarina from her husband-to-be Raimondo (Bernardini and Martinelli 1993b: 294–5). *La vampira indiana* tells the story of a Native-American woman who, 'in order to help her brothers, kills a wealthy landowner and has an innocent man condemned for the crime. But the daughter of the innocent man spies on the Indian woman' and, in the end, justice is made (Bernardini and Martinelli 1993b: 328). In *Il vampiro*, 'a guy wants to marry a girl who is in love with a cousin. A murder is committed and the cousin is imprisoned on a false accusation. The culprit is punished and justice triumphs' (Bernardini and Martinelli 1993d: 280–1). Finally, *La carezza del vampiro* has a young aristocrat saved from the clutches of a money-hungry crook by 'colossal mulatto Maciste' (Martinelli 1991b: 40).
3. The screenplay conceives of *Malenka, la nipote del vampiro* as a supernatural horror with touches of slapstick like the hero's sidekick sneezing after a staked vampire crumbles to dust (de Ossorio 1968). However, in the Italian-dubbed cut approved by the Italian Film Censorship Office and subsequently released in Italian theatres, vampires are just a hoax and no bloodsucking nor staking ever takes place (Nullaosta 54087 1969). The English-dubbed cut called *Fangs of the Living Dead*, which circulated in the Anglophone market in the 1970s, is more faithful to the screenplay, in that it is a straightforward vampire horror culminating in a gruesome staking scene.
4. E.g., Horace Walpole's 1764 *The Castle of Otranto*, Ann Radcliffe's 1797 *The Italian, or the Confessional of the Black Penitents*, James Malcolm Rymer and Thomas Peckett Prest's 1845–1847 *Varney the Vampire; or, the Feast of Blood*, Francis Marion

Crawford's 1880 *For the Blood Is the Life* and Mary Elizabeth Braddon's 1896 *Good Lady Ducayne*.

5. The Italian translator did not work on the English original but on the French edition of 1920, *Dracula, l'homme de la nuit* (same title, same cover art, same misspelling of the author's name as 'Brahm' Stoker). For a detailed study of *Dracula*'s translations in Italian and other languages, see Berni (2016) and Bibbò (2018).

6. The producers' reworking of *I vampiri* led some contemporary reviewers to call the film a 'giallo', i.e. a crime thriller (Anonymous 1957b and 1957d; Centro Cattolico Cinematografico 1957). Incidentally, *I vampiri*'s plot – revolving around a journalist investigating the involvement of an aristocrat family in the murder of some girls, drained of blood and thrown into the Seine – might have been inspired by the real-life Wilma Montesi giallo (in April 1953 the twenty-one-year-old daughter of a carpenter was found drowned on a beach near Rome, and rich and powerful people were accused of her death by muckraking reporters, until all the suspects were acquitted in May 1957).

7. There is no record of these films in the registries of the Italian Film Censorship Office. However, Murnau's *Nosferatu* started being screened in Italian cinema circles in the late 1940s (Anonymous 1948), while Dreyer's *Vampyr* was known to Italian critics since the early 1940s (Viazzi 1940) and its screenplay – actually a movie transcript made from a French film print – was published in Italian translation in the immediate post-war (Buzzi and Lattuada 1948). Finally, it exists a 1936 promotional article launching the Italian edition of Browning's *Mark of the Vampire*: in the article, neither Bela Lugosi nor the words 'Dracula' and 'horror' are mentioned; rather, the selling points are the 'dramatic qualities' of the picture, the action-packed murder-mystery plot and star Lionel Barrymore playing a cunning detective (Anonymous 1936).

8. E.g., *L'Inferno* (Francesco Bertolini, Giuseppe de Liguoro, Adolfo Padovan, 1911), *Malombra* (Carmine Gallone, 1917), *Malombra* (Mario Soldati, 1942) and *Il cappello da prete* (Ferdinando Maria Poggioli, 1944).

9. E.g., *Faust* (Enrico Guazzoni, 1914), *La dama bianca* (Anonymous, 1916), *Il mostro di Frankenstein* (Eugenio Testa, 1920), *Rapsodia satanica* (Nino Oxilia, 1917), *L'altro io* (Mario Bonnard, 1917), *Notte romantica di Dolly, ovvero: Angoscia di Dolly* (Arnaldo Frateili, 1920), *La giovinezza del diavolo* (Roberto Roberti, 1922), *Il cuore rivelatore* (Cesare Civita, Alberto Lattuada, Alberto Mondadori, Mario Monicelli, 1935) and *Il caso Valdemar* (Ubaldo Magnaghi, Gianni Hoepli, 1936).

10. E.g., *Lo spettro* (Gaston Velle, 1907), *La strega di Siviglia* (Anonymous, 1908), *Il fantasma* (L. Adelli, 1909), *Il diavolo zoppo* (Luigi Maggi, 1909), *La ballata della strega* (Luigi Maggi, 1910), *La madre e la morte* (Arrigo Frusta, 1911), *Satana* (Luigi Maggi, 1912), *I rettili umani* (Enrico Vidali, 1915), *La bara di vetro* (Pier Angelo Mazzolotti, 1915), *La sposa dei secoli* (Anonymous, 1916), *L'uomo dall'orecchio mozzato* (Ubaldo Maria del Colle, 1916), *'E scugnizze* (Elvira Notari, 1917), *Kalida'a la storia di una mummia* (Augusto Genina, 1917), *L'uomo che dormì 130 anni* (Arturo Rosenfeld, 1922), *Incanto di mezzanotte* (Mario Baffico, 1940), *Quel fantasma di mio marito* (Camillo Mastrocinque, 1950) and *La paura fa 90* (Giorgio Simonelli, 1951).

PART I

THE INDUSTRIAL CONTEXT

1. THE ITALIAN FILM INDUSTRY (1945–1985)

SAFE BETS: THE ANDREOTTI SYSTEM AND *MINIMO GARANTITO*

If the overall aim of this monograph is to put filmic texts into context, thereby identifying the cultural instrumentality and national specificity of Italian vampire cinema, the first step is to sketch the industrial context in which the thirty-three vampire movies to be studied were made and consumed. In fact, as a cornerstone of the capital-intensive business of motion pictures, genre movies generally do not pop up out of the blue due to the sheer volition and idiosyncrasies of creative individuals, but are manufactured within, and shaped by, an institutional and economic framework in which national and international factors intertwine. In this sense, Riccardo Freda's account of the genesis of *I vampiri* can be quite instructive if subjected to close scrutiny. Speaking in the early 1970s, the Italian director (quoted in Cozzi 1971: 27–8) stated that he started making horror movies

> because of a bet. I was talking with two producers one day, [Ermanno] Donati and [Luigi] Carpentieri. I said that a film could be made in two weeks, and they replied that it was impossible. I insisted, so they phoned [the owner of production and distribution company Titanus, Goffredo] Lombardo: they explained to Lombardo my proposal and asked if he wanted to distribute the film once it was finished. He accepted without much enthusiasm and I very quickly wrote a screenplay for *I vampiri*, which was shot in twelve days. Then I quit the job because I had an argument with the producers, and they completed the rest of the picture

in two days. The movie was set in Paris but, thanks to the miniatures and tricks I created with cinematographer Mario Bava, we shot it in the courtyard of Titanus studio, in Rome.

In the early 1990s, Freda repeated the anecdote almost word by word, insisting on the low-budget nature of the project: 'I agreed to shoot the movie in about ten days, demanding only Gianna Maria Canale as lead actress, Mario Bava as cinematographer and Beni Montresor as production designer' (quoted in Della Casa 1993: 60). What Freda perfected through countless interviews is the typical retrospective tale about the golden age of post-war Italian cinema, in which skilled craftsmen do battle with the lack of money and time to break new ground (see just about any interview anthologised in Faldini and Fofi 1979 and 1981). And of course, as in the American Western epics favoured by Freda ever since his childhood (Freda et al. 1981: 5–7), there is no happy ending to reward the heroic pioneers: 'There was no audience for horror films at that time in Italy. We hired some ladies to scream their lungs out during a premiere screening of *I vampiri*, but it was a half-fiasco and we laughed about it a lot' (Freda, quoted in Pisoni and Ferrarese [1999] 2007: 43).

Official figures confirm Freda's version. According to the documents submitted to the Italian Show Business Bureau by Donati and Carpentieri, the production of *I vampiri* started on 19 November 1956 with a twenty-day shooting schedule. Due mainly to the choice of shooting in CinemaScope, the estimated budget rose from the initial 97 million lire to 142 million lire – 120 million for the shooting and 22 million for post-production and publicity.[1] Donati and Carpentieri's company Athena Cinematografica invested 16 million lire, and so did Lombardo's Titanus. Additional money came from a 50-million-lira state loan, on which the producers asked an extra 25 million lire after adopting the CinemaScope format. Between 5 April 1957 and 31 March 1964, *I vampiri* collected a mere 125,261,762 lire at the domestic box office (Rondolino and Levi 1967: 128), while the three top-grossing Italian movies first released in 1957 – Titanus productions *Belle ma povere* (Dino Risi, 1957), *Lazzarella* (Carlo Ludovico Bragaglia, 1957) and *Arrivederci Roma / Seven Hills of Rome* (Roy Rowland, 1957) – totalled more than 700 million lire each over the same period (Rondolino and Levi 1967: 119, 123). Perhaps unsurprisingly given the bias against Italian-made fantastic narratives described in the Introduction, the Italian edition of Richard Matheson's 1954 sci-fi/horror novel *I Am Legend*, first published by prestigious Milanese publishing house Longanesi in October 1957 under the Fredaesque title *I vampiri*, became much more popular in Italy than Freda's film.[2] As for foreign distribution, between 1957 and the mid-1960s vampire movie *I vampiri* circulated under various titles and in different cuts in France, West Germany and the US (Curti 2017a: 133–4; Venturini 2019), but neither foreign box-office receipts nor documents relating to international distribution deals are currently in the public domain. Thus, as it can be inferred from the bet anecdote, Freda essentially involved Donati, Carpentieri and Lombardo in a market test: they gambled on something new – an Italian *film del terrore* – and, as far as we know, the experiment did not turn out to be a smash hit anywhere.

If the first Italian-made horror was a lost bet, though, Athena Cinematografica and Titanus were not gambling big money. As remarked by Freda, *I vampiri* had all the key characteristics of a low-budget project: a tight shooting schedule, a crew of technicians expert at cutting costs, no expensive actors (top-billing actress Gianna Maria Canale, a fairly popular sex symbol of Italian adventure cinema since 1948, was paid less than 8 million lire, more or less the same salary as the director). But in order to understand why Donati, Carpentieri and Lombardo poured 32 million lire into a movie whose main box-office appeal was the presence of Canale, and why they ended up laughing about its mediocre revenues, it is necessary to describe the birth of the post-war Italian film industry as a state-subsidised, distribution-driven, rampantly speculative business.

Preoccupied with declining audience figures in the US film market, at the end of Second World War Hollywood studios started dumping hundreds of films from their backlist catalogues[3] on the newly deregulated Italian market, with the effect of precluding Italian films from any chance of wide domestic release (Quaglietti 1980: 52–8). The chain-reaction on almost all sectors of the Italian film industry was dramatic: very few screenings of Italian films, meagre box-office receipts and no profit-making for Italian producers, no capital to invest in filmmaking, a resultant crisis and vast unemployment in one of Italy's most lucrative economic activities. The same thing was happening in post-war France to the point that, in 1946, Italy and France started signing a series of bilateral agreements aiming to 'oppose American prevarication' (Freda, quoted in Tassone et al. 1995: 98) by pooling the two countries' technical/artistic/financial resources and creating a single transnational film market out of two separate national ones (Romanelli 2016: 29–31). American companies, and Hollywood studios *in primis*, were not impressed and simply kept flooding the European market with their movies, effectively maintaining a hegemonic position. This situation was denounced in a 1948 manifesto written by Italian film workers and critics. Besides accusing the Italian government of turning a blind eye to Hollywood's dumping policies and massive export of lire to the US, the document blamed the crisis on the inexistent bank credit for Italian film production (Quaglietti 1980: 55–7). In 1949, after the unrest of the various components of the Italian film industry had reached a boiling point, the Undersecretary to the Presidency of the Council of Ministers – Christian Democrat Giulio Andreotti – was able to pass two laws seeking to break the Hollywood monopoly and boost Italian film production while 'acquiring the maximum consensus among conflicting categories (exhibitors, distributors, producers, facility workers) in order to gain political control over Italian film production' (Baschiera and Di Chiara 2010: 31): law 448 of 26 July 1949, also known as 'leggina', and law 958 of 29 December 1949, also known as 'legge Andreotti'.

Relying on Fascist-era legislation (Corsi 2001: 19–31, 42–51), the system put in place by Andreotti in 1949 made Italian cinema totally dependent on the Italian state. First, the two laws created a state-managed special fund for cinematography fed by a ten-year-fixed, 2.5-million-lira deposit to be paid on each foreign film over 1,000 metres that distribution companies wished to import and dub into Italian. Catching two birds with one stone, Andreotti managed to impose a restriction on Hollywood monopoly[4] and find the resources to provide the bank credit that Italian film workers were asking for. Second,

> a special state commission was created within the Italian Show Business Bureau in order to ascertain the nationality of the films shot on Italian territory. If a given film, in spite of foreign investments and the presence of foreign actors and technicians, was certified to be of Italian nationality, it could obtain two benefits: (1) the mandatory scheduling, as part of a national quota mechanism according to which Italian films had to be screened in Italian theatres for at least 80 days per year; (2) state incentives to production under the form of tax refunds (10% of the Italian box-office gross, plus an extra 8% for films that the state commission deemed artistically valid). (Di Chiara 2009: 23)

This system 'remained virtually unmodified until 1965' (Baschiera and Di Chiara 2010: 31): law 897 of 31 July 1956 simply unified the 1949 laws into a single text, substituting the 10-per-cent-plus-8-per-cent tax refund with an automatic 16 per cent tax refund, and increasing both the dubbing deposit (from 2.5 to 5.5 million lire) and the national quota (from eighty to 100 days). Moreover, according to Argentieri (1974: 207–8), Quaglietti (1980: 223–7) and Corsi (2001: 131–6), the 1949 regulations even survived the end of Christian Democracy's political hegemony as law 1213 of 4 November 1965 – informally named 'legge Corona' after Socialist Achille Corona, the Minister of Tourism and Cultural Activities of the first centre-left governments in the history of the Italian Republic – shares with the leggina and the legge Andreotti an emphasis on state credit and automatic tax refunds (definitively fixed at 13 per cent of the Italian box-office gross).

We can now begin to understand why Donati and Carpentieri, the owners of a tiny production company such as Athena Cinematografica, were so easily convinced by Freda to back experiment in terror *I vampiri*. Not only the film was a low-budget effort but, according to the 1949 laws, 'up to 60% of the estimated budget' (Corsi 2001: 50) could be covered by the state with money from the dubbing deposit of the over 200 foreign films imported every year in Italy from 1 January 1950 onwards. For the loan to be granted, however, the state required a *garanzia* (an assurance to recoup at least part of the investment), and it is here that the role of Titanus becomes important. As stressed by Freda (quoted in Cozzi 1971: 27), Athena Cinematografica did not contact Titanus's head as a producer: '[Donati and Carpentieri] phoned Lombardo [. . .] and asked if he wanted to distribute the film once it was finished'. In other words, Donati and Carpentieri wanted first and foremost to secure their upcoming, unprecedented film a place on the domestic market via Titanus, one of Italy's oldest and most established distribution companies, an owner of movie theatres in the Centre-South of the country, and well-connected in France as well (Di Chiara 2013: 35–92).[5] The equation is simple: striking a distribution deal before production even starts means having a fair chance to recoup the production costs via box-office gross and pay back the state loan necessary to make the movie. What Athena Cinematografica was looking for, though, was not an affidavit. More concretely, Donati and Carpentieri wanted an advance payment from the future distributor of their film under the form of *minimo garantito*.

In the slang of the Italian film business, the expression *minimo garantito* alludes to the very common situation in which a producer asks one or more distributors to finance the shooting of a given film project. More specifically, the *minimo garantito* is the sum of money that an Italian distribution company pays to an Italian production company in order to acquire the national and/or international distribution rights of a film yet to be made. The amount of money transferred from the distribution company to the production company before the shooting (via cash payment or, much more often, via promissory notes) is normally based on the distributor's rough estimate of the minimum amount of net box-office receipts that the finished movie would collect during its theatrical release, hence the expression *minimo garantito*, which means 'guaranteed minimum'.

In order to make *I vampiri*, Donati and Carpentieri asked Lombardo for a *minimo garantito* and they got it, together with the possibility of renting Titanus studio at a very discounted rate for the shooting. Both a producer and a distributor, Lombardo almost certainly reckoned that financing a certified-Italian feature would give him the possibility to avoid paying the dubbing deposit on a foreign film he wished to import in the future, as the leggina allowed for this dispensation and even legalised the trade of dubbing-fee waivers among film companies (Quaglietti 1980: 63; Corsi 2001: 49). Official documents report a 16-million-lira investment by Lombardo followed by the concession of a 50-million-lira state loan, which confirms what scholars have so far written about Italian cinema as a distribution-driven business in which 'producers could obtain money in advance from distributors in exchange for domestic or foreign distribution rights; using these distribution rights as *garanzia*, producers could easily gain access to state credit' (Di Chiara 2009: 25).

Finding a distributor willing to grant the *minimo garantito* and thereby asking for a state loan was only half of the producers' job. The other half consisted in demonstrating to the state commission created by the legge Andreotti that the film was of Italian nationality, to obtain the mandatory-scheduling-and-tax-refunds benefits. The procedure to get an Italian-nationality certificate was more or less the same as the one to ask for a state loan. To access state credit Donati and Carpentieri had already submitted to the Italian Show Business Bureau the following, mandatory documents: the screenplay of *I vampiri* (in order for government officials to enact *censura preventiva*, a preventive censorship discouraging the making of movies that may clash with Christian Democracy ideology);[6] the estimated budget; financial plans to cover said budget; the shooting schedule; a complete list of cast and crew with personal data and contracts thereof (a certain number of Italian workers, including at least two graduates from the Centro Sperimentale di Cinematografia in Rome, had to be employed for the film to qualify as Italian); contracts for the rental of Italian film studios, dubbing facilities and film labs (a minimum number of days was required); contracts relating to possible foreign co-productions and domestic/foreign distribution agreements. After the film was greenlit by the state, shot, edited, dubbed and had obtained from the Italian Film Censorship Office the permission to be publicly screened, the final step for Donati and Carpentieri to take was merely bureaucratic, namely submitting to the Italian Show Business Bureau the cost statement for *I vampiri*, the public-screening permission and proof of first public screening in Italy via the designed distributor.

So, upon *I vampiri*'s premiere in Catania (Sala Roma Cinema) on 5 April 1957, Athena Cinematografica obtained the nationality certificate for the first Italian horror movie, and accessed the mandatory-scheduling-and-16-per-cent-tax-rebates benefits. This is not surprising. Aiming to make the various categories of the Italian film industry prosper only at the conditions of focusing on light escapism and avoiding explicit sexual content and political issues that would have hurt the Catholic principles and centre-right agenda of ruling party Christian Democracy, the highly centralised Andreotti system, with its multiple layers of censorship, targeted the manifestly critical works by Communist, or allegedly Communist, auteurs (Argentieri 1974: 62–127; Quaglietti 1980: 74–94; Forgacs 1990: 103–29; Bonsaver 2014: 69), while leaving genre cinema of all kinds a relative freedom, especially when movies were set in remote historical epochs and/or in foreign countries. Consequently, although ridiculed by government officials at the preventive-censorship stage for its adoption of the tritest clichés from 'certain crude, unrefined, French and English popular literature of the nineteenth century', *I vampiri*'s screenplay was approved and the finished film was passed uncut by the Italian Film Censorship Office as VM16 (forbidden to people under the age of sixteen) (Nullaosta 23894 1957).

The case of *I vampiri* confirms that in Italy, after 1949,

> for an adventurous though inexperienced producer it became very easy to make [genre] movies, also because Italian cinema could count on many well-trained professionals skilled at containing costs. Once a picture had been sold in advance to a distributor, it was relatively easy for its producer to have access to the governmental loan fund. Then, as a rule, the producer actually made the movie using about half of the original estimated budget, keeping the rest as his wages; the distributor was left to face the uncertainties of the market. (Baschiera and Di Chiara 2010: 31)

In view of this state-patronised anti-risk cushion, and of the producers' tendency to 'generate profits not by investing money but by subtracting it from the film's budget' (Bizzarri 1957: 1380), Freda's anecdotes can finally be put into the right perspective and *I vampiri* defined as a minor, low-risk speculation: in Italy both small producers like Athena Cinematografica and big companies like Titanus were encouraged to invest in film production for purely financial reasons, as state loans and tax refunds on box-office receipts 'always assured a minimum margin of profit, even if the film barely managed to cover its production expenses' (Corsi 2001: 53). Indeed, an issue of cultural magazine *Il ponte* contemporary to the Italian premiere of Freda's film featured an essay titled *Cinema senza industria (storia economica di dodici anni)* ('Cinema without industry, an economic history of the past twelve years'), heavily criticising the 1949 laws for handing Italian film production over to companies owning nothing but their names, speculators who make films without risking anything from their own pockets:

> In the 1954–1955 season, the impressive number of 200 Italian film production companies was recorded: a real 'pulverisation' of the productive sector. Basically, [. . .] a production company was born for each new film to be made. Between 1953 and 1954, everybody wanted to 'play the game', and perhaps they managed to produce one movie, but then they stopped: these initiatives lacked financial, industrial and commercial solidity. In the 1954–1955 and 1955–1956 seasons, 100 companies produced only one film (not one film in each season, but one film during the two seasons). (Bizzarri 1957: 1377–9)

In the very same issue of *Il ponte*, Moscon (1957: 1333) relates of a one-film production company whose name he considers emblematic of the improvised nature of Italian cinema under the auspices of Christian Democracy's legislation. It is the San Gennaro Proteggimi Film, that is to say the 'Saint Januarius [a Catholic saint famous for performing miracles] Protect Me' production company.

Even safer bets: the rise of *filone*-filmmaking after 1958

Given its poor performance on the domestic market, experiment in terror *I vampiri* remained an isolated case for more than two years. The production of horror-themed films in Italy did not catch up until after the international release of the Hammer *Dracula*, whose worldwide box-office success made six Italian or Italo–French vampire movies rush into production between spring 1959 and summer 1960: horror parody *Tempi duri per i vampiri* and five horrors proper – *L'amante del vampiro*, *Il sangue e la rosa*, *Il mulino delle donne di pietra*, *La maschera del demonio* and *L'ultima preda del vampiro*. However, contrary to *I vampiri*, the producers of these films wanted not only to test the Italian market while safely speculating on *minimo garantito*, state loans and tax refunds, but also hoped to do big business in the international market successfully opened up by Hammer. This attempt to play in the major league (to be accounted for in greater depth in Chapter 2) cannot be understood without explaining the notion of *filone*-filmmaking as exemplified by the late-1950s and early-1960s peplum boom, and detailing the national and international mechanisms that made the 1950s a crucial decade for the Italian film industry – the moment in which it began to go international and conquer its niche in the seemingly impenetrable US market after neorealist one-time hits *Roma città aperta / Rome, Open City* (Roberto Rossellini, 1945) and *Riso amaro / Bitter Rice* (Giuseppe De Santis, 1949) (Wagstaff 1998: 75–8).

Once again, the starting point is the mid-1940s. Ever since the end of Second World War, the US domestic film market had been shrinking, due to TV competition and the emergence of new forms of leisure. All this, 'combined with the drop in Hollywood's largest export market (the UK, from which Hollywood was taking 25% of its receipts)', meant that 'Italy (which gradually replaced the UK as the largest European market) became a progressively more important export market for the Americans' (Wagstaff 1998: 74). Indeed, we have seen how Hollywood majors tried to monopolise Italian screens via dumping between 1945 and the early 1950s. Meanwhile, the anti-trust Paramount Decree of 1948 forced US producers-distributors-exhibitors Twentieth Century-Fox, MGM, Paramount, Warner Bros. and RKO to let go of their theatre chains, making it harder for their films to find a stable place on the domestic market. Hollywood majors therefore became increasingly concerned about the high costs of in-studio shooting and post-production, and decided to focus their financial efforts on making a few star-filled, spectacular films on the cutting edge of technology like war, Biblical and western epics (far more expensive than run-of-the-mill genre production, but granting secure, exorbitant revenues worldwide), leaving the production of genre-oriented B-movies to small, independent companies, whose output majors could always decide to exploit from the distribution side (Conant 1985; Guback 1985). With the aim to maximise profits by keeping production costs as low as possible, American B- and TV-movie companies soon started outsourcing part of their genre film production in foreign countries such as England, where taxes, labour and facilities were cheaper compared to the US (see the Hammer case study in Heffernan 2004: 43–62; Meikle 2009: 1–47), and so did Hollywood majors in Italy, beginning in 1951 with MGM's epic *Quo Vadis* (Mervyn LeRoy, 1951).

The year and the choice of Italy are hardly surprising: lengthily negotiated by the Christian Democrats and the Motion Picture Association of America, a 'special norm' was approved in 1951, forbidding 'the export of 50% of the gross made in Italy by every foreign film, thus forcing Hollywood majors to invest part of their income in Italian film productions', Italian film distribution and works of national interest such as buildings and infrastructures (Baschiera and Di Chiara 2010: 31).[7] Investments in Italian cinema proved to be so lucrative for American companies facing the shrinking of the US market and the post-Paramount-Decree restructuring that they continued well into the 1970s, even if the gross-export ban was permanently lifted in 1963, when the Motion Picture Association of America obtained the full liberalisation of the Italian market, the second biggest market in the Western world for number of tickets sold from the late 1950s to the early 1980s, and for number of active movie theatres throughout most of the 1950s, 1960s and 1970s (Quaglietti 1980: 252–4; Corsi 2001: 124–5). Basically, ever since the early 1950s, American companies understood that any investment in film production in Italy could be recouped with interest simply by finding local business partners through whom the benefits of the Andreotti system could be accessed (de Grazia 1998: 28). Investing in the distribution of Italian films in Italy and abroad was also convenient for US companies and created profitable production-distribution synergies:

> American distributors in Italy used successful 'national' films as a driving force for the success of their whole film catalogue: in 1958–1959, for instance, Warner Bros.'s highest-grossing film in Italy was [Italo–French co-production] *Europa di notte / European Nights* (Alessandro Blasetti, 1959). European film industries made up for Hollywood's decrease in film production with their genre films, co-produced at low cost (by France and Italy at first, soon joined by West Germany, Spain and others). Exports were 'encouraged' by the prestige of Italian art films (e.g., Luchino Visconti and Michelangelo Antonioni, whose works were financed by American companies). (Wagstaff 1999: 859)

The consequences of the infiltration of American capital in film distribution in Italy are analysed further below, when the late-1970s crisis of the Italian film industry is discussed. What is crucial, now, is to establish the impact of Hollywood's 1950s runaway productions on the development of Italian cinema, and the role American companies played in its internationalisation.

The inception of the so-called 'Hollywood on the Tiber' in 1951 had a devastating effect on the productive sector of the Italian film industry, at least initially. Constrained by the blocked-gross regulation and attracted by the possibility of exploiting well-equipped studios, cheap labour and a good climate for location shooting all year round, *Quo Vadis* and other American runaway productions began to 'occupy Cinecittà' for very long periods 'with an unprecedented number of technicians and extras, totally disproportionate for Italian standards', thus causing 'a generalised rise in film production costs' that made it extremely difficult for Italian producers to shoot films in Italy (Corsi 2001: 67). In the long run, though, this rise in production costs proved beneficial, in that it 'forced Italian producers to [. . .] choose projects conceived not only for the domestic market, but also for foreign markets'. Indeed, 'the more serious among Italian producers' learned a lot from Hollywood's technical lesson and industrial workflow, and employed American blocked capital 'for ambitious projects aiming to make Italian cinema known internationally, as a producer of both art films and spectacular, highly entertaining commercial movies' (Corsi 2001: 68–9).

However, the consecration of Italian cinema in the world market as a provider of spectacular entertainment did not come with lavish A-pictures like Technicolor epic *Ulisse* / *Ulysses* (Mario Camerini, 1954), produced with American capital by Carlo Ponti and Dino De Laurentiis for the Italian company Lux, and featuring Kirk Douglas and Silvana Mangano (De Laurentiis's wife and an international star since the 1949 release of *Riso amaro*). Rather, it came with 300-million-lira quickie *Le fatiche di Ercole* / *Hercules* (Pietro Francisci, 1958), produced by tiny Italian company OSCAR with money from Italian producers-distributors Galatea and Lux, mostly obtained through the *minimo garantito* and state-credit mechanisms already described for *I vampiri*. Shot in Eastmancolor and Dyaliscope by cinematographer Mario Bava, and starring an American bodybuilder with minimal acting experience, Francisci's poverty-row version of *Ulisse* proved extraordinarily successful, both in Italy and the US: 'in the *mercato di profondità*', that is to say the low-ticket-fare *seconda* and *terza visione* theatres located in Italy's metropolitan peripheries and small villages, 'the film made 700 million lire in a relatively short period', while thanks to the international contacts of Galatea, *Le fatiche di Ercole* was sold for 'a relatively low price' to Embassy Pictures's head Joseph Levine, who redubbed it and turned it into a USD$12 million hit 'by investing in a publicity campaign of massive proportions'. The great performance of the Italian film on the US market brought to 'an alliance between medium-size American companies and Italian genre cinema' (Di Chiara 2016a: 55–6).

The ingredients of peplum – the 'low-budget superspectacle formula' able to guarantee high box-office revenues proportional to low production costs (Spinazzola 1985: 324–5) – had been found. Thematically, after a series of historical-mythological films with female protagonists epitomised by *Fabiola* (Alessandro

Blasetti, 1949) and *Teodora, imperatrice di Bisanzio* / *Teodora, Slave Empress* (Riccardo Freda, 1954), there was a return to the muscleman films of the 1910s and 1920s popularised all over the world by the marvellous adventures of gentle giant Maciste and other hulking heroes (Spinazzola 1965a; Newman 1986a: 20–2). On the production side, there was the employment of 1950s Italy's pool of skilled writers, directors and technicians, recycling in assembly-line circumstances plots, actors, extras, studio sets, natural sceneries, costumes, props and even footage – the shooting process dramatically sped up by the Italian common practice of post-shoot dubbing (Della Casa and Giusti 2013: 21–46). On the financing side, Italian producers could count on *minimo garantito*, on state patronage, on European co-productions and now, after the success of *Le fatiche di Ercole* in the US, on 'American distributors willing to buy films cash, sight unseen, on a one-off, fixed-price basis, under the form of advance money, before the film was actually shot' (Di Chiara 2016a: 57). As for distribution, a distinction needs to be made between Italian, European and American markets. On the domestic market, pepla exploited the huge network of inexpensive-admission-fare *seconda* and *terza visione* theatres reaching even the remotest Italian villages and their massive, working-class, low-income public hungry for colourful, spectacular entertainment, so that the commercial life of each movie could be prolonged up to five years after its premiere in the pricey *prima visione* theatres located in large city-centres (Spinazzola 1963: 77–9). On the European market, and especially in France, muscleman films were successful among popular audiences and highbrow cinephiles alike (Della Casa 2001b: 312–4; Gili 2010), while on the American market they drew the interest of both TV-syndicators hungry for colour programming and medium- or small-size neighbourhood theatres and drive-ins, whose owners had been facing 'a chronic shortage of product for much of the year' due to the post-Paramount-decree 'curtailment of production from the major studios [. . .] combined with the studios' practice of "bunching" major releases together at the late summer and holiday seasons' (Heffernan 2004: 65).

Aiming to take advantage of the above, after *Le fatiche di Ercole*, dozens of pepla were rushed through production and into distribution by Italian companies of all sizes, from the unprofessional speculators described by Bizzarri (1957) to long-standing firms Lux and Titanus (Della Casa 1986 and 1989; Salotti 1986). As reported by Spinazzola (1965a: 271), the majority of the eighty-something historical-mythological films made and released in Italy between the 1957–1958 season and the 1962–1963 season made more than 300 million lire at the domestic box office, enough money to break even and start making profits, even without the money from foreign distributors. The production of pepla definitively stopped in 1965, after all possible combinations of scenarios and characters had been exhausted by the overproduction of the previous years. At the same time, by 1965 pepla had lost their grip on the international public due to oversupply, and the already-low production costs had to be cut so much by producers in order to make a profit on shrinking foreign pre-sales, *minimo garantito* and state loans that it was no longer possible to guarantee a well-crafted product to interest audiences in the first place.

Speaking more in general, from *Le fatiche di Ercole* onwards, the Italian film industry mostly relied on the intensive exploitation of a given commercially successful film, Italian or otherwise, by churning out dozens of low-cost imitations – more or less creative variations on the themes established by the originary film quickly adding up to create a *filone* ('gold lode'), that is to say a short-lived cycle of movies displaying macroscopic similarities in plots, characters, settings, actors and so on (Wood 2005: 11–12; Noto 2011: 104–10). A *filone* tended to be born and grow hypertrophically by following three main strategies: the copycat mimicking (providing more of the same, with just enough changes to the winning formula of the originary film to avoid lawsuits for copyright infringement), the crossbreeding (combining the most popular elements of two or more different *filoni* into one movie, for instance by having the muscleman heroes of peplum fight pirates, cowboys, dinosaurs, aliens, vampires and witches . . .), and the parody (a particular kind of crossbreeding with comedy in which the clichés of a given *filone* are played for laughs, laid bare and ridiculed). In constant search for a balance between product imitation and product differentiation, these three strategies allowed Italian producers and distributors to extract as much profit as possible from each season's box-office hits, before the inevitable coming of market saturation.

Indeed, from 1958 until the mid-1980s, the 'pattern of Italian commercial cinema reveals an overlapping succession of generic cycles' piggy-backing on popular trends (Newman 1986a: 20). Besides pepla, there was a plethora of (1) erotic-exotic doc/mock/shockumentaries, i.e. compilations of piquant variety numbers and/or travel reportages, launched by the 1959–1961 success of Blasetti's *Europa di notte* and *Il mondo di notte* / *World by Night* (Luigi Vanzi, 1960) among the bourgeois audiences of *prima visione* theatres located in the industrialised cities of Northern Italy (Mandarà 1963; Morandini 1964; Risé 1964; Spinazzola 1985: 315–23); (2) post-Hammer-*Dracula* Gothic horrors and vampire films especially (see Chapter 2); (3) cheap spy movies imitating the James Bond saga (Newman 1986b: 51–2; Diak 2014); (4) grim, gunfight-filled spaghetti westerns launched by surprise smash hit *Per un pugno di dollari* / *A Fistful of Dollars* (Sergio Leone as Bob Robertson, 1964), and slapstick, fistfight-filled fagioli westerns epitomised by top money-maker *Lo chiamavano Trinità . . .* / *They Call Me Trinity* (Enzo Barboni as E. B. Clutcher, 1970), a most successful, early-1970s attempt to reinvigorate the by-then declining spaghetti western *filone* through heavy doses of comedy (Newman 1986b: 52–3; Wagstaff 1992; Frayling 1998; Pezzotta 2008; Fisher 2011; Manzoli 2012: 121–42);[8] (5) *decam-erotici*, i.e. sex comedies set in the Middle Ages, produced by the dozen after the huge commercial success of *Il Decameron* / *The Decameron* (Pier Paolo Pasolini,

1971) and *I racconti di Canterbury / The Canterbury Tales* (Pier Paolo Pasolini, 1972) (Nakahara 2004; Manzoli 2012: 179–84). Not to mention a whole series of gialli, *poliziotteschi* ('cop thrillers'), nazisexploitation, demonic-possession, cannibal, zombie and postapocalyptic movies, creature features, macaroni combat and, again, a few muscleman films after *Conan the Barbarian* (John Milius, 1982) proved to be a worldwide hit (Mora 1986; Newman 1986c; Della Casa 1990; Curti 2006, 2013 and 2019; Renga 2011; Mendik 2015; Baschiera 2016; Ehrenreich 2017; Kannas 2017; Platts 2017; Fisher 2019).

The reasons behind this progressive 'metamorphosis of genre cinema into *filoni* cinema' (Pitassio 2005: 36) should be clear by now. First, the *minimo garantito* mechanism made most Italian producers into simple organisers of made-to-order films distributors thought would sell well (Lo Foco 1984: 23–8; Corsi 2005; Monetti 2008). Contextually, as the majority of Italian producers were not investors but speculators subtracting money from the film's budget, all the economic risk fell upon distributors (Ventavoli 1992: 104–9; Baschiera and Di Chiara 2010: 31), who were thus even more motivated to finance movies of established appeal on the public.[9] Second, thriving on the tax refunds on domestic box-office gross offered to certified-Italian films, Italian distributors-financiers and producers-organisers were encouraged to play it safe and follow well-tested formulas, so that their output would at least break even on its domestic market. Third, both the informal joint participations with US companies and the formal co-production agreements between Italy and various European countries allowed for the extension of the Andreotti system to the international film industry, giving Italian producers-organisers plenty of opportunities to creatively finance movies by addressing foreign distributors and their specific needs. Finally, as both serious producers and adventurers learned in the heydays of the so-called 'Hollywood on the Tiber', it was always better to exploit leftover sets and props from an A-picture through several B-movies instead of just one, since assembly-line work, serial standardisation and constant recycling made economies of scale possible (Della Casa 2001a: 297–300; Menarini and Noto 2005).

From a numerical point of view, the institutional and economic framework put in place in 1949 by Giulio Andreotti boosted Italian film production over the next quarter of a century, in synergy with European co-productions and American investments. The goal of making more than 100 Italian films in one year without resorting to European co-production agreements was reached quite soon, in 1951, and again in 1952, 1953, 1954, 1961, 1962, 1963, 1964, and uninterruptedly from 1967 to 1980 included (the all-time record of 203 '100% Italian' films was set in 1976). If we take both '100% Italian' films and co-productions into account, from 1951 to the mid-1960s, Italian film production figures rose steadily, peaking in 1964 with 290 movies made (155 co-productions) (Nowell-Smith et al. 1996: 158–9). The only perceptible drops were recorded in 1955–1956, undoubtedly due to the climate of uncertainty regarding the extension of the 1949 laws, and in

1965, when production fell from 290 to 203 films (109 co-productions) (Nowell-Smith et al. 1996: 158–9) as a reaction to both the overproduction of 1964 and the lengthy parliamentary negotiations leading to the approval of the legge Corona in November 1965. From 1965 to 1976 included, Italian film production maintained a rate of more than 200 films made per year, with a peak of 280 (111 co-productions) in 1972 (Nowell-Smith et al. 1996: 159), when two *filoni* boomed at the same time – the fagioli western and the *decamerotico*. However, all the historians of Italian cinema quoted so far agree that, from 1949 to 1976 included, the productive sector of the Italian film industry experienced an economic bubble fed by state aids and foreign investments. Apparently a sign of extraordinary growth, at closer inspection the post-1949 production boom proved to be nothing but the trading of long-term industrial planning for immediate gain via rampant speculation. First, 'between 1953 and 1959' there were '391 production companies active in Italy, 265 of which [. . .] were born and died around a single project, to try their luck with an all-in bet' (Corsi 2001: 65). Second, as reported by Quaglietti (1980: 223), 715 Italian production companies contributed to the production of the 1,063 movies of Italian nationality made from 1960 to 1965. As the 1965 legge Corona extended the 1949 system indefinitely, throughout the peplum, the Gothic horror, the spaghetti western, the superspy, the giallo and other *filoni*, the pulverisation and the precariousness of the productive sector first noted by Bizzarri (1957) were confirmed to be 'an inborn, intrinsic characteristic of the Italian film industry, [. . .] even if the people hiding behind the names of the various companies always were more or less the same', going bankrupt and changing business name to avoid paying creditors (Corsi 2001: 65).

Coda: the bubble bursts

The cynical, rapacious approach to film production as a gold-rush-like exploitation of legislative immobility and passing fancies in both the Italian and the world market is perfectly summarised in a 1969 interview with Mario Bava – a man who, as a technician and film director, made at least one movie for every existing genre, except pornography. When asked if he was optimistic or pessimistic about his future in the Italian film industry of the 1970s, he replied that he was simply content with surviving: 'I am a pessimistic . . . optimist. At worst, I will just have to change movie genre. What matters to me is to last' (quoted in Castelli and Monego 1969: 50). Yet, a few years after Bava's optimistic statement, the bubble burst. From the 237 movies (34 co-productions) made in Italy in 1976, production dropped to 165 movies (23 co-productions) in 1977; from 165 to 143 movies (24 co-productions) in 1978; from 143 to 103 movies (24 co-productions) in 1981; from 103 to 89 movies (8 co-productions) in 1985, stabilising from that moment on around an average 110 movies per year, co-productions included (Nowell-Smith et al. 1996: 159–60). Leaving aside the significant drop in co-productions that started with the 1973 revision of the Italo–French bilateral agreements (Romanelli 2016: 36–41), and considering figures relating to '100% Italian' films only, two facts immediately stand out: 119 films were made in Italy both in 1978 and 1952, and throughout the 1980s and 1990s the Italian film industry could hardly put together 100 films per year. That is to say, production-wise, from the late 1970s onwards the Italian film industry has regressed to pre-*filoni* levels.

Figure 1.1   Mario Bava emerging from a grave on the set of *La maschera del demonio* (photo by Osvaldo Civirani available at Archivio Centrale dello Stato – Archivio fotografico Civirani (film) – 098 Maschera del demonio La – 098–0483).

This productive crisis – which led, in the 1980s and 1990s, to a drastic curtailment in the production of genre films other than comedies featuring popular TV entertainers (Corsi 2005) – has been variously explained by scholars. Typically, their starting point is the steady decline in movie-theatre attendance that began in 1956, after the Italian all-time record of 819 million tickets sold was reached in 1955 (Quaglietti 1980: 252). If the decline in attendance – mainly due to Italians beginning to spend their free time with TV and forms of entertainment other than cinema, and to spend their money on consumer durables rather than on leisure (Manzoli 2012: 86–8, 91–3; Penati 2015) – was not immediately matched by a decline in total box-office receipts, it is because, from 1957 onwards, the movie-ticket price was constantly raised by exhibitors in the attempt to compensate for the gradual loss of spectators. Quaglietti (1980: 252) provides compelling data: while the number of tickets sold dropped from the 790 million of 1956 to the 319 million of 1978, box-office receipts went from 116 billion lire in 1955–1956 to 375 billion lire in 1975, as the average ticket price skyrocketed from the 142 lire of the mid-1950s to the 706 lire of the mid-1970s. However, the constant price rise quickly exceeded the Italian inflation rate, to the point that, in 1973–1974, exhibitors reached

> the limit of the 'inelasticity' of demand. When, starting in 1975, the number of tickets sold began to decrease at the rhythm of 100 million units per year, every 'compensation' became impossible and the vertiginous increase in ticket prices caused by the exhibitors' panic turned against exhibitors themselves, and against the Italian film industry as a whole. (Corsi 2001: 119)

In fact, since Italian film production was generally financed by distribution via *minimo garantito*, the post-1975 contraction in exhibitors' profits, with its estimated loss of 32 billion lire between 1976 and 1977 in spite of substantial increases in ticket price (Quaglietti 1980: 252), determined a contraction in production investments by distributors and therefore a decrease in the overall number of films made. Given that the collapse of demand described by Corsi (2001: 119) coincided with the 1976 breaking of the Italian State TV monopoly, the various categories of the Italian film industry were quick to blame the interconnected crisis of cinemagoing and film production on the massive and totally unregulated broadcast of films by private TV companies in late-1970s and early-1980s Italy (see the interviews anthologised in Bettetini 1981), although more studies of Italian TV programming along the lines of Menduni (2005) and Barra (2015: 108–35) are needed to substantiate this accusation.[10]

Writing from an anti-imperialistic perspective, some commentators integrate the above by shifting attention from the post-1955 decrease in cinema attendance and panicked reaction of exhibitors to the monopolistic aims of Hollywood majors over the Italian film market. According to Contaldo and Fanelli (1979: 11–15, 22, 27–9, 41–65, 72–89) and Lo Foco (1984: 20, 27, 30–2), the post-1945 infiltration of US capital in film distribution in Italy led over time to the striking of a series of partnership deals between American distributors and Italian exhibitors to secure the exploitation of American films at all levels of the Italian market. Following a marketing strategy dictated by the Hollywood conglomerates of the early 1970s, starting with the Italian release of *The Godfather* (Francis Ford Coppola, 1972) in September 1972, the owners of the biggest theatre chains in Italy made it so that the most probable box-office hits of a given season (namely Hollywood blockbusters, controversial European auteur cinema and films featuring popular Italian comedians – most of which were distributed, and often partly or entirely financed, by American companies) were put into circulation for a very short time-span and only in *prima visione* theatres. Since this film-event marketing strategy allowed for arbitrary price alterations up to 2,000 lire per ticket and brought about a very rapid recoup of initial investments, by the mid-1970s all the new, most anticipated films were exploited intensively in the *prima visione* circuit for one season only, rather than extensively from the *prima visione* to the low-ticket-fare *mercato di profondità* over the course of many years. As a consequence, starting from the mid-1970s, *seconda* and *terza visione* theatres lost a significant part of their already-shrinking audience to the *prima visione* colossuses. Deprived of both A-pictures and well-crafted B-movies, which had become an exclusive of *prima visione* exhibitors (who got them via partnership agreements with prominent distributors-financiers), the movie theatres of urban peripheries and small villages came to depend on no-budget, very low-quality, purely speculative *filoni* exploits, until *seconda* and *terza visione* screening venues either closed down or were taken over by theatre-chain owners, refurbished and turned into *prima visione* theatres.[11] In such oligopoly/monopoly conditions, the most powerful (mostly American) distributors-financiers active in Italy decided to focus their productive efforts on big-investment movies, causing an enormous increase in the average cost of filmmaking and consequently curtailing low-cost productions. The simultaneous disappearance of *seconda* and *terza visione* theatres and of countless medium- and small-size production companies making low-budget films for the *mercato di profondità* seems to be the reason behind the decrease in production for the year 1977, and behind the withering of Italian genre cinema during the following decades.

NOTES

1. If not otherwise stated, the production data and preventive censorship information concerning post-war Italian films come from the Italian Show Business Bureau fonds at the Archivio Centrale dello Stato in Rome. The shelf marks of the files that have been consulted for the monograph are provided in Appendix B.

2. It is unlikely that Longanesi named the Italian translation of Matheson's novel after Freda's half-fiasco film. It is more probable that, sometime in 1956, the filmmaker got news that a novel called *I vampiri* was to be published by Longanesi and decided to beat the editorial colossus on time: as reported by Curti (2017a: 4), Leo Longanesi, co-founder of the publishing house, was a close friend of Freda's.
 3. The import of American films in Italy ceased from 1 January 1939 to Liberation because of a dispute between the Italian Fascist government and Hollywood majors over state monopoly (Corsi 2001: 28–9).
 4. Yet, as Quaglietti (1980: 61) astutely remarks, by the end of the 1940s Hollywood majors' wartime backlogs were almost exhausted and monopolising Italian screens through dumping was no longer possible anyway.
 5. The casting of French actor Antoine Balpêtré – a member of the renowned Comédie Française – in the role of the Frankensteinian mad scientist proves that the producers thought of selling *I vampiri* on the French market from the very beginning.
 6. Preventive censorship on screenplays was introduced in 1919–1920 during the Kingdom of Italy's centre-left government presided by Francesco Saverio Nitti (Argentieri 1974: 22), and further strengthened under Fascism with law 2125 of 30 November 1939 (Quaglietti 1980: 24).
 7. It is important to stress that this special norm was a 'law outside the law' (Treveri Gennari 2009: 58), having nothing to do with European co-production regulations: 'the flows of American capital and personnel to Italy were defined as "joint participations", an ambiguous term encompassing any kind of artistic and financial exchange, whether legal or illegal' (Corsi 2001: 69). Consequently, it is impossible to know exactly how much money American companies actually invested in Italy.
 8. The term 'fagioli western' ('beans western') is meant to echo the cine-culinary expression 'spaghetti western'. It derives from a famous scene of the aforementioned *Lo chiamavano Trinità . . .* , in which the title character devours a gigantic pan of beans and a loaf of bread before telling the bewildered innkeeper that 'The beans were crap anyway'.
 9. The idea was to 'go only for safe bets' also when part of the budget consisted of money actually invested by the producers themselves. This is because most production companies were so small that they could only make one film at a time, and were therefore unable to 'cover loss-making productions with the proceeds of profitable ones' (Wagstaff 1992: 250).
10. The uncritical adoption of a cinema-versus-TV approach obscures the important synergies between the two media, and in particular the fact that public and private TV channels have been heavily investing in the production of Italian cinema since the second half of the 1970s (Cereda and Lopez 2005; Corsi 2005; Monteleone 2005; Zagarrio 2008; Barra and Scaglioni 2016 and 2017).
11. According to Tagliabue (2005: 352), 11 per cent of Italian cinemas were *prima visione* theatres in 1976; in 1985, over 92 per cent.

2. ITALIAN VAMPIRE CINEMA (1956–1975)

THE MARK OF THE HAMMER *DRACULA*

November–December 1956 saw the shooting of Riccardo Freda's *I vampiri* and Hammer's *The Curse of Frankenstein* (Terence Fisher, 1957), with the Italian release of the former in April 1957 pre-dating by a month the British release of the latter. October–November 1957 saw the Mexican release of *El vampiro* (Fernando Mendez, 1957), produced by Mexican actor Abel Salazar to exploit the domestic success of Frankensteinian rip-off *Ladrón de cadáveres / The Body Snatcher* (Fernando Mendez, 1956), and the shooting of *El ataúd del vampiro* (Fernando Mendez, 1958) and the Hammer *Dracula*. Meanwhile, in the US, Universal's pre-1948 horrors began to be broadcast to syndicated TV by Columbia in a highly successful package known as Shock Theater (Clarens 1968: 171–2). For these reasons, 1956 and 1957 are seen as the landmark years of a 'Gothic revival' that involved Italian and Mexican film production companies, Hammer and its Hollywood silent partners Warner Bros., Universal and Columbia, soon joined by American International Pictures, which inaugurated its Edgar Allan Poe cycle in 1959–1960 with *The Fall of the House of Usher* (Roger Corman, 1960) (Worland 2014). Contrary to the Mexican and Anglo-American film industries, churning out horror movies on an assembly-line basis ever since 1956–1957 (Heffernan 2004: 43–62, 90–112; Meikle 2009: 25–116; Vitali 2016: 77–120), the Italian film industry did not immediately join the trend: lacking a horror-hungry national audience and the international perspectives opened up by Pietro Francisci's peplum *Le fatiche di Ercole* in 1958,

I vampiri remained an isolated incident for more than two years, to the point that, as the Italian film press of the early 1960s (Anonymous 1960c and 1960f; Fofi 1963) and all horror scholars from Mora (1978) to Di Chiara (2016b) remark, it is more appropriate to consider Fisher's *Dracula* as the actual progenitor of Italian horror cinema.

The Hammer *Dracula*'s co-financier and worldwide distributor Universal submitted the movie to the Italian Film Censorship Office on 7 November 1958, under the title *Dracula il vampiro*. The censorship commission reviewed the film on the very same day (which was quite unusual given the government officials' busy schedules) and denied it the public-screening permission 'because the movie contains scenes, events and sequences that are truce, repugnant and shocking' (Nullaosta 28085 1958). As it was its right, Universal appealed the ban, stating that *Dracula* had already been 'screened in several countries around the world without creating any particular sensation in the audiences' and was in no way different from 'other similar films' approved for public screening in Italy (Nullaosta 28085 1958). As for the second claim, the reference probably was to *The Curse of Frankenstein*, released in Italy by Warner Bros. to critical indifference and a moderate public success, after having been approved without cuts in October 1957 (Nullaosta 25288 1957). Following the *Dracula* ban, Universal negotiated with the Italian Film Censorship Office cuts for thirty metres of film:

> Delete the scene in which Dracula enters the library, screaming; tone down the scene in which Dracula shoves the vampire woman to the ground; tone down the scene in which Dracula sleeps in his coffin; delete the close-ups of the vampire woman in her coffin; tone down the killing and transformation of the vampire woman; tone down the killing of Lucy in her coffin; tone down the scene in which Dracula attempts to bite the Doctor; tone down Dracula's final disintegration. (Nullaosta 28085 1958)

Upon the execution of the above, on 19 November 1958, the movie was granted the public-screening permission: just like *I vampiri* and *The Curse of Frankenstein*, *Dracula* was deemed dangerous for minors and therefore rated VM16 (forbidden to people under the age of sixteen).

An in-depth look at trade paper *Cinematografia d'oggi* allows us to get a sense of the cultural climate surrounding horror movies in late-1950s Italy. The September 1958 issue featured the article *'Films del terrore' per controbattere la televisione?* ('Terror films in order to beat TV?'), one of the first reflections on the Anglo-American Gothic revival of the late 1950s from an industrial point of view. In the article, Italian film industry people were warned that, as a reaction to the post-war shrinking of the US film market, Hollywood made an

Figure 2.1 'The greatest, most sensational film of all times': advertisement for the Italian release of the Hammer *Dracula*.

agreement with Hammer to flood 'screens all around the world' with a 'wave' of movies showing horrifying images that TV could not show (Anonymous 1958a). Under this light, the demands to cut footage of Christopher Lee pushing a woman to the ground and lying in a coffin can be seen as something more than just the work of overzealous Christian Democrats concerned about wife-beating and the sanctity of Catholic funerary rituals. In all likelihood, by butchering a huge international money-maker, the Italian Film Censorship Office wanted to send out to powerful American distributors the message that sensationalist *films del terrore* were not welcome, and to discourage local imitations of the Anglo-American horror wave. In addition, a review in the December 1958–January 1959 issue of *Cinematografia d'oggi* advised Italian exhibitors against renting *Dracula*, as 'the acting performances, the dialogues and colour photography are of no use to this undoubtedly terrifying film' (Anonymous 1958–1959). A more emphatic urging for Italian exhibitors and moviegoers of Roman Catholic religion to stay away from Fisher's movie came from the Vatican film censorship office:

> *Dracula* is made with superficiality and ostentation of bad taste. It is difficult to see in a single film so many horrible things, disgusting scenes, sadistic and superstitious acts; all this in a morbid atmosphere that not even the blatant ingenuousness and absurdity of the plot manage to mitigate. Forbidden. (Centro Cattolico Cinematografico 1959a)

Faced with Christian Democracy's veiled threats and the Vatican's open ostracism, Universal organised the Italian premiere of *Dracula* two weeks before Christmas, from 12 to 17 December 1958, in two well-known *prima visione* theatres in Rome – one located in the heart of the city (Metropolitan Cinema) and one in a popular neighbourhood just outside the old-town centre (Capitol Cinema). Albeit generally received with sceptical (L. P. 1959; Lan. 1959; P. 1959; Vice 1959), if not downright scathing (Anonymous 1958b; Ghelli 1959; Verdone 1960), comments by Italian critics of all religious/political credos, mainly highlighting the film's vulgarity, lack of pathos and technical deficiencies, *Dracula* proved to be a box-office success during its premiere week (Ferraù 1958) and 1959 tour around the country. Since the Vatican ban would prevent the film from being screened in thousands of parish cinemas and provincial theatres owned/run by devout Catholics, the commercial exploitation of *Dracula* probably took place in the pricey, urban industrial circuit of *prima* and *seconda visione* theatres rather than in the deep market. Sustained by a creative advertising campaign adorning cinema foyers with candles, black drapes, funeral garlands and a cardboard coffin (De' Rossignoli 1961: 113), *Dracula* 'earned about 600 million lire, ranking as the twenty-eighth highest-grossing film at the Italian box-office in the 1958–1959 season' (Pezzotta 2014: 35) and launching a vampire craze that took the Italian media sphere by storm.

First, in the wake of *Dracula*'s release, newspapers started nicknaming any sex offender, burglar and juvenile delinquent a vampire (De' Rossignoli 1961: 349, 358–9). As for periodicals, by late 1960 virtually every magazine had published at least one article on vampirism, the specific subject dependant on the publication's area of expertise. For instance, showbiz monthly *Sipario* featured an article about youth gangs inspired by vampire movies and horror comics

(Magli 1959), while in medical magazine *Progressi di terapia* there was an article on physician John Polidori, author of *The Vampyre* (Anonymous 1960d). In this cultural climate 'radio drama *Vampiro*', featuring vampires being staked and dying screaming, was broadcast 'twice over the course of just two months' on Italian State Radio (De' Rossignoli 1961: 347). On Italian State TV, much more popular and closely controlled by censorship (Forgacs 1990: 108–16; Scaglioni 2015), monsters could only be played for laughs so comedians Ugo Tognazzi and Raimondo Vianello parodied Dracula during prime-time variety show *Un, due, tre* (De' Rossignoli 1961: 348). This was followed by veteran superstar of the Italian show business Renato Rascel performing a vampire skit during TV quiz show *Il musichiere*, as part of the promotional campaign for Steno's comedy of terrors *Tempi duri per i vampiri* (Della Casa and Giusti 2014: 85). The Italian music industry immediately jumped on the horror bandwagon too, thanks to composers Bruno Martino and Bruno Brighetti, who authored several tongue-in-cheek horror-themed songs (Magazù 1960). In particular, Martino's *Dracula cha-cha-cha* became a hit during summer 1959, spawned a 1960 French version and featured prominently in the soundtrack of both *Tempi duri per i vampiri* and Rome-set Hollywood drama *Two Weeks in Another Town* (Vincente Minnelli, 1962) (Curti 2015: 34). As for variety theatre, in 1959 a revue called *Un juke-box per Dracula* was put into production by vaudeville headliners Sandra Mondaini, Raimondo Vianello and Gino Bramieri, and achieved great success (Anonymous 1960a). Similar shows subsequently popped up in almost every theatre and music hall around the country, and even in night clubs of dubious fame (De' Rossignoli 1961: 351). But nowhere was Italy's vampire craze evident as in the publishing and film industries, that often joined forces to make money out of the horror trend.

As noted by Pezzotta (2014: 34–5) and Camilletti (2018: 41–8), in 1959 and 1960 Italian publishers flooded the market with horror literature, and especially with vampire stories. In July 1959 Milanese colossus Longanesi printed a new translation of Stoker's *Dracula*, updating the Italian editions of 1922 and 1945 mentioned in the Introduction. Although avoiding any reference to Hammer on the cover and in the preface, the title of the Longanesi edition was *Dracula il vampiro*, the one chosen by Universal for the Italian release of Fisher's film. The same thing happened in May 1966, when small, Milan-based publishing house Sugar reprinted the 1945 edition of Stoker's *Dracula*, put a picture of Lee on the cover and called the book *Dracula il Principe delle Tenebre*, a literal translation of the title of *Dracula: Prince of Darkness* (Terence Fisher, 1966), released in Italy in early 1966 as *Dracula, Principe delle Tenebre* (in January 1966 Longanesi had already reprinted its 1959 edition under the old title *Dracula il vampiro*). In 1960 three horror anthologies were published, among which was established Milanese publisher Feltrinelli's *I vampiri tra noi: 37 storie vampiriche*, edited by Ornella Volta and Valerio Riva, and boasting a preface by Roger Vadim in an attempt to cross-promote Vadim's in-the-making, *Carmilla*-inspired film *Il sangue e la rosa*. The trend continued into the 1960s, with book-length studies such as Emilio De' Rossignoli's *Io credo nei vampiri* (printed by improvised publisher Luciano Ferriani in 1961) and Volta's *Il vampiro* (published by Sugar in 1964, after the success of the original French-language edition of 1962), and with horror anthologies such as *Frankenstein and Company: prontuario di teratologia filmica* (edited by Volta and published by Sugar in 1965). Moreover, 'the success obtained at the Italian box-office by Fisher's *Dracula* in early 1959 [. . .] convinced a few "adventurous" small publishers based in Rome' and already active in the war, crime and sci-fi genres 'to print horror-themed pulp novels and distribute them in newspaper stands all over Italy' (Cozzi and Bissoli 2012: 9–10). These pulp novels were penned by Italian writers under English, German or French pseudonyms and tended to cannibalise the works of the renowned foreign authors translated and published by Milanese colossuses Mondadori, Rizzoli, Longanesi and Bompiani. As a result, the *KKK* and *I racconti di Dracula* series were born, in June 1959 and December 1959 respectively.

The *KKK* series, which kept publishing horror novels once or even twice a month until March 1972, was the brainchild of the Vicario brothers (Marco and Alfonso, owners of film production and distribution company Atlantica Cinematografica) and of journalist Leonia Celli, who, through their connections in the film business, started acquiring the screenplays of the foreign horror films to be distributed in Italy in the early 1960s. The deal was simple: the publisher got horror scripts for free from film distribution companies and sold novelisations of such screenplays; in return, film distributors obtained free pre-release advertising for their movies on the cover of the novels. Perhaps not coincidentally, the initial retail price of a *KKK* issue was 150 lire, just like the average film-ticket price in 1959–1960. The novelised films were not many though[1] and, besides the odd short story collection or novella by Poe, Robert Louis Stevenson, Wilkie Collins, Edward Bulwer-Lytton and Robert Bloch, the vast majority of *KKK* novels were horror potboilers (many of them featuring vampires) by Rome-based writers disguised under foreign-sounding aliases and getting from the Vicarios 60,000 lire per manuscript (Cozzi and Lombardi 2013: 17–155). On the other hand, the *I racconti di Dracula* monthly series, which went on until 1981, published only original novels penned by Italian writers under foreign pseudonyms earning 55,000 lire per manuscript. As the title implies, the main subjects were vampires, together with witches, ghosts, mad scientists and serial killers. According to the series' publisher Antonino Cantarella, a Sicilian baron with experience in film production, the pulp novels targeted commuters travelling by train, hence the cheap price (120 lire) and length-limit (125 pages) (Cozzi and Bissoli 2012: 9–24, 73–89).

Given the horror trend, another small Roman publisher, Editoriale Nova, decided to break new ground and import the horror genre into the then-flourishing *fotoromanzo* industry. Born to an immediate success in 1947, the *fotoromanzo* was a comic book of sorts, telling a story through written text (in captions and balloons) and black-and-white or colour images (a series of photographs specifically taken to match an original script, or stills taken from an existing movie). Whether based on an original script or adapting existing films, the plots of 1940s and 1950s *fotoromanzi* invariably revolved around star-crossed lovers, exotic adventures, biographies of saints and patriots (Sullerot [1970] 1977; De Berti 2000: 109–16; Bravo 2003: 13–66). As throughout the 1950s 'producing a *fotoromanzo* story to be printed in black-and-white cost less than 500,000 lire' (Anelli 1979: 86–7), in February 1961 Editoriale Nova's editor-in-chief Umberto Paolessi and journalist Giorgio Boschero – the latter also active as a writer for *I racconti di Dracula* under the pseudonym Joe H. Bosk (Cozzi and Bissoli 2012: 337) – launched a *fotoromanzo* series with colour covers and black-and-white pictures called *Malìa* ('evil spell, charm'), entirely devoted to horror stories and sold in newspaper stands for 100 lire per issue. Initially *Malìa* dealt mainly with vampire narratives written and photographed by the in-house editorial team. However, to cut the already-low black-and-white *fotoromanzo* production costs, agreements with Italian film distributors were soon struck and Editoriale Nova started using plots and stills from American, Mexican, British, French, Spanish and Italian horrors or thrillers dating from the 1940s to the mid-1960s. Italy's first horror *fotoromanzo* series was discontinued in February 1967 because the late 1960s saw an increase in paper and printing costs that expelled small publishers from the market (Anelli 1979: 86–7), and because of the progressive waning of the vampire craze to be discussed further below.

Naturally, in the wake of the Hammer *Dracula*'s success, Italian and American distributors started importing in Italy as many foreign vampire films as possible. The Italian Film Censorship Office reacted by issuing bans, with the result of preventing *The Leech Woman* (Edward Dein, 1960) and a few other low-budget vampire exploits from circulation, because the aforementioned distributors generally did not have the time and/or the money to appeal the pronouncement, edit a new version and have it reviewed a second time (Curti and Di Rocco 2014: 78). In a period in which very old films like the 1941 *Dr. Jekyll and Mr. Hyde* were being re-released (see ads in the late-1958 and early-1959 issues of *Cinematografia d'oggi*), the less wealthy among Italian distributors circumvented state bans by unearthing Italian-dubbed prints of horror-themed Hollywood B-movies from the 1940s and re-releasing them under new titles containing the buzzword 'Dracula'.[2] The foreign vampire films from the late 1950s and early 1960s approved for public screening in Italy were all forbidden to minors, generally after the removal of truculent shots from the trailers[3] and, in some cases, from the movies themselves, as the Italian Film Censorship

Office was against bloody violence and graphic depictions of staking in particular.[4] It is thus that Steno's *Tempi duri per i vampiri* – the first attempt by Italian film producers to cash in on the Hammer *Dracula* – was not a horror proper but used Gothic clichés for laughs according to a tradition that, as we have seen in the Introduction, dated back at least to Giuseppe Palomba's 1812 opera buffa *Vampiri* and Angelo Brofferio's 1827 comedy *Il vampiro*.

Italian vampire cinema from 1959 to 1965

If the most fantastic and gruesome scenes of Freda's *I vampiri* were discarded by the producers in favour of a police-investigation subplot (see the Introduction), the screenwriters of *Tempi duri per i vampiri* went even further in the rejection of straightforward horror. Aware of the meagre receipts gathered by *I vampiri* on the domestic market, Steno and his collaborators decided to parody Hammer's box-office hit, moving the bloodthirsty aristocrat from Mitteleuropa to the *bel paese* and adding vaudeville actor and singer Renato Rascel's slapstick antics, which were repeatedly proven successful at the Italian box office throughout the 1950s, most recently in gangster-film spoof *Rascel-fifì* (Guido Leoni, 1957) and war-movie spoof *Rascel marine* (Guido Leoni, 1958). As a matter of fact, ever since the commercial success of *Fifa e arena* (Mario Mattoli, 1948) – a parody of *Blood and Sand* (Rouben Mamoulian, 1941) starring vaudeville headliner Totò – it became a common strategy for Italian film producers to hire popular theatre comedians (e.g., Ugo Tognazzi, Raimondo Vianello and Walter Chiari in the 1950s and early 1960s, and Franco Franchi and Ciccio Ingrassia in the 1960s and early 1970s) to parody Italian or foreign box-office hits (D'Amico 1985: 53–73, 91–6, 136–43; Menarini 2001: 16–25, 57–65).

Adopting the Ultrascope-Ferraniacolor-Technicolor format, and appropriating elements from the then-booming summer holiday *filone* of Italian film comedy (featuring bikini-clad beauties in gorgeous Italian sceneries and centred on characters 'looking for love, or at least a fling') (Fullwood 2015: 76),[5] *Tempi duri per i vampiri* went into production in spring 1959, with a sixty-two-day shooting schedule including location shoot in the Ligurian Riviera. Film direction was entrusted to Steno, who could boast a long experience in movie parodies as a writer of the Gothic-tinged detective-film spoof *C'è un fantasma nel castello* (Giorgio Simonelli, 1942) and the aforementioned *Fifa e arena*, and as a writer and director of sci-fi spoof *Totò nella Luna* (Stefano Vanzina as Steno, 1958). The estimated budget of *Tempi duri per i vampiri* was 257 million lire, which Italian production companies CEI-Incom, Mountfluor Films and Maxima Film planned to cover with a state loan of 140 million lire and an investment of 117 million lire (CEI-Incom also was the film's distributor and the owner of the studio where interiors were to be shot). Rascel was cast as the male lead for 30 million lire, while recently risen international horror star Christopher Lee and *Le fatiche di Ercole*'s female lead Sylva Koscina were hired for 3 and 3.5 million lire respectively, in the small roles of vampire Baron Roderico of Bramfürten and a rich tourist. The idea was that of making a timidly transnational product, as testified by the investment-recoup plan that the producers submitted to the Italian Show Business Bureau: Italian box-office receipts and tax refunds would grant a minimum income of 250 million lire, and selling the film abroad would yield a minimum return of 40 million lire. While little is known about foreign sales,[6] the plan certainly worked on the domestic market, as *Tempi duri per i vampiri* ended up costing 192 million lire (post-production included) and was a hit in the *prima visione* circuit between October 1959 and January 1960 (Anonymous 1960e), which led to another horror parody being rushed into production by CEI-Incom, *Il mio amico Jekyll / My Friend, Dr. Jekyll* (Marino Girolami, 1960), starring Ugo Tognazzi and Raimondo Vianello.

A sustained production of vampire horrors started in late 1959, when Bruno Bolognesi's tiny, improvised production company Consorzio Italiano Films decided to make *L'amante del vampiro* to capitalise on the Hammer *Dracula*'s success in Italy and around the world. As reported by screenwriter Ernesto Gastaldi,[7] *L'amante del vampiro* cost around 40 million lire and was financed through *minimo garantito* by a regional distributor. Additional money was brought by actors Walter Bigari and Gino Turini on the condition that they would play leading roles. The casting of French actress Hélène Rémy suggests that Bolognesi either presold or hoped to sell the movie in France, where Fisher's *Dracula* was enjoying a huge box-office success and critical praise among cinephile circles (Boullet 1962; Caen 1962; Le Bris 1962a and 1962b; Tavernier 1963). *L'amante del vampiro* was shot over the course of three weeks in December 1959, with a cast including friends and lovers of director Renato Polselli and the production team. Given the shoestring budget, cast and crew never set foot in the Istituto Nazionale Luce studio mentioned in the opening credits, and spent three weeks living in a small hotel close to the real-life location where interior scenes were shot, Palazzo Borghese in Artena – a cost-cutting strategy that would soon become typical of the Gothic horror *filone*.

Indeed, *L'ultima preda del vampiro* was produced in summer 1960 by Nord Film Italiana under very similar circumstances. Written and directed by *I vampiri*'s co-scenarist Piero Regnoli, the film was mainly shot on location in and around Palazzo Borghese, recycling props and artistic and technical cast from *L'amante del vampiro*. In the documents submitted to the Italian Show Business Bureau, the production company declared a four-week shooting schedule and an estimated budget of 50 million lire covered by the Italian distributor's *minimo garantito* (20 million lire), by an investment from Nord Film Italiana (7 million lire) and by an unspecified financier (15 million lire). The rest came from Regnoli (4.7 million lire), leading actor Bigari (1 million lire) and production managers Umberto Borsato and Tiziano Longo (2.3 million lire) in exchange for a share of the future profits. In the end the film cost about 37 million lire (post-production included), more or less the salary that Rascel got to star in *Tempi duri per i vampiri*.

Between Polselli's and Regnoli's ultra-low-budget efforts, three much more professional vampire films were made in Italy in the wake of *Dracula*'s international success: Vadim's *Il sangue e la rosa* (put into production in November 1959), Giorgio Ferroni's *Il mulino delle donne di pietra* (shot in February–March 1960) and Mario Bava's *La maschera del demonio* (shot over the course of an alleged six weeks in spring 1960). With a budget of 340 and 161 million lire respectively (post-production and publicity excluded), *Il sangue e la rosa* and *Il mulino delle donne di pietra* were Italo–French co-productions aiming to craft a spectacular product to be distributed internationally. Specifically, *Carmilla*-inspired *Il sangue e la rosa* was a fifty–fifty co-production between Rome-based Documento Film and French producer Raymond Eger, with Documento Film's 170 million lire mainly coming from a 93-million-lira *minimo garantito* by Paramount (which took care of distribution in Italy) and from 62-million-lira-worth pre-sales to foreign distributors. Shot at Cinecittà studios and in the Roman countryside, the movie boasted: (1) the screenwriter-director who married and divorced Brigitte Bardot, and made her an international sex symbol with worldwide box-office hit *Et Dieu . . . créa la femme / . . . And God Created Woman* (Roger Vadim, 1956); (2) scope and Technicolor photography; (3) Hollywood actor Mel Ferrer and Italian model/actress Elsa Martinelli. Similarly transnational but less lavish a production, *Il mulino delle donne di pietra* made use of Eastmancolor photography (a process much cheaper than Technicolor), widescreen ratio and a cast of Italian, French and German talents to tell a story mixing *I vampiri*'s scientific vampires, the mad sculptor from Michael Curtiz's *Mystery of the Wax Museum* and André De Toth's *House of Wax*, the mad surgeon from *Les yeux sans visage / Eyes without a Face* (Georges Franju, 1960) and the Gothic atmospheres of both Hammer and Carl Theodor Dreyer's *Vampyr*. 30 per cent of the total budget came from French investors, who paid for French actors and location shooting in the Netherlands, while the rest of the money came from an investment by Italian production company Wanguard Film and its associates, plus a 40-million-lira *minimo garantito* and 20 million lire given on credit by the Cinecittà studios where the film was shot.

On the contrary, Bava's directorial debut *La maschera del demonio* was a '100% Italian' production – its title probably meant to echo *House of Wax*'s and *The Curse of Frankenstein*'s Italian-release titles *La maschera di cera* and *La maschera di Frankenstein*. The first treatment penned by Bava, titled *Il Vij* and dated 1 September 1959, called for a faithful adaptation of Nikolaj Gogol's 1835 short story *The Vij* nestled in a 1950s-set frame story about a newlywed couple lost in the woods (Gomarasca et al. 2004: 20), but over the course of many revisions the story-within-a-story structure was dropped, the original evil gnome was turned into a female vampire-witch and the plot changed accordingly, until it bore very little resemblance to Gogol's tale. The film was produced by tiny production company Jolly Film and producer-distributor Galatea, which after the success of its B-movie *Le fatiche di Ercole* had been specialising in pepla and low-cost rip-offs of successful foreign genre films, including Freda's sci-fi/horror hybrid *Caltiki il mostro immortale*, an imitation of *The Quatermass Xperiment* (Val Guest, 1955), *X the Unknown* (Leslie Norman, 1956) and *The Blob* (Irvin S. Yeaworth Jr., 1958) made for a mere 110 million lire (post-production and publicity included). As a result, *La maschera del demonio* was shot in black-and-white at Titanus studio rather than in colour at the more prestigious Cinecittà studios like *Il sangue e la rosa* and *Il mulino delle donne di pietra*. Yet, *La maschera del demonio* was made less quickly and less cheaply than usual for Galatea's standards. According to Venturini (2001: 138), for the sake of perfecting dolly shots, widescreen compositions and lighting, the production granted Bava an extra week of shooting and the initial budget of 100 million lire (post-production and publicity included) was raised to 145 million lire. As declared in the financial plan submitted to the Italian Show Business Bureau, such money came from a 65-million-lira investment by Galatea (60 million lire were *minimo garantito* by Italian distributor UNIDIS), on top of which an 80-million-lira state loan was requested.

After the Italian Gothic horror production boom of 1960, Bava's colour triptych *I tre volti della paura* and Antonio Margheriti's black-and-white supernatural love story *Danza macabra* were the only vampire horrors from the early 1960s that enjoyed a decent budget. Planned as a 333-million-lira seventy–thirty co-production between Italy (100 million lire from Emmepi Cinematografica and Galatea, plus a 160-million-lira state loan) and France (Galatea's French subsidiary Société Cinématographique Lyre), *I tre volti della paura* was actually made for about 206 million lire (post-production and publicity excluded), while eighty–twenty Italo–French co-production *Danza macabra* cost 190 million lire (post-production and publicity excluded), with 44 million lire by Parisian company Leo-Lax Film, a 50-million-lira *minimo garantito* from Italian distributor Lux and an investment by producer Giovanni Addessi's near-bankrupt company Vulsinia Film. In both cases, the biggest cheques were written to rent facilities and equipment, and to hire well-known foreign actors (15.6 million lire for Boris Karloff and 2.8 million lire for Mark Damon in *I tre volti della paura*; 8 million lire for Barbara Steele and 7 million lire for Georges Rivière in *Danza macabra*), while the shooting process was heavily based on artisanal skills leading to massive time and cost savings. *I tre volti della paura*, for instance, was almost entirely shot in Titanus studio and its episode *I Wurdalak*, adapting Aleksey Tolstoy's 1839 vampire novella *La famille du Vourdalak*, recycled the crypt-set from *La maschera del demonio* (Pezzotta 2013: 57–8). *Danza macabra*, on the other hand, exploited existing sets from a period film of Addessi's that had been finished before schedule, and it was shot at breakneck speed over the course of fifteen days using multiple-camera setups for each scene (Margheriti, quoted in Fazzini 2004: 50–1).

All the other vampire horrors from the early 1960s – Roberto Mauri's *La strage dei vampiri*, Freda's *L'orribile segreto del Dr. Hichcock*, Camillo Mastrocinque's *La cripta e l'incubo*, Polselli's *Il mostro dell'Opera*, Mario Caiano's *Amanti d'oltretomba* and Massimo Pupillo's *La vendetta di Lady Morgan* – followed the Polselli–Regnoli mode of production instead. That is to say, they were financed mainly through *minimo garantito* and shot in real-life locations because the producers had rented the cheapest Italian film studios only to obtain the Italian-nationality certificate and connected benefits. Costing 96 and 141 million lire respectively (post-production included), *L'orribile segreto del Dr. Hichcock* and *La cripta e l'incubo* were the most expensive films in the group, undoubtedly because the former made use of Barbara Steele, Robert Flemyng and Technicolor photography, and the latter cast Christopher Lee in a 12-million-lira supporting role.

L'orribile segreto del Dr. Hichcock is another collaboration between Freda and producers Ermanno Donati and Luigi Carpentieri, who in the early 1960s had renamed their company Panda Cinematografica and had started making pepla (Di Chiara 2009: 137–8). Given Alfred Hitchcock's enormous popularity in Italy, due to the broadcast of *Alfred Hitchcock Presents* on Italian State TV since January 1959 and the Italian release of worldwide hit *Psycho* (Alfred Hitchcock, 1960) in the 1960–1961 season, Donati and Carpentieri commissioned Ernesto Gastaldi the script for a Hitchcockian thriller cum necrophiliac twist and hired Freda to direct it as fast as possible in a Roman villa (Curti 2017a: 177–89). According to the financial plan submitted by Donati and Carpentieri to the Italian Show Business Bureau, the budget consisted mostly of *minimo garantito* from distributor Warner Bros. (75 million lire), plus 35 million lire from 'banks, suppliers, associates and third parties'.

Carmilla-inspired *La cripta e l'incubo* was a seventy–thirty Italo–Spanish co-production that exploited the appeal of horror star Lee to obtain a substantial *minimo garantito*, and then proceeded to relegate him in a minor role to keep the budget as low as possible. Indeed, according to *La cripta e l'incubo*'s financial plan, most of the money came from a deal with an Italian distributor (Imperialcine or UNIDIS) and from an investment by Italian production company MEC Cinematografica, which was itself probably a distributor able to secure some advance money from partner theatres at the regional level. With this money and the Spanish quota, the film was shot with great economy 'on an existing natural set, in and around the Castle Piccolomini in Balsorano, [. . .] cast and crew also accommodated in the [. . .] manor in order to cut costs' (Curti 2015: 129).

Adopting MEC Cinematografica's strategy, regional distributor Carlo Caiano founded production company Cinematografica Emmeci and tried to persuade the Italian Show Business Bureau to greenlight a European co-production to finance his son Mario's *Amanti d'oltretomba*, starring Steele reprising her double role of ingénue and vengeful revenant from *La maschera del demonio*. Upon several rejections, Cinematografica Emmeci eventually resigned to have the movie shot at breakneck speed in Villa Parisi in Frascati, on an investment of 81 million lire (post-production and publicity included).[8] Made in the same year, *La vendetta di Lady Morgan* cost a little more (86 million lire, post-production and publicity included), was almost entirely shot in and around Castle Chigi in Rome and ended up being the one and only film tiny company Morgan Film produced during its brief existence. The other two vampire horrors – *La strage dei vampiri* and *Il mostro dell'Opera* – were both produced by regional distributors and shot in spring–summer 1961, for 52 and 62.5 million lire respectively (post-production included). Inexpensive film studios were hired by the production companies but hardly, if ever, used: the former movie was shot in and around a real-life castle in Lazio, while the latter, a fusion of the Hammer *Dracula* and Gaston Leroux's 1909–1910 novel *The Phantom of the Opera*, was mostly shot in a real-life theatre in Umbria.

In order to maximise profits in times of vampire craze, some pepla set the bloodsuckers against popular musclemen Ercole (*Ercole al centro della Terra* and *Ercole contro Moloch*), Maciste (*Maciste contro il vampiro* and *Maciste e la regina di Samar*) and the like (*Roma contro Roma*). SPA Cinematografica's *Ercole al centro della Terra* borrowed its title from *Journey to the Center of the Earth* (Henry Levin, 1959) and, inspired by *Tempi duri per i vampiri*, paid Lee 3.4 million lire to play the small role of a bloodthirsty usurper from Hades. Thanks to the combined appeal of horror star Lee and the huge popularity of historical-mythological films in Italy and abroad, the film secured a 107-million-lira advance from Italian and German distributors, and was subsequently shot, edited, dubbed and launched with great economy, for a total 169 million lire (17.4 of which went to English bodybuilder Reg Park for playing Ercole). *Ercole al centro della Terra* was to be titled *Ercole contro i vampiri* (Continenza and Tessari 1961), but film company Ambrosiana Cinematografica registered the title *Maciste contro il vampiro* first and then managed to shoot and release a vampire-themed peplum before SPA Cinematografica. *Maciste contro il vampiro* made up for the absence of Hammer's Dracula by casting American Gordon Scott – the popular 1950s Tarzan – as Maciste (12.3 million lire), and by greatly investing in a Middle-East-like setting inspired to *Il ladro di Bagdad / The Thief of Baghdad* (Bruno Vailati, Arthur Lubin, 1961). *Maciste contro il vampiro* cost 330 million lire (post-production included), covered by *minimo garantito* (from distributor Dino De Laurentiis, in whose state-of-the-art Dinocittà studios the film was partly shot), deferred payments to Italian and Yugoslavian suppliers and a hefty state loan (Ambrosiana

Cinematografica asked for 260 million lire in its 450-million-lira financial plan). The other three vampire-themed pepla were all made for about 140–160 million lire each (post-production and publicity included): Gordon Scott vehicle *Ercole contro Moloch* and *Maciste e la regina di Samar* were seventy–thirty Italo–French co-productions (the Italian part of the budget mainly came from *minimo garantito* and foreign pre-sales), while Galatea – the company that found the gold lode of peplum in 1957–1958 and was bound to disappear with the production crisis of 1964–1965 (Venturini 2001: 14–33) – patched *Roma contro Roma* together with footage from its previous pepla and a plot centred on political conspirators worshipping a vampire goddess (as usual for Galatea, money mostly came from Italian distribution and state credit).

In 1966 the production of vampire films (horror or otherwise) stopped in Italy, to be resumed only in 1969. Besides the general decrease in Italian film production after record year 1964, this was due to the intertwining of national and international factors. As for national factors, the hypothesis that the Italian government used its powers to prevent vampire movies from being made in Italy is to be discarded. First, although much derided for their lack of originality and verisimilitude at the preventive-censorship stage,[9] all the vampire movies that asked for the Italian-nationality certificate were greenlit by the Italian Show Business Bureau. If comments on excessively gruesome screenplays were made by government officials, as in the case of *Il mulino delle donne di pietra*, a reassuring letter signed by production delegates was enough to get the shooting started.[10] Second, as far as the Italian Film Censorship Office was concerned, only *L'amante del vampiro* – the first, non-parodic *Dracula* rip-off – was hindered, as the censors granted it a VM16 rating only after the removal of 'all the close-ups of the vampire', which were judged 'truce and repugnant' (Nullaosta 31701 1960). *Tempi duri per i vampiri* and the vampire-themed pepla got an all-ages-admitted rating, like almost every parody and muscleman film that preceded them. The other vampire films were simply rated as forbidden to minors (VM16 if the film was made before 1962; VM14 or VM18 after a new rating system was implemented with law 161 of 21 April 1962). Cuts were asked only in relation to female nudity,[11] which would have happened to any movie in 1950s and early-1960s Italy, regardless of genre and country of origin, while prints of Italian films destined to foreign markets were allowed to be much more sexually explicit, as shown by the French versions of *L'ultima preda del vampiro* and *Danza macabra* (Piselli and Guidotti 1989: 88; Piselli et al. 1996: 73, 81, 88; Gomarasca et al. 2002: 41). In view of all this, the national factors behind the interruption of vampire film production in Italy from 1966 to 1968 included should be sought in market dynamics rather than in state intervention.

Since in the post-1949 Italian film industry distribution normally fed production, the analysis should start from box-office figures.[12]

Table 2.1 Censorship and box-office data for 1956–1965 Italian vampire films.

Title	Italian Film Censorship Office rating	Vatican censorship rating	Release period (distributor)	Box-office gross in lire
I vampiri	VM16 (Nullaosta 23894 1957)	Adults only, with reservations (Centro Cattolico Cinematografico 1957)	April 1957-March 1964 (Titanus)	125,261,762 (Rondolino and Levi 1967: 128)
Tempi duri per i vampiri	All ages admitted (Nullaosta 30310 1959)	Forbidden (Centro Cattolico Cinematografico 1959b)	October 1959-March 1964 (CEI-Incom)	530,445,618 (Rondolino and Levi 1967: 151)
L'amante del vampiro	VM16 (Nullaosta 31701 1960)	Forbidden (Centro Cattolico Cinematografico 1960a)	May 1960-March 1964 (Rome International Films)	104,590,561 (Rondolino and Levi 1967: 156)
Il mulino delle donne di pietra	VM16 (Nullaosta 32613 1960)	Forbidden (Centro Cattolico Cinematografico 1960b)	August 1960-March 1964 (Cino Del Duca)	159,588,021 (Rondolino and Levi 1967: 164)
La maschera del demonio	VM16 (Nullaosta 32584 1960)	Forbidden (Centro Cattolico Cinematografico 1961a)	August 1960-March 1963 (UNIDIS)	137,673,316 (Rondolino and Levi 1967: 173)
Il sangue e la rosa	VM16 (Nullaosta 33435 1960)	Forbidden (Centro Cattolico Cinematografico 1961c)	January 1961-March 1964 (Paramount)	207,228,361 (Rondolino and Levi 1967: 168–9)
L'ultima preda del vampiro	VM16 (Nullaosta 33364 1960)	Forbidden (Centro Cattolico Cinematografico 1960c)	November 1960-March 1964 (Film Selezione)	72,193,134 (Rondolino and Levi 1967: 221)

(Continued)

Title	Italian Film Censorship Office rating	Vatican censorship rating	Release period (distributor)	Box-office gross in lire
Maciste contro il vampiro	All ages admitted (Nullaosta 35277 1961)	Not recommended (Centro Cattolico Cinematografico 1961b)	August 1961-March 1964 (Dino De Laurentiis)	495,006,611 (Rondolino and Levi 1967: 187)
Ercole al centro della Terra	All ages admitted (Nullaosta 35906 1961)	Adults only (Centro Cattolico Cinematografico 1962b)	November 1961-March 1964 (Imperialcine)	397,623,049 (Rondolino and Levi 1967: 185)
La strage dei vampiri	VM16 (Nullaosta 36600 1962)	Forbidden (Centro Cattolico Cinematografico 1962a)	February 1962-March 1964 (regional distribution)	36,205,638 (Rondolino and Levi 1967: 219)
L'orribile segreto del Dr. Hichcock	VM18 (Nullaosta 37710 1962)	Not recommended (Centro Cattolico Cinematografico 1962c)	June 1962-March 1964 (Warner Bros.)	139,011,326 (Rondolino and Levi 1967: 219)
Ercole contro Moloch	All ages admitted (Nullaosta 41880 1963)	Morally mature adults only (Centro Cattolico Cinematografico 1964a)	December 1963-June 1965 (Euro International Films)	254,599,067 (Rondolino and Levi 1967: 259)
I tre volti della paura	VM14 (Nullaosta 40988 1963)	Forbidden (Centro Cattolico Cinematografico 1963)	August 1963-March 1964 (Warner Bros.)	103,503,195 (Rondolino and Levi 1967: 248)
Roma contro Roma	All ages admitted (Nullaosta 42091 1964)	Adults only, with reservations (Centro Cattolico Cinematografico 1964b)	February 1964-June 1965 (Cineriz)	102,285,381 (Rondolino and Levi 1967: 266)

Title	Italian Film Censorship Office rating	Vatican censorship rating	Release period (distributor)	Box-office gross in lire
Danza macabra	VM18 (Nullaosta 40624 1963)	Forbidden (Centro Cattolico Cinematografico, 1965b)	February 1964–June 1965 (Globe Films International)	100,673,013 (Rondolino and Levi 1967: 257)
Maciste e la regina di Samar	All ages admitted (Nullaosta 43266 1964)	Adults only (Centro Cattolico Cinematografico 1965a)	June 1964–? (Atlantis Film)	219,721,000 (Baroni 1995: 128)
La cripta e l'incubo	VM14 (Nullaosta 42808 1964)	Not recommended (Centro Cattolico Cinematografico 1964c)	May 1964–June 1965 (regional distribution)	49,127,896 (Rondolino and Levi 1967: 257)
Il mostro dell'Opera	VM18 (Nullaosta 43135 1964)	Forbidden (Centro Cattolico Cinematografico 1968)	June 1964–? (regional distribution)	7,476,000 (Baroni 1995: 139)
Amanti d'oltretomba	VM18 (Nullaosta 45399 1965)	Forbidden (Centro Cattolico Cinematografico 1965c)	July 1965–December 1965 (regional distribution)	20,559,000 (Rondolino and Levi 1967: 272)
La vendetta di Lady Morgan	VM14 (Nullaosta 45744 1965)	Forbidden (Centro Cattolico Cinematografico 1966)	December 1965–? (INDIEF)	61,000,000 (Baroni 1995: 162)

PART I THE INDUSTRIAL CONTEXT

Evidently, only the movies in which vampires were a surplus attraction in an already-tested winning formula became a commercial success, that is to say managed to gather box-office receipts that – after taxes and the exhibitors' and distributors' shares – exceeded production costs: Renato Rascel star vehicle *Tempi duri per i vampiri* and pepla (with the exception of *Roma contro Roma*, which was released when the *filone* was already waning due to oversupply). As for vampire horrors, none managed to replicate the 600-million-lira success of the Hammer *Dracula*. *L'amante del vampiro*, *L'ultima preda del vampiro* and *L'orribile segreto del Dr. Hichcock* might have turned out to be slightly profitable on the domestic market but, if this actually happened, it was due more to the meagreness of production investments than to the greatness of box-office returns. All the other vampire horrors failed to break even and make profit upon their release on the Italian market. The case of *Il mostro dell'Opera* – submitted to the Italian Film Censorship Office and released in 1964, but shot in spring 1961 under the title *Il vampiro dell'Opera* – sums it up pretty well. With its belated release due to producer Ferdinando Anselmetti's financial problems, its title change and its box-office fiasco, the film shows that, after the 1959–1961 vampire craze, Italian audiences' 'interest in Dracula's makeshifts had waned' and 'native bloodsuckers did not take root: Dracula worked much better as a trademark' for pulp novels and *fotoromanzi* (Curti 2015: 135), as the butt of the joke in Italian State TV's advertising show *Carosello* (see for instance the 1965 commercial *L'ispettore Bramiè: La fine del vampiro*), or as a stage costume for beat/rock band I Corvi.

True, in most cases the producers-organisers of Italian vampire horrors had already made their profit by appropriating part of the *minimo garantito* and state loans. Not to mention the fact that financial risk could be cushioned via European co-production agreements and, in the Andreotti system, the producers of certified-Italian films could count on both transferable dubbing-fee waivers and tax rebates on domestic box-office receipts for extra earnings. Yet, the key question posed by the above box-office data remains: why distributors kept on feeding the production of Italian vampire horrors if, ever since *I vampiri*, such movies repeatedly proved at best mediocrely successful at the Italian box office? Given the films' production history previously outlined, one could say that distributors-financiers were gambling little money since the *minimo garantito* corresponds to the minimum amount of net box-office receipts that a distributor expects to make from a given film. However, from the businessman's point of view, this kind of speculation involving products with limited appeal on the domestic market – and excluded from circulation in the vast parish cinema circuit by the Vatican censorship – was quite risky, as distributors-financiers had to wait years for their films to pass from *prima* to *terza visione* theatres in order to finally get low box-office receipts and therefore very little tax refunds from the state.[13]

To paraphrase what has been written about the Gothic horror *filone* as a whole (Pironi 1977; Troiano 1985 and 1989; Mora 1986; Della Casa 1990, 2000 and 2001c; Pitassio 2005), within the context of the Italian film industry, the early-1960s vampire horrors were a marginal phenomenon in terms of number of films made, and inconsequential in terms of box-office receipts. Contrary to pepla and, after 1964, spaghetti westerns – which sold countless tickets in both Italy and the world market – Italian horrors were 'domestic films made for export' (Di Chiara 2016b), in view of their release in continental Europe (mainly Francophone and German-speaking countries) and in the American drive-in circuit and syndicated TV. In the latter case, as explained by Lucas (2007: 281–328), *La maschera del demonio* was a trailblazing movie. Picked up for North American distribution by American International Pictures after a promotional screening in Rome, Bava's directorial debut was shortened, redubbed and rescored by AIP, and released in US theatres as *Black Sunday*, in February 1961, in the wake of the success of Fisher's *Dracula* and AIP's own Poe cycle. Having quickly become the highest-grossing film of the season for AIP, *Black Sunday* led to several production-distribution agreements being struck between the American company and Galatea. In fact Galatea later financed *I tre volti della paura* with money from AIP's UK-based subsidiary Alta Vista (Arkoff 1995: 20; Heffernan 2004: 134–53; Pezzotta 2013: 57–62; Curti 2015: 78–86), and it is possible that AIP was also behind *Roma contro Roma* as Galatea's vampire-themed peplum was released theatrically and on syndicated TV in the US by AIP.[14] More generally, the US success of both the late-1950s Hammer Gothic and *Black Sunday* encouraged American independent distributors and TV syndicators to buy at fixed price and often rework *I vampiri*, *L'amante del vampiro*, *Il mulino delle donne di pietra* (whose foreign-distribution rights were owned by Galatea), *L'ultima preda del vampiro*, *La strage dei vampiri*, *L'orribile segreto del Dr. Hichcock*, *La cripta e l'incubo*, *Danza macabra* and other non-vampiric Italian horrors (Heffernan 2004: 229–61; see also most of the entries in Curti 2015) – one-off payments in US dollars providing Italian producers-organisers and distributors-financiers with ample margins for profit given the exiguity of production costs.

This is exactly what kept Italian horror cinema (vampire-themed or otherwise) alive from the early 1960s to the half of the decade, and also the main reason why Italian producers repeatedly cast English-speaking, internationally bankable stars such as Lee and Steele. After 1965, when in view of ever-shrinking profits AIP decided to end its Poe cycle and Hammer's 1966 *Dracula: Prince of Darkness* failed to become a worldwide smash hit like its 1958 predecessor, Italian horror producers saw a contraction in their foreign end markets and production was halted. Equally crucially, as Curti (2011: 44–5) remarks, by early 1966 the extraordinary domestic gross and very good sales in Spain and West Germany of Sergio Leone's *Per un pugno di dollari* convinced

Italian production and distribution companies of all sizes to dive into another *filone*, the spaghetti western. In Italy, the waning interest in horror films on the Anglophone market contributed to the disappearance of both Galatea, at the forefront of fantastic cinema ever since 1957–1958, and the *Malìa* series, which between 1961 and 1966 had published several *fotoromanzi* based on AIP's Poe cycle and on the made-for-export Italian Gothic horrors of 1960–1965. As for the *KKK* and *I racconti di Dracula* series, which would remain in business until 1972 and 1981 respectively, from around 1963 their stories started dealing more and more with sex crimes and serial killers rather than with Gothic paraphernalia (Cozzi and Bissoli 2012: 11–23; Cozzi and Lombardi 2013: 81–155), testifying to the fact that the vampire craze in Italy ended even before Hammer put the 1966 Dracula-sequel into production.

Italian vampire cinema from 1969 to 1975

The production of vampire films involving Italian companies restarted in 1969 with thirty–thirty–forty Italo–Spanish–West German co-production *Il Conte Dracula*, made for 346 million lire between the Eastern coast of Spain, Munich and Tirrenia studios in Tuscany (for Italian production company Filmar the estimated budget of 317 million lire rose unexpectedly due to a dramatic devaluation of lira in 1970–1971 and bankruptcy was the inevitable next step). A self-proclaimed faithful adaptation of Stoker's novel, *Il Conte Dracula* was directed by Spaniard Jesús Franco and starred Christopher Lee, who got 30 million lire for the trouble of finding time in his busy schedule. After that, six Italian films tapping into the vampire mythology would make use of co-production agreements in order to cushion financial risks, pool artistic resources and provide a spectacular product that could sell well in both continental Europe and the Anglophone market: Aldo Lado's *La corta notte delle bambole di vetro* (Italy, Yugoslavia, West Germany), Margheriti's *Nella stretta morsa del ragno* (Italy, France, West Germany), Ferroni's *La notte dei diavoli* (Italy, Spain), Jorge Grau's *Le vergini cavalcano la morte* (Italy, Spain), Alain Jessua's *L'uomo che uccideva a sangue freddo* (Italy, France) and Paul Morrissey's *Dracula cerca sangue di vergine . . . e morì di sete!!!* (Italy, France).

Little can be written about the production of *La corta notte delle bambole di vetro*, as the film's file is missing from the Italian Show Business Bureau fonds at the Archivio Centrale dello Stato in Rome. According to Lado (quoted in Švábenický 2014: 34–40), his directorial debut *La corta notte delle bambole di vetro* was produced by Italian Enzo Doria, who by the early 1970s had specialised in supporting young, aspiring or emerging filmmakers like Marco Bellocchio, Silvano Agosti, Salvatore Samperi and Liliana Cavani. For Prague-set *La corta notte delle bambole di vetro* Doria's help was crucial to find Yugoslavian partners to obtain the permission to shoot in Eastern Europe, mostly in Zagreb and Ljubljana (very few scenes were shot in Italian studios, which were rented just to obtain the Italian-nationality certificate). Similarly scarce are the information about *Le vergini cavalcano la morte* and *L'uomo che uccideva a sangue freddo*, because the Italian production companies involved were minority partners whose main input was the payment of a *minimo garantito* to secure distribution rights in Italy: as for *Le vergini cavalcano la morte*, the Italian investment covered 30 per cent of the 154-million-lira final cost; as for *L'uomo che uccideva a sangue freddo*, Italian distribution colossus Medusa Distribuzione covered 20 per cent of the 870-million-lira final cost. More details are available on the other three co-productions *Nella stretta morsa del ragno*, *La notte dei diavoli* and *Dracula cerca sangue di vergine . . . e morì di sete!!!*.

As reported in official documents, *Nella stretta morsa del ragno* was a sixty–twenty–twenty Italo–French–West German co-production put together by Produzione DC7, a company owned by the Addessi brothers, Furio and Raffaele. The estimated budget for the forty-one-day shooting in Dinocittà studios was almost 430 million lire, but the actual cost of the movie cannot be determined due to the Addessi brothers' failure to submit the cost statement to the Italian Show Business Bureau (Produzione DC7 went bankrupt in 1973). The works of Lippi and Codelli (1976: 178) and Palmerini and Mistretta (1996: 73) help us to reconstruct the history of this troubled co-production. In the late 1960s Margheriti teamed up with then-retired producer Giovanni Addessi (father of Furio and Raffaele, who acted as front men only) and with German actor-producer Peter Carsten to cash in on the spaghetti western trend, and made the relatively successful *E Dio disse a Caino . . . / And God Said to Cain* (Antonio Margheriti as Anthony Dawson, 1969), starring Carsten and Klaus Kinski. After the box-office fiasco of the Margheriti-Carsten co-production *L'inafferrabile invincibile Mr. Invisibile / Mr. Superinvisible* (Antonio Margheriti as Anthony M. Dawson, 1970), Margheriti found himself in financial troubles and was convinced by Giovanni Addessi to direct *Nella stretta morsa del ragno*, a colour remake of *Danza macabra* starring Carsten and Kinski among others.

Slovenia-set *La notte dei diavoli*, on the other hand, was shot in about one month, mostly in real-life locations in the Lazio region, around the Bracciano lake. The movie cost almost 162 million lire, 70 per cent of which came from a 30-million-lira *minimo garantito* by Italian distributors, and from the funds of Italian production companies Filmes Cinematografica and Due Emme Cinematografica (the latter co-owned by Roberto Maldera, who not coincidentally obtained an important acting role in the film). *La notte dei diavoli*, however, seems to be based on an idea by the Spanish co-producer, Eduardo Manzanos Brochero, credited as the sole author of the treatment (Manzanos Brochero 1971) and praised by the functionaries of the Italian Show Business Bureau for imbuing his vampire tale with 'an atmosphere of anguish and suspense that positively sets the work apart from similar initiatives whose pathos [. . .] often falls into the ridicule'.

As written by Curti (2017b: 80–4, 116–19), production-wise *Dracula cerca sangue di vergine . . . e morì di sete!!!* was quite unique a case. Following the *succès de scandale* of *Trash* (Paul Morrissey, 1970) upon its Italian release in early 1972, producer Carlo Ponti invited Morrissey to Cinecittà studios to improvise a Frankenstein movie (*Il mostro è in tavola . . . barone Frankenstein*, or *Flesh for Frankenstein*) and a Dracula one (*Dracula cerca sangue di vergine . . . e morì di sete!!!*, or *Blood for Dracula*), to be shot back-to-back in 3D over the course of seven weeks, on a total budget of USD$700,000 coming from Ponti's Compagnia Cinematografica Champion and its French associates. The two movies (whose estimated budgets submitted to the Italian Show Business Bureau amount to 220 and 230 million lire respectively) were shot from March to May 1973 under the direction of Morrissey and his tutor Margheriti, the latter receiving a solo director credit in the Italian prints of the films for reasons relating to the obtaining of Italian-nationality certificates. For technical issues, only the Frankenstein movie was shot in 3D, on existing sets from Italo–American low-budget horror *Lady Frankenstein* (Mel Welles, 1971), while *Dracula cerca sangue di vergine . . . e morì di sete!!!* recycled much of its twin film's cast, crew, props and costumes, and also made use of Villa Parisi, a classic set of Italian horrors from Caiano's *Amanti d'oltretomba* to *Le notti del terrore / Burial Ground* (Andrea Bianchi, 1980) and beyond.

As for the '100% Italian' vampire films of the 1970s, accurate production figures cannot be provided due to the lack of cost statements in the relevant files preserved in the Italian Show Business Bureau fonds at the Archivio Centrale dello Stato in Rome. Judging from the available official documents and from the films themselves, it is however safe to assume that budgets were either low (Lucio Fulci's *Il cav. Costante Nicosia demoniaco, ovvero: Dracula in Brianza*, which probably secured a decent *minimo garantito* from Titanus by choosing a parodic register and by casting star comedian Lando Buzzanca in the title role) or, in the majority of cases, close to non-existent (Filippo Walter Ratti's *La notte dei dannati*, Corrado Farina's *. . . Hanno cambiato faccia*, Riccardo Ghione's *Il prato macchiato di rosso*, Polselli's *Riti, magie nere e segrete orge nel Trecento . . .* and Luigi Batzella's *Il plenilunio delle vergini*). For instance, made at the beginning of the decade that saw Italian inflation reach its peak, . . . *Hanno cambiato faccia* was planned as a 97-million-lira feature but, according to Farina (quoted in Guarneri 2019a), it ended up being shot on a mere 50 million lire chipped in by the director and other members of cast and crew united in the cooperative Filmsettanta. Not to mention *La notte dei dannati* and *Il prato macchiato di rosso*: the former recycled the soundtrack of Amando de Ossorio's 1969 *Malenka, la nipote del vampiro* and was shot back-to-back with erotic drama *Erika* (Filippo Walter Ratti as Peter Rush,

1971) (same screenwriter, director, crew, leading actors and interiors, and same production company, Primax Film, which went bankrupt in early 1971, soon after the two-in-one shooting wrapped up);[15] the latter was a project whose financially precarious, scraped-together nature is attested by obtrusive, plot-embedded product placements for Chivas Regal and winemaker Testa.

Following the 1960s Italian Gothic horror tradition, the five shoestring-budget, '100% Italian' vampire films made little or no use of the cheap studios hired by the producers. Shooting mostly took place in real-life locations such as historical and modern buildings in small provincial towns (*La notte dei dannati* and *Il prato macchiato di rosso*), in villas and office spaces owned by friends (... *Hanno cambiato faccia*) (Farina 2016: 124–5), or in Castle Piccolomini and Palazzo Borghese (*Riti, magie nere e segrete orge nel Trecento* ... and *Il plenilunio delle vergini*), already used in the previous decade for vampire horrors *L'amante del vampiro*, *L'ultima preda del vampiro* and *La cripta e l'incubo*. Indeed, the Italian vampire films from the 1970s not only cast 1950s and 1960s stars on the wane (Lucia Bosé, Rossano Brazzi, Mickey Hargitay, Nino Castelnuovo, Mark Damon, Sylva Koscina and Pierre Brice), but were also made by the same people who pioneered Italian Gothic horror in 1959–1965. *L'amante del vampiro* and *Il mostro dell'Opera*'s director Polselli wrote, produced and directed *Riti, magie nere e segrete orge nel Trecento* ... via his company GRP Cinematografica, while *La notte dei diavoli* and *Nella stretta morsa del ragno* were directed, respectively, by sexagenarian veteran Ferroni of *Il mulino delle donne di pietra* fame and by jack-of-all-trades Margheriti of *Danza macabra* fame. Mixing Stoker's 1914 posthumous short story *Dracula's Guest* with references to the Nibelungs saga and to William Peter Blatty's 1971 best-seller *The Exorcist*, *Il plenilunio delle vergini* was written and directed by Batzella (a supporting actor in *La strage dei vampiri*), and its production managed by Walter Bigari (the male lead of *L'amante del vampiro*, *L'ultima preda del vampiro* and *La strage dei vampiri*) and Ralph Zucker, 'an American citizen of Jewish origin [. . .] who in 1958 tried his luck in Italy' (Curti 2015: 149) and ended up producing a few films, among which *5 tombe per un medium / Terror-Creatures from the Grave* (Massimo Pupillo as Ralph Zucker, 1965) and *Il boia scarlatto / Bloody Pit of Horror* (Massimo Pupillo as Max Hunter, 1965), both starring Bigari.

Italian box-office figures varied wildly, as shown by the table below. Yet, they never got close to those of *Ultimo tango a Parigi / Last Tango in Paris* (Bernardo Bertolucci, 1972), *Malizia / Malicious* (Salvatore Samperi, 1973) and the other top money-makers of the 1970s (see the season-by-season reports in Rondolino 1975, 1976 and 1977), not even when vampire films were distributed by established companies like Medusa Distribuzione and Titanus, granting access to the highly lucrative, oligopolised/monopolised *prima visione* circuit of the 1970s.

Table 2.2 Censorship and box-office data for 1969–1975 Italian vampire films.

Title	Italian Film Censorship Office rating	Vatican censorship rating	Release period (distributor)	Box-office gross in lire
Il Conte Dracula	VM14 (Nullaosta 62939 1973)	Morally controversial, ambiguous (Centro Cattolico Cinematografico 1974)	September 1973-August 1975 (INDIEF)	83,751,000 (Rondolino 1975: 160)
La notte dei dannati	VM18 (Nullaosta 58702 1971)	Forbidden (Centro Cattolico Cinematografico 1973a)	September 1971-August 1975 (King)	80,170,000 (Rondolino 1975: 123)
...Hanno cambiato faccia	VM18 (Nullaosta 57934 1971)	Forbidden (Centro Cattolico Cinematografico 1972a)	July 1971-August 1975 (Garigliano)	26,190,000 (Rondolino 1975: 122)
La corta notte delle bambole di vetro	VM14 (Nullaosta 58956 1971)	Forbidden (Centro Cattolico Cinematografico 1972c)	October 1971-? (Overseas Film Company)	181,249,000 (Baroni 1996: 58)
Nella stretta morsa del ragno	VM14 (Nullaosta 58787 1971)	Morally controversial, ambiguous (Centro Cattolico Cinematografico 1971)	August 1971-August 1975 (Panta Cinematografica)	228,636,000 (Rondolino 1975: 123)
La notte dei diavoli	VM14 (Nullaosta 60050 1972)	Forbidden (Centro Cattolico Cinematografico 1972b)	April 1972-August 1975 (PAC)	136,383,000 (Rondolino 1975: 141)

Title	Italian Film Censorship Office rating	Vatican censorship rating	Release period (distributor)	Box-office gross in lire
Le vergini cavalcano la morte	VM18 (Nullaosta 62852 1973)	Forbidden (Centro Cattolico Cinematografico 1975b)	Summer 1973–? (regional distribution)	45,798,000 (Baroni 1996: 112)
L'uomo che uccideva a sangue freddo	VM14 (Nullaosta 61865 1973)	Forbidden (Centro Cattolico Cinematografico 1975a)	February 1973–August 1975 (Medusa Distribuzione)	675,365,000 (Rondolino 1975: 176)
Il prato macchiato di rosso	VM18 (Nullaosta 61372 1972)	Forbidden (Centro Cattolico Cinematografico 1976)	March 1973–? (regional distribution)	32,205,000 (Baroni 1996: 93)
Riti, magie nere e segrete orge nel Trecento...	VM18 (Nullaosta 60795 1972)	Forbidden (Centro Cattolico Cinematografico 1975c)	January 1973–August 1975 (regional distribution)	45,732,000 (Rondolino 1975: 173)
Il plenilunio delle vergini	VM18 (Nullaosta 62028 1973)	Forbidden (Centro Cattolico Cinematografico 1973b)	March 1973–August 1975 (regional distribution)	81,630,000 (Rondolino 1975: 165)
Dracula cerca sangue di vergine... e morì di sete!!!	VM18 (Nullaosta 64499 1974)	Forbidden (Centro Cattolico Cinematografico 1975e)	63 days in the 1975–1976 season (Gold Film)	32,161,000 (Rondolino 1976: 87)
Il cav. Costante Nicosia demoniaco, ovvero: Dracula in Brianza	VM14 (Nullaosta 67018 1975)	Forbidden (Centro Cattolico Cinematografico 1975d)	280 days in the 1975–1976 season (Titanus)	201,147,000 (Rondolino 1976: 86)

Predictably, the highest-grossing film was *L'uomo che uccideva a sangue freddo*, distributed by a prominent company and featuring huge star Alain Delon. Given the aforementioned unavailability or incompleteness of production data, it is difficult to establish which movies were commercially successful. At the same time, a comparison with the Italian box-office receipts of the 1960s cannot be made, due to the vertiginous increase in ticket prices described in Chapter 1. However, some hypotheses on the consumption of such films can be brought forward by dividing the movies into two categories, according to their marketing strategy.

Italian vampire films from 1969 to 1975 were either straightforward horrors (in which case they nostalgically harked back to late-1950s and early-1960s vampire movies) or hybrids mixing the vampire myth with genres or *filoni* that were popular in the late 1960s and early 1970s. Nostalgic horrors were not many: *Il Conte Dracula* (a poverty-row imitation of early Hammer Gothic), *Nella stretta morsa del ragno* (a colour remake of *Danza macabra*), *La notte dei diavoli* (a feature-length remake/update of the Aleksey-Tolstoy-inspired *I Wurdalak* segment from *I tre volti della paura*, with occasional references to George Romero's 1968 hit *Night of the Living Dead*)[16] and *Le vergini cavalcano la morte* (a fictionalised Erzsébet Báthory biopic mixing *I vampiri* with Hammer's female-vampire cycle of the early 1970s).[17] Conceived for a transnational Euro-American market just like their 1950s–1960s antecedents, *Il Conte Dracula*, *Nella stretta morsa del ragno*, *La notte dei diavoli* and *Le vergini cavalcano la morte* premiered in Italy between summer 1971 and autumn 1973, that is to say after both the Italian release of Hammer's 1968–1970 Dracula movies *Dracula Has Risen from the Grave* (Freddie Francis, 1968), *Taste the Blood of Dracula* (Peter Sasdy, 1970) and *Scars of Dracula* (Roy Ward Baker, 1970), and an early-1970s Italian re-release of horror classics like Curtiz's *Mystery of the Wax Museum*, De Toth's *House of Wax*, Fisher's *Dracula* and *Dracula: Prince of Darkness* (Castelli 1970a and 1970b). In this cultural environment, it is likely that in Italy *Il Conte Dracula*, *Nella stretta morsa del ragno*, *La notte dei diavoli* and *Le vergini cavalcano la morte* gathered their modest receipts among horror aficionados that first discovered the genre in the late 1950s and early 1960s. Indeed, 1969 saw both a brief renaissance of the horror *fotoromanzo* (e.g., the 1970–1971 *Suspense* and *Wampir* series, based on classical-Hollywood, Hammer, AIP, Mexican and Italian Gothic horrors) and the birth of Italy's first horror (sub)culture magazine, monthly *Horror*, which kept publishing only until October 1972, but on whose pages – alongside historical articles on Universal monsters, German Expressionism, Gothic literature and Hammer – a critical cult of Freda (Cozzi 1971), Bava (Castelli and Monego 1969; Cozzi 1970–1971) and Margheriti (Cozzi 1970) was started.[18]

As for the hybrid vampire films, *Dracula cerca sangue di vergine . . . e morì di sete!!!* and *Il cav. Costante Nicosia demoniaco, ovvero: Dracula in*

Brianza mixed vampire lore with comedy, as it became quite popular all over Europe after *Dance of the Vampires* (Roman Polanski, 1967) and its many imitators like de Ossorio's *Malenka, la nipote del vampiro, Gebissen wird nur nachts / The Vampire Happening* (Freddie Francis, 1971), *Old Dracula* (Clive Donner, 1974), *Tendre Dracula / Tender Dracula* (Pierre Grunstein, 1974), *Dracula père et fils / Dracula and Son* (Édouard Molinaro, 1976) and *Las alegres vampiras de Vögel* (Julio Pérez Tabernero, 1976). If in *Dracula cerca sangue di vergine . . . e morì di sete!!!* references to Roman Polanski and his deadpan humour went as far as casting him in an uncredited cameo, Fulci's decision to tell the story of a laughable Brianza-based Dracula might have had more to do with the hope to repeat the success of horror parodies *Young Frankenstein* (Mel Brooks, 1974) and *L'esorciccio / The Exorcist: Italian Style* (Ciccio Ingrassia, 1975) at the Italian box office than with the desire to pay tribute to the Polish director (Albiero and Cacciatore 2004: 159–64). The screenplay of *Il cav. Costante Nicosia demoniaco, ovvero: Dracula in Brianza* in fact includes a long sequence parodying William Friedkin's *The Exorcist* (Fulci and Avati 1975), and in the finished film Ciccio Ingrassia – director and protagonist of *L'esorciccio* – appears in the small role of a witch doctor. In Fulci's movie there are only two noticeable references to Polanski's oeuvre: a gag showing homosexual vampire Sperandeu being rejected by the heterosexual protagonist (a nod to *Dance of the Vampires*) and the ending in which said protagonist contemplates his monstrous child (a nod to the final scene of 1968 hit *Rosemary's Baby*).

While *La corta notte delle bambole di vetro* combined *Rosemary's Baby* (the satanic conspiracy) with the Dario-Argento-like giallo *filone* inaugurated in 1970 with *L'uccello dalle piume di cristallo* (an American abroad investigates on a series of murders), . . . *Hanno cambiato faccia, L'uomo che uccideva a sangue freddo* and *Il prato macchiato di rosso* injected exploitation with the political engagement of post-1968 European auteur cinema via the vampire-bourgeoisie equivalence.[19] *La notte dei dannati, Riti, magie nere e segrete orge nel Trecento . . .* and *Il plenilunio delle vergini*, on the other hand, used vampirism as an excuse to string together softcore sex scenes, bringing to the extreme consequences the mix of bloodsucking and eroticism displayed in Hammer's late-1960s and early-1970s vampire films (the 1970–1971 Karnstein trilogy especially), in the Jean Rollin 1968–1971 vampire tetralogy, in *Les lèvres rouges / Daughters of Darkness* (Harry Kümel, 1971), in *Vampyros Lesbos* (Jesús Franco as Franco Manera, 1971), and in the widely read, adults-only, Italian comic-book series *Jacula* (1969–1982) and *Zora la vampira* (1972–1985).

It is not by chance that, among the 1969–1975 Italian vampire movies, *La notte dei dannati, Riti, magie nere e segrete orge nel Trecento. . .* and *Il plenilunio delle vergini* were the only ones facing serious censorship issues, in spite of a more relaxed approach to female nudity and heterosexual lovemaking on the part of the Italian Film Censorship Office after 1968. *La notte dei dannati* and *Il plenilunio delle vergini* were required to tone down lesbian scenes (the latter was also ordered to remove the shots in which the male lead kisses the lower parts of Countess Dracula) (Nullaosta 58702 1971; Nullaosta 62028 1973), while *Riti, magie nere e segrete orge nel Trecento*. . . obtained a public-screening permission only in appeal, after an initial ban due to the 'incoherent series of sadistic sequences meant to stimulate the lowest sexual instincts by mixing exasperated cruelties and degenerate eroticism' (Nullaosta 60795 1972) – a scathing review echoed by Vatican censors, who labelled the movie a 'nonsensical [. . .] porno-horror' (Centro Cattolico Cinematografico 1975c). Moreover, it is not by chance that lesbian-themed *Nella stretta morsa del ragno* and the three erotic horror films listed above were advertised in adults-only Italian magazines like *Cinesex*, *Cinestop* and *BigFilm*, where sensationalist plot synopses were accompanied by several pictures of naked actresses, often taken from scenes shot for the export market only (Anonymous 1971; Giustiniani 1971; Baviera 1972; Santevril 1972).[20] In fact, in view of the new trends in horror cinema set between the late 1960s and the early 1970s by *Night of the Living Dead*, *Rosemary's Baby*, *L'uccello dalle piume di cristallo* and *The Exorcist*, the place of Italian vampire films in the domestic and the world market came to depend solely on female nudity and simulated sex scenes (Curti 2017b: 1–4), until production was halted in 1975, about one year after Hammer finally ended its dragging Dracula cycle with wuxia-horror sans Lee *The Legend of the 7 Golden Vampires* (Roy Ward Baker, 1974).

Towards a culturally specific monsterology

As explained in the Introduction, for most of the nineteenth and the twentieth centuries, the Italian intelligentsia followed the *auctoritas* of Giacomo Leopardi, Alessandro Manzoni and Benedetto Croce, championing rationalism, classicism and realism as the true expressions of the Italian character. It is therefore unsurprising that, from the immediate post-war period until well into the 1970s, Italian film critics and intellectuals more in general focused on neorealism and its heritage, either ignoring fantastic narratives as escapist and thus culturally meaningless, or at best simplistically labelling them as a cathartic working through of Cold-War-era fears of impending atomic disaster (Fruttero 1960; De' Rossignoli 1961: 359–61; Miotto 1961; Eco 1964; Batini 1968: 5–6). In particular, ever since the premiere of Italy's first experiment in terror *I vampiri*, Italian Gothic horrors were dismissed by the contemporary Italian film press as 'the feeble echoes of a catacombic, Romantic Decadentism that never took root in our country' (Anonymous 1957a), degraded cultural sub-products whose primary reason for existence was economic, namely cashing in on successful foreign prototypes (Anonymous 1960c and 1960g; Fink 1960 and 1966; Quarantotto 1960, 1965 and 1969; Zanotto 1961; Brega 1963; Fofi 1963). One left-wing critic even went as far as calling Freda's *Caltiki il mostro immortale* and the horror-themed 'film "magliari"' ('counterfeit-foreign films') that followed a 'monster' growing 'cancer-like' within the national film industry, threatening the 'economic-organisational autonomy' and 'cultural autonomy' of Italian cinema (Pirro 1965: 38–9).

This bias was so deep-seated in Italy that the people involved in the making of such critically despised movies largely agreed with the press on both the *disimpegno* (escapism and cultural meaninglessness) and the foreignness (imported and derivative nature) of Italian fantastic cinema. As for the issue of *disimpegno*, many of the directors whose work is studied in the present monograph were candid about considering their films as audio-visual entertainment to be sold to a mass audience for profit rather than as an outlet for social commentary. Looking back at his directorial debut *La maschera del demonio*, Bava said:

> Since in that period [the Hammer] *Dracula* had just been released, I thought of making a horror movie. [. . .] It was the first film I directed, and it was a very serious matter, because if the movie did not perform well [at the box office] my career was over [. . .]. The film made five billion [*sic*] at the US box office and I became a director. (Quoted in Della Casa 1995: 27)

The down-to-earth, careerist perspective was shared, among others, by Polselli ('When you work in commercial cinema you must first of all make films that are cost-competitive and have the potential to make money') (quoted in Fazzini 2004: 57), Margheriti ('I am a slave for my producers. A prostitute. If it is for money, my answer is "Yes"') (quoted in Curti 2017b: 38), and Fulci ('Social comments are always out of place in a fantasy film, which should be all the more enjoyable for having nothing in common with the mass of films made by amateurs who take up social standpoints because they are not experts at making films') (quoted in Palmerini and Mistretta 1996: 59).

As for the issue of foreignness, Bava once again summed up the situation by stating that, before the late-1950s release of the Hammer *Dracula*, he 'did not even know vampires existed. [. . .] Here [in Italy] we have the sun that chases everything away' (quoted in Pezzotta 2013: 7). The quote is significant, because it highlights one of the bulwarks behind the Italian intelligentsia's dismissal and ridiculing of Italian-made Gothic horrors in the late 1950s and throughout the 1960s: the incompatibility between the sunny atmosphere of the *bel paese* and horror stories such as vampire narratives. For instance, in the 1959 preventive-censorship report on the screenplay of

Il sangue e la rosa, government officials wrote that 'the nebulous character' of the *Carmilla*-inspired plot is more fitting to 'a Nordic saga' than to 'a story set in the sunny Italian climate' – a judgement that echoes not only the 1910s and 1940s Italian reviews of fantastic films quoted in the Introduction, but also Pirro (1965: 39) ('In the Italian landscape [. . .] it is impossible to imagine a truculent vampire story'), Anonymous (1969: 107) ('Can you imagine a story of horror and vampires set in Milan or Palermo? You can? Well, congratulations, you have a very good imagination') and many other 1960s texts identifying Northern Europe as the ancestral homeland of, and the ideal stage for, horror narratives (Fruttero 1960; Rondi 1961a and 1961b; Fofi 1963; Batini 1968: 5–10). Not coincidentally, a substantial amount of Italian horrors from the late 1950s onwards tried to mask, blur or mitigate their Italian origin in view of their domestic release through a wide variety of strategies such as setting the stories abroad; hiring foreign leading actors; using foreign-sounding pseudonyms for Italian producers, screenwriters, directors, cast and crew; constantly referencing foreign literary sources and films; making co-production and joint-participation agreements with other countries (Pitassio 2005; Pezzotta 2014; Baschiera 2016; Di Chiara 2016b). The makers of *La vendetta di Lady Morgan* even went as far as discarding the original, Italian-set ending of the film described in scene 90 of the screenplay: a century after the death of star-crossed lovers Susan and Pierre in rural Scotland, the two meet again in 1960s Rome, reincarnated as tourists visiting the sun-drenched, car-congested Via dei Fori Imperiali (Grimaldi 1965).

Yet, in view of what has been written in Chapters 1 and 2, it is undeniable that the Italian rip-offs of the Hammer *Dracula* and of other foreign vampire films were not slavish plagiarisms. The industrial analysis conducted so far has in fact brought to the fore the national hybridity of Italian vampire cinema, subjected as it was to commercial and ideological pressures at both global and local level. In addition to international/global factors (the late 1950s Gothic revival, the post-war flourish in European co-productions and the post-Paramount-Decree restructuring of the US film industry among others), national/local factors such as distribution-fed production, time- and cost-saving shooting practices, state censorship and state aids definitely shaped the Italian vampire films' form and content, mixing foreign models with distinctively national traits. Within this transnational/glocal framework, the Italian cultural specificities of the thirty-three films included in the corpus will now be analysed in detail. The aim of the following chapters is to show that – in spite of the imitation of foreign templates and the great reliance on profits coming from distribution on the international market – Italian vampire movies tapped into, and more or less distortedly mirrored, Italy's contemporary zeitgeist with regard to gender, socio-economic and political issues.

Notes

1. Only nine, in fact: *The Black Sleep* (Reginald LeBorg, 1956), *The Vampire* (Paul Landres, 1957), Mendez's *El vampiro*, *The Return of Dracula* (Paul Landres, 1958), *The Revenge of Frankenstein* (Terence Fisher, 1958), *The Mummy* (Terence Fisher, 1959), *Doctor Blood's Coffin* (Sidney J. Furie, 1961), *The Sadist* (James Landis, 1963) and *The Gorgon* (Terence Fisher, 1964).
2. An exemplary case is Erle C. Kenton's *House of Dracula* from 1945, first approved for all audiences by the Italian Film Censorship Office in December 1948 under the title *La casa degli orrori* ('The house of horrors') (Nullaosta 4783 1948): in 1961 regional distributor All'Insegna Mediterranea rented out a print of *House of Dracula* to various exhibitors in and around Naples, changing the original Italian title to *Dracula nella casa degli orrori* ('Dracula in the house of horrors'). Since the Italian Film Censorship Office was not notified of the title change, a governmental investigation followed, leading to the distribution company being fined. The title *Dracula nella casa degli orrori* was eventually used for a *fotoromanzo* adaptation of *House of Dracula*, in issue 30 (July 1963) of the *Malìa* series.
3. E.g., Landres's *The Return of Dracula* (Nullaosta 29018 1959), *Curse of the Undead* (Edward Dein, 1959) (Nullaosta 31205 1960) and *The Brides of Dracula* (Terence Fisher, 1960) (Nullaosta 33224 1960). A couple of years earlier, the Italian Film Censorship Office had already required two brief shots featuring skulls and skeletons to be removed from the trailer of *I vampiri* (Nullaosta 23894 1957).
4. E.g., *Blood of the Vampire* (Henry Cass, 1958) (Nullaosta 28463 1959), Landres's *The Return of Dracula* (Nullaosta 29018 1959) and Fisher's *Dracula: Prince of Darkness* (Nullaosta 46568 1966).
5. In Italy, the summer-holiday-themed film comedy blossomed in the late 1940s and early 1950s with *L'imperatore di Capri* (Luigi Comencini, 1949), *Domenica d'agosto* (Luciano Emmer, 1950) and *Bellezze a Capri* (Adelchi Bianchi, 1951), then thrived *filone*-like in the late 1950s and early 1960s with films like *Vacanze a Ischia / Holiday Island* (Mario Camerini, 1957), *Racconti d'estate / Love on the Riviera* (Gianni Franciolini, 1958), *Brevi amori a Palma di Majorca* (Giorgio Bianchi, 1959), *Tipi da spiaggia* (Mario Mattoli, 1959), *Avventura a Capri* (Giuseppe Lipartiti, 1959), *Costa Azzurra* (Vittorio Sala, 1959), *Ferragosto in bikini* (Marino Girolami, 1960), *Scandali al mare* (Marino Girolami, 1961), *I Don Giovanni della Costa Azzurra / Beach Casanova* (Vittorio Sala, 1962), *Una domenica d'estate / Always on Sunday* (Giulio Petroni, 1962), *Diciottenni al sole / Eighteen in the Sun* (Camillo Mastrocinque, 1962) and *Peccati d'estate* (Giorgio Bianchi, 1962).
6. *Tempi duri per i vampiri* circulated on US TV in an English-dubbed, abridged version titled *Uncle was a Vampire*, as part of a 1962–1963 film package put together by Embassy Pictures (Heffernan 2004: 238). The movie also opened in Paris in August 1962, distributed by Procidis (Le Bris 1962c).
7. There is no file regarding *L'amante del vampiro* in the Italian Show Business Bureau fonds at the Archivio Centrale dello Stato in Rome, so the information contained in this paragraph is based on Gastaldi (1991: 176–82) and Guarneri (2019b).
8. With the help of Alberto Grimaldi's Produzioni Europee Associate, the Caianos first organised a 100-million-lira seventy–thirty co-production between Italy and

Spain, which was rejected by the Italian Show Business Bureau for lack of Spanish actors in the cast. Then, the Caianos organised a 150-million-lira seventy–thirty co-production between Italy and West Germany, which was rejected as 'a feigned co-production'. At the same time, the original title *Orgasmo* (Caiano and De Agostini 1964) was changed into the less explicit *Amanti d'oltretomba* ('Lovers from beyond the grave'), echoing the title of issue 10 (November 1961) of the *Malìa* series, *L'amante d'oltretomba*.

9. The preventive-censorship reports on *L'ultima preda del vampiro* and *La cripta e l'incubo* are exemplary: the former 'conscientiously uses all the usual elements to be found in vampire movies, adding only – as a spark of originality – some "vampire cats", which by the way spend the whole film innocuously locked in their cages'; the latter 'depicts events so unlikely that even certain horrifying scenes [. . .] risk falling into the ridicule, or in a totally surrealistic absurdity, thus neutralising [. . .] the horror premise of the film'. The preventive-censorship report on *I tre volti della paura*, in which the film's 'original literary inspiration' is praised for 'dignifying' the conventions of horror cinema, suggests that, in principle, government officials were less contemptuous towards movie adaptations of horror literature.

10. Such a letter was not even necessary for *La maschera del demonio* and *Amanti d'oltretomba*, which were given the benefit of the doubt by government officials in spite of their screenplays being bashed, respectively, as 'so full of witches, vampires, skeletons, ghosts, murders and corpses that [the Hammer] *Dracula* plays like a children's show in comparison' and 'the product of a sick imagination, full of recurrent, obsessive obscenities'. Somewhat surprisingly, government officials praised the screenplay of *L'orribile segreto del Dr. Hichcock* for taking necrophilia as its subject matter, deeming it a very original idea.

11. Producers were forced to cut brief shots featuring bare breasts from *Il sangue e la rosa* (Nullaosta 33435 1960) and *L'ultima preda del vampiro* (Nullaosta 33364 1960), while almost 100 meters of film showing characters kissing, caressing and peeping up skirts were excised from *La vendetta di Lady Morgan* (Nullaosta 45744 1965).

12. None of the Italian vampire movies studied here was ever sold to, and broadcast by, Italian State TV during the 1954–1975 monopoly years. Censorship reasons aside, this was because at that time Italian State TV executives and representatives of the film business agreed on the principle that only a small number of very old (meaning at least five-year-old) films should be televised in Italy in order for TV and movie theatres not to become competitors (RAI 1977: 217–348; Simonelli [1971] 2002). After the breaking of the Italian State TV monopoly in 1976, Italian vampire movies might have been bought and televised by private networks, which in late-1970s and early-1980s Italy were not subject to any censorship or fair-competition regulation. However, if this actually happened, it is impossible to establish how much money the rights owners obtained.

13. According to official documents, *La vendetta di Lady Morgan* was even denied access to the mandatory-scheduling-and-tax-rebates benefits, as in summer 1966 one functionary of the Italian Show Business Bureau found the film 'macabrely stupid and stupidly macabre', went on a one-man crusade against it and had it

14. There is no sign of American investments in *I tre volti della paura* and *Roma contro Roma* in the documents submitted to the Italian Show Business Bureau by Galatea. This is because, as explained in Chapter 1, the flows of American capital and personnel to Italy – the so-called 'joint participations' – were not regulated and checked as rigidly as those of European co-productions.
15. The beginning of the end for Primax Film was its failing to honour a promissory note given to assistant director François Chevreuil and script supervisor Renata Parisi, which led to a lawsuit. The same thing happened in early 1973 to Produzioni Cinematografiche Internazionali Virginia, the production company of *Il plenilunio delle vergini*, protested by film editors Piera Bruni and Gianfranco Simoncelli (the two were hired for 800,000 lire, of which 400,000 was paid cash in advance and 400,000 via a promissory note that was never honoured).
16. The provisional title of *La notte dei diavoli* was *I diavoli sono tra noi* ('The devils are among us') (Manzanos Brochero 1971), a blatant reference to the 1960 Feltrinelli anthology *I vampiri tra noi: 37 storie vampiriche* ('The vampires are among us: 37 vampire stories'), in which the first Italian translation of Aleksey Tolstoy's novella *La famille du Vourdalak* was published. Moreover, as noted by Curti (2017b: 76), in both *Night of the Living Dead* and *La notte dei diavoli* a little girl attacks and kills her mother, and the titular monsters (explicitly called 'living dead' in one scene of *La notte dei diavoli*) assault a person driving a car. Indeed, the title *La notte dei diavoli* ('The night of the devils') sounds like an innuendo to Romero's debut, as the titles *La notte dei dannati* ('The night of the damned') and *La corta notte delle bambole di vetro* ('The short night of the glass dolls') perhaps are.
17. The title *Le vergini cavalcano la morte* ('Virgins ride death') references the Italian-release title of Hammer's *Countess Dracula* (Peter Sasdy, 1971), *La morte va a braccetto con le vergini* ('Death walks arm in arm with virgins'). Incidentally, one of *Le vergini cavalcano la morte*'s screenwriters was Alessandro Continenza, who had already contributed to late-1950s and early-1960s Italian vampire cinema by co-writing *Tempi duri per i vampiri* and *Ercole al centro della Terra*.
18. Curated, among others, by future filmmakers Pier Carpi and Luigi Cozzi, the first issue of *Horror* came out in December 1969, published by Milan-based Sansoni Editore. The year 1969 is all but coincidental: in early 1969 made-for-TV Gothic miniseries started invading Italian State TV, spearheaded by *Jekyll* (Giorgio Albertazzi, 1969) and *Geminus* (Luciano Emmer, 1969) (Curti 2011: 373–95).
19. As written by Della Casa and Giusti (2014: 43–4), the distributors of *La corta notte delle bambole di vetro* initially thought of naming the film *La corta notte delle farfalle* ('The short night of the butterflies') because Argento's 1970–1971 smash hits had an animal in the title. This is probably why the title of Margheriti's remake of *Danza macabra* was changed from *E venne l'alba . . . ma tinta di rosso* ('And dawn came . . . but tinged red') (Unknown 1971) to *Nella stretta morsa del ragno* ('In the firm grip of the spider'). In all likelihood, *Il prato macchiato di rosso*'s ('The red-stained lawn') original title *Vampiro 2000* (Ghione 1972) and *L'uomo che uccideva a sangue freddo*'s ('The man who killed in cold blood') original title *Terapia d'urto*

(Traitement de choc) (Jessua and Curel 1972) were changed to piggy-back on Italo–West German giallo *Sette orchidee macchiate di rosso / Seven Blood-Stained Orchids* (Umberto Lenzi, 1972) and Italian giallo *La bestia uccide a sangue freddo / Cold Blooded Beast* (Fernando di Leo, 1971) respectively.

20. In Italy *La notte dei dannati, Riti, magie nere e segrete orge nel Trecento* . . . and *Il plenilunio delle vergini* also circulated uncut as erotic *fotoromanzi*, in *BigFilm* issue 20 (October 1971), *Cinesex Mese* issue 1 (January 1973) and *Cinestop Attualità* issue 12 (May 1973) respectively.

PART II

VAMPIRE SEX AND VAMPIRE GENDER

3. FEMALE VAMPIRES

BURN WITCH BURN: THE FEMALE VAMPIRES OF 1956–1965

Together with Italy's scant heritage of literary horrors, the parasitic dynamics of *filone*-filmmaking explain why most Italian vampire movies imitate foreign hits, starting from the Hammer *Dracula*. In many cases, however, such 'cinema of imitation' (Baschiera 2016) did not produce slavish plagiarisms, but more or less creative variations on the templates established by foreign vampire films. Indeed, in spite of Italian vampire cinema's imported and derivative nature, ever since the late 1960s historians of the horror film have identified some elements of Italianness in Italian Gothic horrors, namely the centrality of female characters and the influence of the nineteenth-century melodrama on movie plots (Clarens 1968: 190–4; Mora 1978: 289–342; Troiano 1985 and 1989). These seminal suggestions came to dominate current academic discourses about Italian horror, as best exemplified by the thematic analyses of the Gothic horror *filone* put forward by Pezzotta (1997 and 2014), Della Casa (1990, 2000 and 2001c), Di Chiara (2009) and Curti (2011). From Mora (1978: 292), in particular, these four scholars borrow the premise that, instead of focusing on male monsters and male stardom like Universal and Hammer, Italian Gothic horror 'takes as its central figure [. . .] the woman' as the 'catalyst of a moral monstrosity' connected to the typically melodramatic themes of 'sin, guilt and evil (all of them sexually connoted)'. Pezzotta (1997 and 2014), Della Casa (1990, 2000 and 2001c), Di Chiara (2009) and Curti (2011) then proceed to map their assumptions onto the thirty-something horror films made in Italy between 1956 and the mid-1960s and, true to the Manichean 'logic of the excluded middle' that Brooks ([1976] 1995: 18) sees as the key feature of the nineteenth-century melodramatic imagination, split Italian Gothic horror's leading ladies into irreconcilable opposites: hyper-sexed, proactive villainesses (wicked human beings, vampires, witches, ghosts or a combination thereof) and chaste, passive damsels in distress – the two mutually exclusive archetypes generally marked via different hair colour.

Focused on *I vampiri*, *Il mulino delle donne di pietra* and *La maschera del demonio*, the most extensive analysis of the Italian female vampire to date is Di Chiara's (2009: 51–119). Combining semiotics and structuralist anthropology, the author conceives of Italian vampire horrors as sexual morality plays that somewhat differ from the Hammer *Dracula*'s template. Instead of a four-sided triangle in which demon lover Dracula, ineffectual husband Arthur Holmwood and marriage guidance counsellor Van Helsing do battle for the body of sexually frustrated housewife Mina (Hutchings 2003: 60–78), Italian vampire horrors bring to the screen a melodramatic triangle in which a bachelor must choose between the socially forbidden, hedonistic, non-procreative sexuality of a beautiful female vampire and the socially prescribed, marital, procreative sexuality of a good-looking, but rather frigid, angelic virgin. Since the former type of sexuality is explicitly associated to the sterility, non-normativity and so-called 'unnaturality' of necrophilia, gerontophilia, bestiality and lesbianism, the male protagonist's choice ultimately falls on the angelic virgin, and the female vampire is rejected, fought and purged from society. Within this narrative trajectory, detection plays a key role: a riddle in that she seems young, beautiful and good but is not, the monstrous female is a two-faced, deceitful being to be investigated and publicly unmasked before justice is done in the grand finale. The most notable examples are decrepit Erzsébet Báthory imitator Duchess Marguerite Du Grand from *I vampiri* and 200-year-old vampire witch Princess Asa Vajda from *La maschera del demonio*, masquerading as attractive debutante Gisèle and twenty-one-year old, God-fearing ingénue Katia Vajda respectively. Eventually, the villainesses' cover is blown, and Marguerite and Asa meet their end after undergoing the very same accelerated-ageing metamorphosis meant to make the 'inner putrefaction of the character' (Riccardo Freda, quoted in Lourcelles and Mizrahi 1963: 23) visible to the audience.[1]

The pre-ending scene from *La maschera del demonio* in which, after mistaking Asa for Katia, dashing hero Andrej Gorobec accidentally sees what lies underneath the woman's cloak is even more revealing of Italian vampire horrors' attitude towards femininity. In a striking parallel with Canto XIX of Dante Alighieri's *Purgatorio*, where the veils covering the body of an attractive siren are torn to expose a disgustingly stinking belly, Asa's lovely appearances are shown to be a mere cover for a pile of bones and rotten viscera. What Yavneh (2001: 110) writes about the *antica strega* ('old witch') of *Purgatorio* can be transposed word for word to the old witch of *La maschera del demonio*: in a work 'concerned with the "vanitate" of the flesh and its allures [. . .], the Siren's foul belly makes her a figure [. . .] for the threat of [. . .] female sexuality' and 'the menace of a desire that refuses to look beyond the corporeal' (in both Dante's poem and Mario Bava's film the siren is contrasted to the *donna santa*, the saintly woman who is just as beautiful, but *onesta*, pure, incorporeal).

In sum, having to negotiate between commercial imperatives (the need to boost ticket sales through sex and violence) and state and religious censorship bodies forbidding the portrayal of evil under attractive appearances, Italian vampire horrors of the late 1950s and early 1960s worked out a representational code based on a careful mixture of allure and punishment. In compliance with Pope Pius XII's 1955 ruling that cinematic depictions of 'the struggle against Evil and even Evil's temporary victory' are admissible if they 'lead to a deeper understanding of life, of the right path to take [. . .] in judgements and

Figure 3.1   Charnel eroticism: Barbara Steele on the set of *La maschera del demonio* (photo by Osvaldo Civirani available at Archivio Centrale dello Stato – Archivio fotografico Civirani (film) – 098 Maschera del demonio La – 098–0004).

actions' (quoted in Valli 1999: 47), transgression is brought to the screen as embodied by the 'theriomorphic' (Di Chiara 2009: 75), 'non-canonical' (Pezzotta 2014: 36) sexuality of the female vampire only to be violently sanctioned at the end, so that the heteronormative status quo can be reaffirmed, typically via the marriage between the male protagonist and the damsel in distress. This moralistic, cautionary-didactic, Catholic framework explains what Pezzotta (1997: 26) highlights as one of the central features of the Gothic horror *filone*: the focus on the female vampire's face as both an 'object of desire' and a 'target for violence'. The final disfigurement of the villainesses in *I vampiri*, *L'amante del vampiro*, *Il mulino delle donne di pietra*, *La maschera del demonio*, *L'orribile segreto del Dr. Hichcock* and *Amanti d'oltretomba* is meant to ultimately make the female vampires' face as repugnant as their soul, thus fixing the ontological breach that momentarily made Evil desirable.[2]

Focusing on Italian Gothic horror's cathartic qualities like Di Chiara (2009: 51–119), but seeking to link the films to post-war Italy's socio-historical context, Günsberg (2005: 133–72) and Bini (2011a) blend psychoanalysis and Marxism, and examine 'the patriarchal subtext of [Italian horror's] portrayal of femininity in relation to the position of real women [. . .] from the late 1950s to the mid-1960s' (Günsberg 2005: 135). As a result, the films are seen as 'implicitly and explicitly address[ing] the issue of women's gradual emancipation within Italian society', and exposing the 'male fears surrounding female sexuality' brought about by 'the changes in Italian culture that were a consequence of the new consumerist society of the late 1950s' (Bini 2011a: 53). Within this framework, largely echoing Imbasciati's (1969, 1970a and 1970b) studies of sex-and-crime-themed Italian comic-book series like *Satanik* (1964–1974), female vampires would be a metaphor for the New Women of the post-war Italian Republic who, after having entered the job market and obtained active and passive suffrage, started rejecting confinement in the house and the sexually repressive submission to the male as either virgin daughters or (house) wives-mothers. Vampire horrors *I vampiri*, *L'amante del vampiro*, *Il mulino delle donne di pietra*, *La maschera del demonio* and *La strage dei vampiri* are therefore said to 'perhaps more subconsciously than intentionally' (Bini 2011a: 59) play out 'the threat femininity poses to masculinity in terms of problems of differentiation and the dissolution of subjectivity through the invasion of boundaries, incorporation and castration' (Günsberg 2005: 133), and to exorcise male anxieties over powerlessness and emasculation via happy endings 're-establishing masculine supremacy, with "bad" femininity dispatched' by homosocial brotherhoods, 'and "good" femininity ushered off into the domestic realm of a new heterosexual family formation' (Günsberg 2005: 172).

As Krzywinska (1995) and Günsberg (2005: 159–72) astutely note by analysing *Carmilla*-inspired *La cripta e l'incubo*, though, Italian patriarchy's worst nightmare might just not be the femme fatale who seduces and devours men.

In fact, as the most blatant expression of 'an autonomous female eroticism, free from the postulates of the stronger sex' (Troiano 1989: 97), the lesbian vampire of *La cripta e l'incubo* poses much more dangerous a threat in that she embodies a form of gynosociality excluding men altogether. While both Krzywinska (1995) and Günsberg (2005: 159–72) praise the film for allowing the spectator to enjoy the potentially subversive pleasure of seeing the hero stood up in the middle of a love declaration because the heroine prefers female company, their analyses focus on the repressive strategies enacted by the text. Like all the coeval Italian Gothic horrors, *La cripta e l'incubo* adopts the 'patriarchal divide-and-conquer approach' of splitting the female gender into opposing, irreconcilable poles in order to produce a 'fractured [. . .] femininity' that 'is unlikely to cohere socio-politically as a group that is sufficiently empowered to challenge patriarchy'. With gynosociality effectively prevented, female characters end up 'isolated and alienated from each other', so that male characters – who always 'work in homosocial fashion in teams or pairs' – can easily assert their dominance (Günsberg 2005: 160). More specifically, *La cripta e l'incubo* reworks the melodramatic triangle described by Di Chiara (2009: 51–119) and has female protagonist Laura Karnstein torn between the so-called 'normal', 'natural', heterosexual relationship with young scholar Friedrich Klauss (a dashing-hero character absent from Le Fanu's short story but inserted by the screenwriters to enhance the commercial potential of the film) and the so-called 'abnormal', 'unnatural', homosexual liaison with good-looking, monstrous female Sheena. And just as spellbound Laura is about to elope with Sheena, suitor Friedrich, Laura's father and an old relative of the Karnsteins's stake the female vampire, taking Laura back under the control of heteronormative patriarchy.[3]

Bringing to the screen 'feminine threats to masculine identity', Italian vampire horrors from the late 1950s and early 1960s seem to mirror 'the emergence of socio-political female autonomy and self-determination in the face of patriarchal hegemony' (Günsberg 2005: 158–9). Such vampire horrors can then be seen as a mid-twentieth-century Italian updating of the misogynistic taming of the late-nineteenth-century English New Woman that Stoker scholars have traced in the novel *Dracula* (Demetrakopoulos 1977; Senf 1982; Johnson 1984; Byers [1981] 1988; Cranny-Francis 1988; Griffin [1980] 1988; Brennan 1992; Bronfen 1992: 313–22; Stott 1992; Boone 1993; Spear 1993; Craft [1984] 1997; Eltis 2002; Moretti [1983] 2005). In fact, as Troiano (1989: 96) notes, a 'poetics of gynophobia' clearly lurks behind Italian Gothic horror narratives, with its Victorian-era corollary of Madonna/Magdalen dichotomy and all-male Crews of Light bent on the destruction of phallic women.

Mulvey ([1975] 1985) provides a good starting point to investigate the gynophobia underlying the filmic representation of Italian female vampires. The feminist essay on classical Hollywood's narrative and libidinal economy rejects the idea that commercial cinema is just innocuous entertainment and, invoking a political use of psychoanalysis, describes how framing, camera movement and editing cut up women's bodies in order to appease men's castration anxieties and reinforce patriarchy. This ideological aim is achieved by crafting either sadistic-voyeuristic narratives in which women are investigated, demystified, saved/punished by males, or scopophilic ones turning female body parts into a fetish, whose excessive beauty compensates for the threat of castration posed by women's lack of penis. If the sadistic-voyeuristic model perfectly applies to early Italian vampire cinema, as shown by the dynamics of the Gothic horror *filone* highlighted by Pezzotta (1997 and 2014) and Di Chiara (2009: 51–119), it is not so for fetishistic scopophilia, which requires a culturally specific distinction.

For the aforementioned commercial reasons, a large number of Italian vampire movies from the late 1950s and early 1960s devote most of their screentime to the evil bombshell rather than to the asexual, angelic damsel in distress. In addition to breasts,[4] two parts of the villainess's body are repeatedly brought to the spectators' attention: the eyes and the mouth. The interaction between the two erogenous zones located in the face is best exemplified by *La maschera del demonio* and *I tre volti della paura*'s segment *I Wurdalak*, where vampirisation takes place via kiss instead of bite, playing more like a love scene than an act of violence (no blood is shed on camera). In *La maschera del demonio*, Asa lies in a crypt, breathing deeply – posture, costume and framing emphasising the size of her breasts. She tells doctor Kruvajan: 'Come closer! Kiss me! My burnt, dry lips will transform you. You will be dead for mankind, but alive in death!' Terrified yet irresistibly attracted, Kruvajan steps beside Asa's corpse. An extreme close-up of Asa's face follows: it is taken from Kruvajan's point of view and the camera pans from the vampire witch's eyes to her parted lips while slowly zooming into the mouth. Kruvajan and Asa kiss in the subsequent two-shot and, from that moment on, he is her slave. In *I Wurdalak*, vampirised peasant Sdenka is sitting on her bed wearing only a nightgown and tells her human lover Count Vladimiro d'Urfé that 'My lips are dead without your kisses'. Three close-ups of Sdenka's face follow, intercut with two reaction shots of wide-eyed Vladimiro. The female vampire's eyes are highlighted either via zoom in/out or lighting tricks, and their hypnotic effect is shown by making the close-ups blurred, as if onlooking Vladimiro was drunk or feverish. Then, the lovers kiss on the mouth in a two-shot emphasised by zoom and the female vampire's lips slowly approach the man's neck. Evidently, given the Catholic prejudice against female corporality described by Yavneh (2001), in early Italian vampire cinema fetishistic scopophilia does not perform the reassuring function of expressing a mastering of male gaze over females. On the contrary, an excessively beautiful body is the very weapon female vampires use to submit their prey, and its display therefore heightens men's anxieties rather than appeasing/disallowing them, leaving sadistic punishments (and especially those that make women literally and metaphorically lose their face) as the only viable option for patriarchal ideology to assert itself.

While the vampire women's hypnotic gaze can be considered a simple gendered variation of the Universal Dracula's mesmerising look (and perhaps a parodic inversion of the Dantean cliché of noble-minded men falling in love at first sight with the *donna santa*), the focus on the mouth is to be connected to a specifically female archetype, namely the devouring *vagina dentata* first analysed by Bonaparte ([1934] 1971) and subsequently reworked in many of the psychoanalytic and feminist approaches to vampire fiction listed in the Introduction. Although none of the people involved in making vampire movies in Italy was a high-profile intellectual expounding on psychoanalytic theories, the connection is less far-fetched than it may seem at first glance. *Danza macabra*, for instance, opens with character Edgar Allan Poe reciting the 1835 short story *Berenice*, the very same tale that Bonaparte ([1934] 1971: 218–19) labels as a male attempt to overcome castration anxiety in that the protagonist cures himself of his fetishistic obsession for a young woman by depriving her mouth of the teeth that threatened to bite him. This retributive disfigurement is undoubtedly similar to the sadistic punishments inflicted to both the sexy villainesses of the Gothic horror *filone* and the evil matriarchs of vampire-themed pepla *Roma contro Roma* (where centurion Gaio saves the day by plunging his sword into the eye of blood-drinking, cyclops-goddess Oro, whose gaze turns men into brainwashed zombies at her command) and *Maciste e la regina di Samar* (in which the titular muscleman makes the face of a power-hungry alien queen thirsting for the blood of her terrestrial lookalike melt down). Whether the reference to Bonaparte ([1934] 1971) was an unintended by-product of the commercial need to piggy-back on American International Pictures's 1960–1964 Poe cycle, or a calculated attempt to tap into the psychoanalytic debate about vampirism triggered on the Italian press by Servadio (1959), Mazzini Rizzo (1961) and Miotto (1961) among others, it is impossible to establish. Whatever the case, it is not difficult to read the Italian female vampire as a threatening 'womb-gullet' (Creed 1993: 111) ready to bite off the patriarchal phallus: most notably in *L'ultima preda del vampiro* and *La strage dei vampiri*, we are shown women who, after acquiring fangs and a new aggressiveness/appetite, repeatedly try to escape from controlling males such as their husbands, employers and doctors. Tellingly, as we shall see more in detail in Chapter 4, the fanged women from *L'amante del vampiro* and *L'ultima preda del vampiro* show little respect even for the authority of their male vampire partner, who does not hesitate to kill them when he has had enough.

All in all, drawing from a variety of methodologies from semiotics to Marxism-informed psychoanalysis, current scholarship has been portraying the Italian female vampire of the late 1950s and early 1960s as a hyper-attractive dominatrix – a voracious, insatiable sexual predator who uses her physical qualities to overrule men (heterosexual female vampire) or exclude them altogether (lesbian vampire). Attempts to connect this portrait to the Italian zeitgeist, though, have so far produced only very vague discourses centred on male anxieties concerning the female emancipation brought about by the last years of Second World War, the post-war reconstruction and the new affluence of the late-1950s economic miracle. The former two, granting Italian women access to the job market and the right to elect and be elected, are seen as an initial step towards female self-awareness, while neocapitalist modernisation is seen as the decisive cause for women's rejection of traditional patriarchal culture and its limitation of feminine horizons to the choice between angel of the hearth and whore (Günsberg 2005: 133–72; Bini 2011a). In order to provide a detailed account of 1956–1965 Italian vampire cinema from a gender perspective, it is then necessary to investigate more in depth the socio-historical context in which vampire films were produced and consumed.

Gender struggle in post-war Italy

That, in the aftermath of Second World War, Italian men were anxious because Italian women started entering the public sphere of work and politics *en masse* after two decades of home confinement under Fascism is easily demonstrable. For instance, Christian Democrat Angela Maria Guidi Cingolani – the first woman ever allowed to speak in an Italian legislative session – opened her 1 October 1945 speech as a newly elected Consultative Assembly member by reassuring her male colleagues: 'Do not be afraid that women's contribution will be a return to a matriarchy, if such a thing ever existed. We know better than to aspire to that; but even if we did, we certainly could not do any worse than you men have done!' (quoted in Tambor 2014: 3). This is typical of post-war Italy's 'Lost Wave' proto-feminism – an informal, cross-party, female 'movement for women's equality' that, while presenting itself as unthreatening as possible to men's established positions, 'justified itself by the entire society's need to be redeemed and protected from the threats men had unleashed' in the form of totalitarianism and war (Tambor 2014: 3).

Crucially, these were the same years in which Italian women's contribution to Resistance was being downplayed and depoliticised by men and women alike by invoking 'maternal feelings' of care and protection as a core reason for the struggle against Nazi-Fascism, the Catholicism-inspired maternal register being 'the strongest female image on which women could draw and [. . .] the only socially acceptable one in which they could be stronger than men' (Willson 2010: 105). Indeed, the belittling of women was omnipresent in Italian political debates of the immediate post-war. While active and passive female suffrage was granted in 1945–1946, most male politicians were sceptical of adult women's intellectual capabilities. Many members of the Italian Communist Party, in particular, deemed women electors too irrational/sentimental and therefore prone to be controlled by reactionary Catholics, to the point that the party leader was forced to dispel these claims in public speeches (Togliatti [1945] 1965a and [1953] 1965b). As for gender diversity in the Parliament of the Italian Republic, composed of 630 elected deputies and 315 elected senators, female presence was minimal until very recently, a sign of distrust towards female politicians from both electors and fellow party members. In each of the six legislations following one another from spring 1948 to summer 1976, fewer than fifty women obtained a seat in the Chamber of Deputies (forty-five in 1948, thirty-four in 1953, twenty-five in 1958, twenty-nine in 1963, nineteen in 1968 and twenty-six in 1972) and fewer than eleven in the Senate (four in 1948, one in 1953, three in 1958, six in 1963, ten in 1968 and six in 1972). The height of post-war misogyny, however, was reached when occupational issues were at stake.

For Italian women Second World War and the immediate post-war were periods of reversal of traditional gender roles: since most male adults were fighting or hiding, prisoners or dead, women had to fill in the head-of-the-family role and deal with the world outside the house for the first time in their life. As a consequence, after 1945 'a bitter conflict of interest arose between th[e] mass of unemployed men', returning from the front and demanding a reinstatement of the pre-war status quo, 'and the many thousands of women who had worked during Second World War and wanted to hold on to their jobs' and newly acquired economic independence (Ginsborg 1990: 80). The zeitgeist is perfectly summarised by Garofalo (1956: 80–1):

> Articles about the need for women workers to leave their jobs to unemployed males are appearing once again [. . .]. Women are praised for what they have done so far [. . .] but they are basically told: 'Now step aside and go back in the house [. . .]'. [. . .] In speeches and the press, ironical remarks are often made about women who work only to gain some extra money for luxuries like dresses, trips and entertainment, occupying a place that could go to a man who needs to feed his family.

Similarly, whenever the female politicians of the Lost Wave tried to pass laws that – in agreement with the democratic principles of the 1948 Italian Constitution – sought to make the work sphere less of a 'fortress of virility' (Garofalo 1956: 52), they were met by male colleagues, and by male and female public opinion more at large, with pseudo-scientific discourses about women belonging to the domestic sphere as mothers and housewives. For instance, from 1945 until the approval of law 66 of 9 February 1963, female deputies and senators had been struggling to grant their fellow women the right to become judges and diplomats, and to access state examinations awarding civil service jobs, only to be told that females are naturally unfit for such careers. Two reasons were advanced: first, 'in certain days of the month', women transform into irrational menstrual monsters endowed with an uncontrollable 'aggressive libido' (Garofalo 1956: 121); second, the female body is so delicate that it must be spared 'any overwork or strain in order to protect the health of [women's] reproductive system and progeny' (Tambor 2014: 159).

Evidently, the 'binary logic' of 'strictly separate gender roles' and 'the hierarchy implicit in the structure of the traditional patriarchal family unit' that 'were intensely instrumentalised during the Fascist regime [...] carried over into the post-war' (West 2006: 23). In the late 1940s and over the course of the 1950s, domestic manuals still prescribed the Italian woman to be a 'diligent little wife' whose most fulfilling achievement lies in childbearing and managing the household while the husband is 'absent from home almost all day long due to his [breadwinning] work' (West 2006: 24). Gender stereotypes were furtherly reinforced through Catholic propaganda, emanating both from the churches' pulpits and via mass media like the press, radio and, after 1954, TV (the latter two firmly under control of the Christian Democrats after their landslide victory at the general elections of 1948 and 1953):

> The purpose of marriage (and of the family) in the words of *Famiglia Cristiana* (13 October 1946), the leading Catholic popular weekly, was: 'committing oneself to carrying out a great mission in life, that of collaborating with God in perpetuating and multiplying human life'. Women's specific role was the subordinate one of mother and husband's help-mate, with its attendant virtues of modesty, submission and sacrifice. (Allum 1990: 83)

The model was the Virgin Mary, who not coincidentally became the object of a Vatican-sponsored, nationwide cult in the immediate post-war, culminating in Pius XII's 1950 dogma of Mary's Assumption. Things were not different on the far-left side of the ideological spectrum: in spite of the fact that the Italian Communist Party repeatedly denounced female oppression and insisted on female occupation as a key to emancipation (Berlinguer 1954; Longo 1965; Togliatti [1945] 1965a, [1953] 1965b, [1954] 1965c and [1959] 1965d), in real life party members and sympathisers followed a strictly heteronormative, patriarchal model of family and gender relations – one that was identical to that of their right-wing antagonists (Caldwell 1991: 28–50; Bellassai 2000; Tasca 2004).

In the post-war years, the female politicians' struggle to correct the most blatant instances of male privilege touched not only the ideal figure of the wife-mother, the nurturing and selfless Madonna, but also focused on its opposite – Magdalen, the whore, yet another creation of patriarchy. In fact, parallel to the attempt to give Italian women the opportunity to free themselves from confinement in the domestic sphere, there was the attempt to abolish *case chiuse* ('closed houses'), the state-run brothels where adult women could be legally detained under a house-arrest regime for most of the day and allowed to exercise the so-called 'oldest profession'. The debate following Socialist senator Angelina Merlin's 1948 proposal to close down *case chiuse* on grounds that no democratic state could discriminate women and monetise on their sexual exploitation offers invaluable insights on gender issues in the Italian Republic.

All major political forces indicted the inhumanity of the legalised prostitution system, but thwarted the approval of Merlin's bill for ten years. Besides economic interests to be protected, the belated approval was due to the fact that, from the neofascists to the Communists, there was a consensus among male citizens that 'public brothels were important sites of the production and passing down of masculinity in Italy, places of patriarchal identity and certainty. Their management by the state lent legitimacy to th[e] structure of gender definition and hierarchy' that subordinated women to men (Tambor 2014: 126). According to the nationwide Doxa polls of 1949 and 1959, the vast majority of female public opinion was against the abolition of *case chiuse* too: determined to defend howsoever small an influence they gained by conforming to patriarchy's idealised model of femininity, Italian Madonnas agreed with men that sex is postribular fun and love is familial duty, and therefore saw Magdalens as a necessary evil, performing the social function of providing males with the opportunity to let off some steam without the risk of emotional complications that may jeopardise existing or prospective, respectable, procreation-bent marriage bonds (Garofalo 1956: 91–3; Parca [1965] 1977: 48–91, 215–35; Tambor 2014: 108–40). When, after a decade of virulent press campaigns against it, the law was finally approved on 20 February 1958, it had become a symbol of 'women's takeover and destruction of every last space of masculine refuge' (Tambor 2014: 126), and many a man went on record lamenting 'the lost paradise' of *case chiuse* (Parca [1965] 1977: 215). Most importantly, though, by the time the law was approved, it had been appropriated by the Christian Democrats and changed so much that, from a vindication of the absolute equality between sexes, it had become yet another instrument to keep women in their place, under strict police surveillance, subordinate to male authority but idealised as 'the creature[s] of which the poets make angels, to whom Christianity brings the honors of divine maternity' (Tambor 2014: 137).

In spite of the appeals to the sanctity of womanhood and, especially, motherhood, post-war Italy remained for decades a country where, as ruled by the Cagliari Courthouse on 7 November 1961, 'it is not a crime to beat one's wife for correctional purposes' (quoted in Carrano 1977: 77). As a matter of fact, a double standard was in place in Italy and, until very recent times, females could be subjected throughout their whole life to the arbitrary violence of their male tutors, whether fathers, brothers or husbands. For example, article 559 of Codice Penale (introduced in 1930 and upheld by the Constitutional Court in 1961) criminalised and harshly punished female adultery only, while, by the combined effects of article 587 CP and article 581 CP (also introduced in 1930), women could be wounded or even killed by their husbands and/or male relatives with little to no consequences if the female was found out to have an illegitimate carnal relationship bringing shame to the honour of her family: impunity in case of beating not resulting in death, three to seven years in prison in case of murder ostensibly committed in a state of rage and without premeditation. Article 559 CP was abolished in 1968, divorce was introduced in 1970 (and confirmed via referendum in 1974), and the parity between the two spouses in family law was established in 1975, but the dispositions about honour killing contained in article 587 CP were maintained as far as 1981.

As shown by the above discussion of the Italian legislation, the economic miracle of the late 1950s was far from bringing about an instantaneous, radical change in gender issues. At closer scrutiny, it is perhaps more correct to think of the so-called 'boom' and its immediate aftermath as a period in which the dynamics of change clashed against subtle strategies to reaffirm patriarchal traditionalism under different means. This is evident, once again, in the work sphere. State data reveal that, throughout the 1950s, around 6.5 million Italian women (26 per cent of the total female population) were working under a regular contract: on the one hand there was an incentive for employers to hire women because they could be paid less than men for the same job; on the other hand law 860 of 26 August 1950, which guaranteed working women paid maternity leave and other benefits, somewhat curbed female employment (Tambor 2014: 75–107). In the peak years of the economic miracle, from 1958 to 1963, the number of working women increased, showing a trend of female workers leaving jobs in agriculture to take on jobs in industry and services. Afterwards, however, women's employment declined and, during the 1960s, about a million women left the labour force. Besides the higher numbers of young women undertaking full-time education in high school and university, the decline was because 'male wages rose, and, as a result, some women were expelled from the labour market, particularly as the principle of equal pay, agreed in 1960, made employing them less attractive'. At the same time, 'improved male earnings enabled more women to become full-time housewives', and '[t]he pattern increasingly became that women worked when they were young, then left the labour market after the birth of their children, after which they found it hard to return' (Willson 2010: 119).

As the extended, patriarchal, peasant family of the countryside gave way to the city-dwelling, working-class, nuclear family, the main female role model of the 1960s continued to be the housewife (Tasca 2004). This was for three reasons. First, for many women, 'particularly those from peasant backgrounds, the option of dedicating themselves to caring properly for their family and home could seem a conquest [. . .] that had largely only been possible for wealthy women in previous generations' (Willson 2010: 120). Second, 1960s Catholic propaganda kept insisting on Pius XII's 1945 statement that 'every woman's destiny is motherhood' (Willson 2010: 131). Third, from the second half of the 1950s, consumer culture successfully intercepted the desire for security of many an Italian woman who had experienced the hardships of war and reconstruction, and proposed via women's magazine and radio and TV advertisements an attractive figure of the modern Italian woman that did not hurt the Vatican's and the Christian Democrats' principles – the '[*donna*] *tutta casa e famiglia*, smartly dressed, with well-turned-out children and a sparkling house full of consumer durables' paid by instalments with the husband's salary (Ginsborg 1990: 244). As two surveys of 100,000 Italian housewives conducted by the Catholic organisation Centro Italiano Femminile in 1949 and 1964 revealed, though, the dream of being a housewife slowly turned into a nightmare of isolation, loneliness and dissatisfaction on the personal level (Willson 2010: 121–2), while 'the idealized confinement of women to the home in the 1960s served to enclose them in a purely private dimension, and to remove them even more than previously from the political and public life of the nation' (Ginsborg 1990: 244).

Besides pinpointing the exact source of Günsberg's (2005: 133–72) and Bini's (2011a) vaguely defined male anxieties over female invasiveness and aggressiveness, the sketch of the Italian socio-historical context from the mid-1940s to the mid-1960s shows that patriarchal attempts to prevent gynosociality, marginalise and tame the rebellious, post-war New Women were as successful in real life as in the vampire movies analysed in the opening section of the chapter. No matter how scary, cruel and bloodthirsty matriarchy was depicted in vampire horrors and in vampire-themed pepla *Roma contro Roma* and *Maciste e la regina di Samar*, real Italian men had little to fear from their female fellow countrymen. First, the sexist mentality of Italian society was so solid that it was shared by most women as well, as proven by the debate on *case chiuse*. Second, the Lost Wave proto-feminism always was a top-down movement with little follow-up in Italian society, and its egalitarian crusades ended up hijacked by Christian Democrats more often than not. Feminist groups started forming in 1966 (curiously the year the Gothic horror *filone* waned and vampire cinema production came to a halt in Italy) and, as we shall see further below, they gathered political momentum only in the early 1970s. The zeitgeist, then, matches the misogynistic agenda of early

Italian vampire cinema, which not coincidentally developed in an industrial environment controlled by Christian Democracy.

However, the triumph of the institutionalised, 'dominant cultural order' (Hall [1980] 2009: 169) sanctioned by the punishment of the villainesses must not overshadow the complexity of the female monster. With the exception of the matriarchs from *Roma contro Roma* and *Maciste e la regina di Samar*, and of lesbian Julia from *Danza macabra*, female vampires are never portrayed as pure, perverted wickedness. On the contrary, a careful analysis of the filmic texts allows identifying some cues that the (overwhelmingly) male screenwriters[5] and (exclusively) male directors may have inserted for spectators to develop a certain sympathy towards the villainess so that, while appeasing the anxieties of Italian men, Italian women's woes and sorrows under patriarchy could also be highlighted. Acknowledging this 'mixture of adaptive and oppositional elements' (Hall [1980] 2009: 172) makes it possible to nuance the monolithic portrait of the Italian female vampire painted by academics so far and problematise taken-for-granted assumptions on Italian vampire cinema as an all-out misogynistic cultural manifestation.

Hard to be a woman: the female vampires of 1956–1965 revisited

A timidly feminist side of Italian vampire horrors from the late 1950s and early 1960s emerges if the cautionary-didactic, Manichaean dynamics of the nineteenth-century French stage melodrama dissected by Brooks ([1976] 1995) are traded for the specificities of Italian melodrama, and especially the cinematic melodrama codified in the immediate post-war by director Raffaello Matarazzo in a series of box-office hits like *Catene / Chains* (1949), *Tormento* (1950) and *I figli di nessuno / Nobody's Children* (1951). Contrary to French stage melodrama's 'moral polarization and schematization' (Brooks [1976] 1995: 11–12), in Italian melodrama 'the figures of the Virgin and the Whore are often found in the same woman', because for Italian authors and audiences pathos does not lie in the peripeties leading to the final triumph of Good over Evil, but occurs when the narratives 'complicate any easy moral condemnation and dwell instead on suffering as a redemptive state and a route to compassion' (Bayman 2014: 45). If we apply this suggestion to Italian Gothic horror, the female vampire remains a villainess to be executed for the greater good of society, but her evil deeds are, if not excused, at least justified by very human feelings of either hate or love that are presented to the spectator within a revenge or tragic-love plot.

Il sangue e la rosa, *La maschera del demonio* and *La cripta e l'incubo* are illustrations of the former type of storyline. While *Il sangue e la rosa*'s villainess is the ghost of an eighteenth-century woman tormenting the 1960s descendants of the man who shamelessly betrayed her love, Asa Vajda and Sheena Karnstein wreak havoc in nineteenth-century Central-Eastern Europe to exact revenge on their family for the wrongs they suffered centuries earlier in their mortal life within a misogynistic society ruled by their male relatives. It is never clear if, prior to their death at the hand of the inquisitors, Asa and Sheena really were vampire witches as they were accused to be: by setting their trial and execution during the period of early-modern witch hunts made infamous by *Vredens dag / Day of Wrath* (Carl Theodor Dreyer, 1943), Arthur Miller's 1953 play *The Crucible* and its Italo–French film adaptation *Les sorcières de Salem / The Crucible* (Raymond Rouleau, 1957), the filmmakers automatically cast doubts on the validity of the accusations.[6] Furthermore, there are no witnesses, no evidence of crime, no confessions – during the trial, the spectator can only listen to an all-male jury's verdict of culpability and see two young women as they face a horrible death with the dignity, defiance and faith in resurrection of a Christian martyr. Asa is dressed in white like Ingrid Bergman in *Giovanna d'Arco al rogo / Joan of Arc at the Stake* (Roberto Rossellini, 1954) and about to be burnt alive, Sheena almost completely naked and crucified: both refuse to recognise the legitimacy of the court, invoke higher powers and curse the judges.[7] As has been written apropos of the later Hammer horror *Dracula: Prince of Darkness*, in *La maschera del demonio* and *La cripta e l'incubo*, too, 'the image that should speak to us of the conquest of institutionalized good has a latent subversive content: it shows [. . .] males overpowering and symbolically violating a struggling, screaming female' (Prawer 1980: 258). Sheena makes it explicit right after hearing from her fellow Karnsteins the death sentence punishing her for unspecified 'sacrilegious crimes'. Echoing the opening scene of Middle-Age-set peplum *Maciste all'Inferno / The Witch's Curse* (Riccardo Freda, 1962), written by *La maschera del demonio*'s screenwriter Ennio de Concini and revolving around a lustful judge using his position to have a woman who rejected him executed for witchcraft, Sheena says: 'You kill me unjustly! But you will pay for your sins!' The apex of melodrama Italian-style, however, is reached in the tragic-love plots of *I vampiri*, *Il mulino delle donne di pietra* and *La maschera del demonio*, where female vampires seek to realise the impossible dream of living a so-called 'normal' life, loving and being loved just like anybody else.

Let us start from the opening scene of *La maschera del demonio*, with Princess Asa Vajda tied to a stake next to the lifeless body of her lover Javutich. The all-male jury of prelates – dubbed 'the Sacred College of the Primates of Moldavia' – is led by Asa's brother Griabi, who sentences the woman to death with the following words:

> I, Great Inquisitor Griabi, second-born in the lineage of the Princes of Vajda, condemn you and, as your brother, I disown you. Many a crime you have committed in order to satisfy your satanic love for Devil's servant Igor Javutich. May God have mercy on your soul!

Besides the very vague accusations, what is interesting to note is the genealogical reference: if Griabi is the second-born, then his sister is presumably the eldest in the family and, given the aristocratic custom of keeping family assets undivided, the sole heir to the Vajda's fortune, which suggests that the Great Inquisitor might have exploited the religious hysteria of the times to get rid of Asa and her partner for inheritance reasons.[8] Whatever the case, once Asa and Javutich return from the dead, their objective does not seem to be vengeance *tout court*. Rather, they seek the blood of the nineteenth-century Vajdas as a means to rejuvenate and make up for lost time, which makes them piteous, slightly sympathetic characters along the lines of lovelorn Imhotep from Universal's 1932 *The Mummy*, not least for tear-jerking monologues like the one pronounced by newly resurrected Javutich as he caresses Asa's corpse:

> You have pulled me out of the earth that was as heavy as lead on my body, Asa. Now you are not alone any more. I will bring Katia to you and she will be your prey. [. . .] Through her, you will live again. You will talk and smile like her, and we will live again, as in the old days.

Duchess Marguerite Du Grand from *I vampiri* and Elfi from *Il mulino delle donne di pietra* would stop at nothing to fulfil their dreams of love, too. Their villainy therefore acquires a shade of tragic grandeur mixing moral reprobation with awe-like respect and, perhaps, compassion, as in the Italian melodramatic imagination the reasons of the heart are commonly perceived as uncontrollable, 'all-too-human and eternal passions' (Raffaello Matarazzo, quoted in Casadio 1990: 8), and much more dignified a motive than lust or greed. In her prime, Marguerite was madly in love with a married man, Pierre Lantin senior, and, once rejected, she used her wealth and social position to ruin the Lantins. Now, in mid-1950s Paris, decades after her beauty faded, she has her henchmen feed her the blood of innocent schoolgirls to regain her lost youth and seduce Pierre Lantin junior (a portrait of Pierre Lantin senior is hanged in Marguerite's bedroom, next to the bed, symbolising her everlasting romantic obsession). Although viciously evil for the whole film, in the end we are informed by a policeman that 'the Duchess died confessing her crimes', which hints at a repentance *in extremis* and a minimum of hope for the safety of her soul.

Elfi, on the other hand, suffers from a rare disease that kills her every time she is under emotional strain, so she is forced to spend the best years of her life as a recluse in her family house, in company of her hyper-protective father and a shady, lustful doctor, who revive her with transfusions of fresh female blood. It is the feeling of having being unjustly wronged 'by a blind and cruel fate' (Matarazzo, quoted in Casadio 1990: 8) over which she has no control that, in a typically melodramatic fashion, makes her a pity-inducing, somewhat sympathetic victim as well as a cruel perpetrator. For instance, as she sadistically teases bound-and-gagged angelic virgin Liselotte, Elfi reveals her deep emotional wounds and fragility:

> I am so afraid of thunder! When I was a child, I always hid under the bed . . . Were you afraid too? No? It is because you have never been all alone like me, in this dark, gloomy house. Maybe you already knew Hans and you took refuge in his arms during storms . . . Shivering in his arms must have been tremendously exciting!

For all its privileging of the Madonna over the Magdalen, *Il mulino delle donne di pietra* is far from providing a portrait of the female vampire as absolute evil. Rather, the screenwriters and the director seem to air the idea that the blame for fallen women's misfortunes should be put, at least partially, on the very same overemphasis on female virginity and moral double standard that Garofalo (1956) and Parca ([1959] 1966 and [1965] 1977) consider a bulwark of post-war Italy's oppressive patriarchal mentality. At the beginning of the movie, Hans enjoys a sexual encounter with sex bomb Elfi (she is first seen emerging from vagina-shaped curtains, wears a scarlet nightgown and utters femme-fatale lines like 'It is I who want you!') only to realise how pure and beautiful is the love of his virginal sweetheart Liselotte, who forgives all his faults without asking questions and agrees to marry him. This 'implicitly underlines a moral male-oriented judgement: better a modest life companion than a passionate lover who could not even offer her virginity' (Curti 2015: 52), which is confirmed by the film's treatment submitted to the Italian Show Business Bureau: 'Embittered for having yielded to the call of the flesh and having fallen against his will into Elfi's trap, Hans finds peace in his childhood friend Liselotte's pure love' (Unknown 1959). As Di Chiara (2009: 103) writes, then, 'Hans's behaviour is that of the young, petty-bourgeois stock-character who, after an adventure with an already "compromised" woman, goes back to his girlfriend to get married'. However, *Il mulino delle donne di pietra* does not promote the male-oriented narrative as unproblematically and enthusiastically as the treatment and the moralistic framework sketched by Italian horror scholars would lead us to believe.

Indeed, one-third of the way through the film, in the highly melodramatic scene in which Hans breaks up with one-night stand Elfi, she makes some good points before bursting into hysterics and dropping dead on the floor:

> I love you, Hans. I love only you, do you understand? Even if other men before you took advantage of my loneliness . . . of my lack of experience . . . But maybe you are blaming me for this? You are unfair. If you only knew how horrible is my life, all alone in my room!

In short, under patriarchy, once a woman gives in to passion and falls (loses her virginity out of the wedlock), she is branded as a whore and becomes a pariah of sorts. Contrary to men – who are free to satisfy their sexual appetites at any one time and, if virgin, are allowed to fall without suffering any consequence – unmarried, non-virgin women are excluded from the number of the respectably marriageable and become an easy target for unscrupulous men who promise redemption via marriage in exchange for sex with no intention of keeping their part of the bargain after coitus. As a matter of fact, desperate with her outcast status, the compromised woman would even be the first to offer men sex, like Elfi does with Hans, in the attempt to convince the sexual partner to marry her and make a so-called 'honest woman' out of her.

The tragic-love narratives of *I vampiri* (symptomatically retitled *Quella che voleva amare*, 'She who wanted to love', for its August 1958 *fotoromanzo* release in issue 31 of *I vostri film*), *Il mulino delle donne di pietra* and *La maschera del demonio* allow putting forward three interconnected points. First, in spite of their academic reputation of transgressive, promiscuous man-eaters, the most well-known Italian female vampires from the late 1950s and early 1960s are quite romantic and decidedly monogamously minded, their dream being the same as that of the damsels in distress on which they feed: living with a man *more uxorio*, happily ever after. The only difference between the two female opposites lies in the means by which they try to win over their beloved, that is to say in the conflict between carnality and purity, with the latter always triumphant – except in *Il sangue e la rosa* (whose ending suggests that Leopoldo Karnstein's angelic bride is possessed by villainess Millarca), *I Wurdalak* and *Danza macabra* (where vampirised damsel in distress Sdenka and undead adulteress Elisabeth eventually get to live forever with the young man they are in love with).[9]

Second, if damsels in distress are little more than screaming ornaments waiting to be saved and married by the dashing hero, vampire women do not fare much better from a female-empowerment point of view: they, too, live in a condition of total dependence to men, as shown by the fact that the monstrous female is easily disposed of by the good guys once her male servants and/or lovers are defeated (*I vampiri*, *La maschera del demonio* and *L'orribile segreto del Dr. Hichcock*), switch allegiance (*L'amante del vampiro*) or lose interest in her (*La strage dei vampiri*). In other words, with the exception of Sheena from lesbian-themed *La cripta e l'incubo*, female vampires embrace rather than reject the heteronormative mentality of post-war Italy according to which the members of the so-called 'weaker sex' must put themselves under the protection of the supposedly 'stronger sex' in order to survive – the power of the vampire dominatrix being the sum of male manpower and intellect she can co-opt through sex appeal and/or the black arts. And indeed, trapped under patriarchy, both damsels in distress and villainesses ultimately end up voicing the same feelings of frustration, entrapment, powerlessness, worthlessness and isolation that, according to Ginsborg (1990: 244) and Willson (2010: 121–2), plague the Italian post-war housewife. Elfi, as we have seen, laments her imprisonment and loneliness in the familial home several times over the course of *Il mulino delle donne di pietra*, and so do Laura in *La cripta e l'incubo* ('Almost nobody ever comes here. This castle is like a tomb . . . ') and Katia in *La maschera del demonio*:

> I feel so desperate and lonely here! [. . .] What is my life? Bitterness and grief, something that is destroyed little by little and nobody ever rebuilds. It wastes away day after day, like this garden, which is dying away like my aimless existence![10]

The case of *L'amante del vampiro*'s vampire Countess Alda, who, like Duchess Marguerite Du Grand, is more afraid that the lack of blood would make her look her real age than kill her, brings us to the third point, namely that female vampires give a great importance to their physical aspect, obsessing about youthful looks and beauty. Other notable examples come from *Amanti d'oltretomba* (in which decrepit servant Solange agrees to be an accomplice in a brutal double murder to reacquire youth via blood transfusion and marry her master) and *L'orribile segreto del Dr. Hichcock* (in which the title character tries to make up to his first wife Margaretha for mistakenly burying her alive by feeding her the blood of his second wife Cynthia, so that Margaretha – grotesquely aged due to the shock of premature burial – will get back her good looks). Not coincidentally, in an early-1960s nationwide poll, 'physical qualities' ranked absolute first choice as an answer Italian adult males gave to the question 'What is the most valuable characteristic in a woman?', with '21% of the votes' (Parca [1965] 1977: 118), thus showing at work 'the dictatorship of beauty', that is to say the patriarchal dogma according to which beauty is the only weapon for a woman to catch a male protector and make it in life (Garofalo 1956: 29).

By bringing to the fore the vindictive and tragic sides of early Italian vampire cinema, common assumptions about the Gothic horror *filone* have been problematised, and the female vampire presented as an all-too-human being melodramatically caught between sexual rebellion/transgression (pre- or extra-marital sex, recreational rather than procreative intercourse, so-called 'abnormal' sexual behaviours, excessive beauty, matriarchy) and hyper-identification with traditional patriarchal values (marriage, monogamy, dependency/submission to the male, overemphasis on female youth and beauty). Such nuanced and contradictory portrayal, though, is hardly due to a feminist sensibility on the part of screenwriters and directors. Rather, it is most likely a by-product of the *filone*-filmmaking mode of production described in Chapters 1 and 2.

First, as all *filoni* exploits, the Italian vampire movies of the late 1950s and early 1960s generally were written and shot at breakneck speed, and revised/reworked by people with different tastes and agendas at different stages of pre-production, production and post-production, which is bound to result in changes in register within the film, if not plain inconsistencies. Second, for the almost totality of the people making genre cinema in Italy, the main motive for working on a project was financial gain, and therefore the aim was to craft a movie obliging popular narrative formulas, established cultural stereotypes and censorship diktats, so that many spectators would go to see it (especially in a huge film market such as the Italian one, where the state also granted to producers tax refunds proportional to box-office receipts). Under this light, the sexy, uninhibited, slightly sympathetic villainess of Italian Gothic horror – a much rounder character than the passive damsel in distress – could have been conceived both as eye candy for male spectators and a hook for strong female identification, in order to broaden the audience as much as possible. The countercheck to the above considerations is provided, by way of counterpoint, if we move on to investigate the portrayals of female vampires in post-1968 Italian cinema.

A MISSED SEXUAL REVOLUTION: POST-1968 FEMALE VAMPIRES

As 'bastardised excrescences' of the Gothic revival triggered in 1957–1958 by Hammer (Curti 2011: 300), the Italian vampire horrors made after 1968 generally adopt the narrative *topoi* codified in the late 1950s and early 1960s. First of all, they reprise the sexually connoted moral dichotomy between villainesses and damsels in distress emphasised via hair colour (for example, wayward brunette Lucy versus blonde wife-to-be Mina in *Il Conte Dracula*, and red-headed, promiscuous Countess Dracula versus raven-haired, virgin chambermaid Tanya in *Il plenilunio delle vergini*). A minimal variation to this scheme is provided by *La notte dei dannati*, where blonde Danielle is already happily married when she crosses path with a dark-haired vampire witch, which makes her a madame in distress rather than a damsel in distress. Second, while under the influence of the 1968–1971 Jean Rollin vampire tetralogy, of Hammer's 1970–1971 Karnstein trilogy and of Harry Kümel's and Jesús Franco's 1971 film-scandals *Les lèvres rouges* and *Vampyros Lesbos* the late-1960s and early-1970s Italian female vampires become even more proactive and forward in soliciting sex from male and females alike, their woman-in-peril counterparts maintain the passivity of the late 1950s and early 1960s, so that decisive actions are once again entrusted to either a male hero (*La notte dei dannati*, *La notte dei diavoli*, *Il plenilunio delle vergini* and *Dracula cerca sangue di vergine . . . e morì di sete!!!*) or homosocial brotherhoods (*Il Conte Dracula*, *Le vergini cavalcano la morte* and *Riti, magie nere e segrete orge nel*

Trecento . . .). Third, in the denouement, many post-1968 Italian vampire horrors tend to focus on the punishment of evil women through disfigurement, purifying fire, staking or other bodily mutilations (*Il Conte Dracula, La notte dei dannati, La notte dei diavoli, Le vergini cavalcano la morte* and *Il plenilunio delle vergini*), although there occasionally are sardonic, unhappy endings that, just like in early-1960s entries *Il sangue e la rosa, I tre volti della paura* and *Danza macabra* and in Roman Polanski's 1967 *Dance of the Vampires*, let vampires have it their way (. . . *Hanno cambiato faccia* and *Nella stretta morsa del ragno*) or doom the male protagonist right after evil is defeated (*Il plenilunio delle vergini* and *La notte dei diavoli*).

The main difference between the Italian vampire horrors of 1956–1965 and those of 1969–1975 lies in the latter's abundance in female nudity and lack of nuance in the representation of the villainesses. From an industrial perspective, this is explained by the fact that – inspired by the international success of Anglo-American, Francophone, West German and Spanish sexy/horror hybrids in the late 1960s and early 1970s, and aided by a relative relaxation of the Italian Film Censorship Office over the course of the second half of the 1960s – Italian horror began to target adult males by relying more and more on sensationalist sexual content at the expense of plot and character development, and even narrative coherence, as denounced in the censorship reports for *Riti, magie nere e segrete orge nel Trecento* . . . cited in Chapter 2. Tellingly, the only post-1968 female vampires who are given a minimum of characterisation are those played by Lucia Bosé and Milena Vukotic – two ageing actresses who, by the early 1970s, had little sex appeal to show off, if compared to their much younger co-stars Ewa Aulin, Silvia Dionisio, Dominique Darel and Stefania Casini. Vukotic, in particular, played a middle-aged *racchia* ('ugly woman') in the hyper-successful comedy *Venga a prendere il caffé . . . da noi / Come Have Coffee with Us* (Alberto Lattuada, 1970) and, in spite of a full-frontal-nudity photoshoot in Italian monthly *Playboy* (Blasetti and Frontoni 1976), found herself typecast in the role ever since.

In *Le vergini cavalcano la morte*, forty-one-year-old, former Miss Italia 1947 Bosé exploits her fading beauty to play Erzsébet Báthory II, a nineteenth-century Marquise who resorts to bathing in blood like her infamous ancestor to regain youth and the sexual attentions of her estranged husband Karl. When her plan fails, guilt-ridden after commissioning several murders and killing Karl in a fit of jealousy, Báthory II confesses her crimes and takes full responsibility in front of the authorities, just like Duchess Marguerite Du Grand from *I vampiri* did *in articulo mortis*. In the last shot of *Le vergini cavalcano la morte*, we see the Marquise walled up in her room by court order, mummified in front of a mirror, forever bound to contemplate her decaying face. In *Dracula cerca sangue di vergine . . . e morì di sete!!!*, on the other hand, thirty-eight-year-old Vukotic plays the small role of unattractive spinster Esmeralda Di Fiore: due to being a virgin, she is vampirised by Dracula and, after he is executed, she commits suicide by impaling herself on the same stake that killed her demonic husband. These are the only two female vampires who can compare to the villainesses of the late 1950s and early 1960s as far as psychological depth, inner turmoil and tragic grandeur are concerned. As for the rest, the characterisation of post-1968 female vampires is flattened, if not dumbed down, as shown most blatantly in *La notte dei dannati* and *Il plenilunio delle vergini*.

Borrowing from *La maschera del demonio* and *La cripta e l'incubo*, *La notte dei dannati* is centred around Tarin Drôle ('Strange Nose'), a woman executed for witchcraft in 1650 who periodically returns from the dead to exact revenge on the descendants of her executioners, the family of the Princes of Saint Lambert, leading the male Saint Lamberts to madness and drinking the blood of the female Saint Lamberts to continue her existence as young and beautiful Rita Lernod. Contrary to the early-1960s templates, though, no flashback of Tarin Drôle's execution is provided to cast doubts on the validity of the seventeenth-century inquisitors' accusations. Moreover, the villainess is given little dialogue and spends most of her screentime coveting beautiful young females, mangling or caressing their exposed breasts. As a matter of fact, *La notte dei dannati* starts as a revenge-from-beyond-the-grave horror but soon becomes a sexual-triangle narrative of the *Les lèvres rouges* or *Vampyros Lesbos* kind in which, for unexplained reasons, the vampire witch insinuates herself between detective Jean Duprey and his wife Danielle (neither of whom belongs to the Saint Lambert family). Showstopping softcore interludes abound in *Il plenilunio delle vergini* as well. Here, a threadbare plot revolving around twin brothers Franz and Karl Schiller looking for the ring of the Nibelungs around the village of Ladracu is fleshed out to the minimum requirement of eighty minutes by Countess Dracula's sexual exploits with evil twin Franz and zombie chambermaid Lara, and by the final orgiastic ritual of sex and blood. Not coincidentally, the screenplay of the film calls for the subtitle *Eros Vampiros* – a clear nod to *Vampyros Lesbos* – to appear in the opening credits (Batzella 1972).

That after 1968 the female vampire had become a synonym for pure, bloodthirsty and sex-starved evil is confirmed by the 1970s adults-only Italian magazines advertising some coeval vampire films from Italy and abroad. In an article about *Le frisson des vampires / The Shiver of the Vampires* (Jean Rollin, 1971) titled *Voglio la vampira che mi piace tanto* ('I want the female vampire whom I like so much'), for instance, it is noted that 'a brand new vampire figure' is 'trending today' – a version of the vampire that, compared to previous big-screen incarnations, is 'revised and corrected, or, to better put it, revised and corrupted, transformed into a charming female creature hungry for blood and sex' (Rey 1971: 1). A launch article for *Il plenilunio delle vergini* focusing on its star Rosalba Neri, the actress 'that more than any other has become "the undressing leading lady" of Italian cinema' (Santevril 1972: 8), similarly quips that 'Rosalba – naturally, given the times we live in – rather than blood seeks (you bet it!) sex' (Santevril 1972: 6). The piece then lauds director Luigi Batzella for having the end credits roll right after the death of Neri's character, as the movie makes no sense without the 'panoramic and expressive curves' of 'the vampire Countess thirsty for blood (and sex!)' (Santevril 1972: 11). Finally, the publicity blurb puts special emphasis on *Il plenilunio delle vergini*'s sapphic scenes, for example on the covers of *Cinesex Attualità* issue 13 (November 1972) and *Cinestop Attualità* issue 12 (May 1973), where the taglines 'Rosalba Neri ... più lesbica che mai!' ('Rosalba Neri ... more lesbian than ever!') and 'Lesbo-vampira assatanata' ('Horny lesbo-vampire') appear in blood-red block letters.[11]

The joke about the updating and spicing up of classic horror figures is recycled in a launch article for *La notte dei dannati* unambiguously titled *Sesso nelle tenebre* ('Sex in the darkness'):

> Black magic is now spreading everywhere. Until a few years ago, it was practised only by small congregations in England – the adepts grouped around efficient and extremely knowledgeable, yet decrepit and ugly, witches. It is only natural, then, that their followers were few. But, in a short turn of years, sexual commodification penetrated even in this dark zone of Western subculture. The average age of witches drastically dropped [...] and their attractiveness grew enormously: today a black magic priestess must be a beautiful-bodied, twenty-year-old girl (during the rituals, nakedness is mandatory just like formal dress at the Nobel Prize ceremony). (Giustiniani 1971: 74)

Perhaps inspired by the fact that the subject of 'the first full-frontal-nudity picture ever to appear in an Italian popular magazine' was Gothic-horror-*filone* star 'Barbara Steele [...] in a photoshoot female photographer Elisabetta Catalano made in 1967, for *Playmen* issue 1' (Pezzotta 2014: 44), an article advertising *Requiem pour un vampire / Requiem for a Vampire* (Jean Rollin, 1971) even proposes a direct connection between the so-called 'sexual revolution' of the late 1960s and vampire cinema, in that they both are bent on liberating people by breaking centuries-old taboos about carnal pleasures and the representation of sexuality (Circi 1972). Full-frontal female nudity and lovemaking without inhibition or remorse are the main attractions also in the horror-themed, adults-only, Italian comic-book series of the late 1960s and early 1970s, as best exemplified by the adventures of female vampires Jacula and Zora, whose namesake series spanned from 1969 to 1982 and from 1972 to 1985 respectively, and sold an average 60,000 copies per issue in the first years, when production expenses were 50 lire per copy and the retail price 200 or 300 lire (Pettarin 1980; Curti

2011: 307–12). 'Finally, I can love without restraint!', says a naked girl lying on a tomb during a vampire sabbath in *Jacula* issue 1 (March 1969), symbolically announcing the death of the Catholic-patriarchal obscurantism and welcoming a new era of sexual freedom and female self-fulfilment. A sketch of the contemporary historical and socio-cultural context is therefore needed to assess the claims about the inherently subversive quality of post-1968 Italian vampire cinema and, especially, to shed light on its gender politics.

As already mentioned, in Italy feminist groups started forming in 1966, bringing together the predominantly upper-middle-class, university-educated women who constituted the target audience of the first Italian editions of second-wave-feminism manifestos like Simone de Beauvoir's 1949 *Le deuxième sexe* and Betty Friedan's 1963 *The Feminine Mystique*, published between 1961 and 1965. The pathfinder was the collective Demau ('Demystification of authority') in Milan, followed in the early 1970s by Rome-based Rivolta Femminile ('Female revolt'), Milan-based Liberazione Femminile ('Female liberation'), Trento-based Cerchio Spezzato ('Broken circle'), Padua-based Lotta Femminista ('Feminist struggle') and a few others. As a matter of fact, a characteristic of Italian feminism was 'its diffusion through a number of diverse groups' operating in different cities – 'varied realities' (Bono and Kemp 1991: 4) that were seldom in contact with each other and strongly suspicious 'of all formally constituted parties, which were seen as entrenchments of male authority' (Bono and Kemp 1991: 10). Proud of their non-institutional basis, Italian feminist groups adopted as an operating principle the idea that the personal is political and, through the theoretical tools of 1960s-1970s French psychoanalysis, elaborated a philosophical practice known as *autocoscienza*, consisting of 'independent, small groups of women, meeting to discuss issues of all kinds on the basis of personal experience' (Bono and Kemp 1991: 9). Seeking freedom in sexual difference rather than equality at men's conditions, the most radical Italian collectives even declared that 'we [women] communicate only with women' (Rivolta Femminile [1970] 1991: 40). In their writings, Italian feminists – and especially the members of Rivolta Femminile and Lotta Femminista – criticised Marx's dialectic materialism for ignoring women's unpaid labour within the house and accused Marxist revolutionary theory of being patriarchal: women liberation 'does not lie in achieving economic independence' and is not to be postponed until after the proletarian revolution, like the Italian Communist Party had been saying ever since its foundation in 1921, but must be achieved in the here and now by 'destroying the institution [of the family] which made [women] into slaves even after slavery had been eliminated' (Lonzi [1970] 1991: 52).

According to historians, the origins of 1970s Italian feminism are less connected to the creation of the 1966 Demau collective than to the Italian student movement of 1968: 'many of the women involved in the "new" feminism of the 1970s came out of the experience of 1968, with its strong anti-institutional bias, and were or had been members of extraparliamentary [left-wing] groups' (Bono and Kemp 1991: 10). The birth, demands and impact of the Italian student movement will be explored in Chapter 6. For now, suffice it to say that the youth revolt that exploded in Italian universities in 1967–1968 catalysed the 1960s male and female teenagers' ever-growing restlessness about traditional gender roles: the authority of the father over sons and daughters was fiercely questioned, the family was charged with the sexual enslavement of females, and slogans exalting personal freedom and free love were shouted. As in 'other Western countries, many Italian women first became politicised through the sit-ins and mass debates of the student movement', criticising 'authoritarian ideas (including the "authoritarian family")' and calling for 'greater sexual freedoms', then 'rebelled against it' (Willson 2010: 151) upon realising that, for their male fellow protesters, the much-called-for sexual freedom simply meant that women should make themselves available at any time to meet men's sexual needs, on pain of being called frigid, lesbian, old-fashioned, reactionary or a combination thereof (Segre 1982). This explains why 1970s feminists, exasperated by and disgusted with their former male comrades' die-hard sexism, insisted on *autocoscienza* and the importance of gynosociality rather than on male–female dialogue.

Although never widespread at mass level, very loosely structured and fragmented in a myriad local sections, the Italian feminist movement gained some momentum from the early 1970s to the early 1980s, when a series of parliamentary debates and referenda touched upon issues like legalising contraceptive pills, divorce and abortion, which were seen as potentially instrumental to liberate women from the century-old stereotype of the (house) wife-mother. In spite of the fact that in Italy the laws on divorce and abortion were passed in far less radical a form than the one many feminists hoped for (Caldwell 1991: 51–101), the Italian feminist movement quickly entered collective imagination as synthesised by its slogan 'Tremate, tremate, le streghe son tornate!' ('Tremble with fear, the witches are back!'), meant to underline the aggressiveness of 1970s feminist militants, who – contrary to the moderate, non-threatening proto-feminists of the Lost Wave – purported to literally scare men off their privileges.[12] The witch analogy, however, proved a double-edged sword for Italian feminists, because it was immediately used by their ideological rivals to derogatorily depict the Italian feminist movement as a coven of nagging, often ugly and past-their-prime women who conspired against constituted order out of sexual frustration, mostly to take revenge on the men they could not win over.

Moving from the socio-cultural context back to the filmic texts, only two post-1968 Italian vampire movies can be said to bend the austere sexual morality of the Gothic horror *filone* codified in the late 1950s and early

1960s, and embrace the countercultural mindset of the student-protest years. In . . . *Hanno cambiato faccia* and *Il prato macchiato di rosso*, the theme of the conflict between the so-called 'good' and the so-called 'bad' femininity is reworked to make hyper-sexed hippy characters a *bona fide* positive model: the former film contrasts a red-headed hippy girl's joyous embracing of sex as healthy, uncomplicated fun with a brunette vampire secretary's view of sex as a duty and a means to an end; the latter contrasts a cute, brunette hippy's sexual attraction to her partner with a blonde, lame, vampire-like, upper-class woman's incestuous relationship with her neo-Nazi brother. As for the rest, given both the dependence of the Italian vampire output of 1969–1975 to early-1960s narrative models and the one-dimensionality of 1970s vampire women, post-1968 Italian vampire cinema leans heavily towards an all-out misogyny whose aim is twofold – to exorcise the old fears of the immediate post-war (many 1970s male characters still end up willy-nilly serving a vampire dominatrix, as shown by *La notte dei dannati*, *La notte dei diavoli* and *Le vergini cavalcano la morte*) and the new anxieties about 1970s feminists, who were struggling to build a society where females could survive without a male protector if they so desired.

Perfectly capable of getting by without any help from men, the powerful vampire witches of horrors *La notte dei diavoli*, *La notte dei dannati* and *Il plenilunio delle vergini* lend themselves particularly well to incarnate the 1970s patriarchal stereotype of the feminist *strega* in all its shades, from the old maid jealous of other people's familial happiness to the impenitent or reformed lesbian. In *La notte dei diavoli*, an extended peasant family (consisting of an old patriarch, his submissive young wife and two kids, plus the patriarch's slightly younger brother and his three grown-up children) is threatened by a wurdalak in the Slovenian backwoods. Conforming to contemporary sexist slander against feminists, the wurdalak is not a highwayman like in Aleksey Tolstoy's *La famille du Vourdalak* and *I tre volti della paura*'s segment *I Wurdalak*, but a middle-aged, unmarried woman of unremarkable physical qualities who lives alone in the wilderness, plotting to destroy the family unit barricaded in the ancestral house. As for motivations, the screenwriters and the director strongly imply that she acts out of sexual frustration and envy: her aim is to separate the old patriarch from his attractive young wife, and it is only after the vampirised patriarch is dispatched by his relatives that the wurdalak unleashes her fury on the rest of the family, as a revenge of sorts. In *La notte dei dannati*, on the other hand, the all-female orgiastic rituals officiated by vampire witch Tarin Drôle/Rita Lernod might be seen as a parody of *autocoscienza* meetings, while the lesbian villainess's rejection of males as inadequate sexual partners (she kills her husband the Prince of Saint Lambert and subsequently starts chasing young women around, including married Danielle) could be a sexploitative dramatisation of the Italian feminists' radical stance that 'wom[e]n must not be defined in relation to man' (Rivolta Femminile [1970] 1991: 37) and should communicate only among themselves.

The most misogynistic vampire horror, however, is *Il plenilunio delle vergini*. This is not so much because Countess Dracula is executed by hero Karl in the finale, as a punishment for her lesbian escapades and for her taking on a penetrative, masculine role during heterosexual intercourse ('It is almost like it is she who is possessing him, now', aptly comments a caption in the May 1973 *fotoromanzo* adaptation of the movie, in *Cinestop Attualità* issue 12, as the naked Countess refuses the receptive missionary position and mounts on top of her male partner to penetrate him with her fangs). As we have seen when discussing state and religious censorship bodies in Italy, identifying evil with non-normative sexuality and violently sanctioning it were inescapable conditions for industry people who sought to make money by challenging the boundaries of the visible. The apex of misogyny in *Il plenilunio delle vergini* is actually reached one hour into the movie, when the Countess, after many decades of widowhood livened up only by lesbian ménages, finally has sex with a man in the person of consummate playboy Franz: so wonderful is the experience that the Countess calls him 'the living reincarnation of my husband Count Dracula', decides to marry Franz and share with him the immortality and omnipotence granted by the ring of the Nibelungs. Besides exemplifying what Zimmerman ([1981] 2004: 78) calls the 'heterosexual context' of the lesbian vampire film – that is to say the flattering of male viewers' egos by showing a man 'stepping in to separate two women and thus prove his superior prowess, [. . .] his sexual potency and his masculine superiority' – Countess Dracula's character arc is a stark illustration of the sexist idea that what women really want is not equality/emancipation/freedom/power but a virile husband able to satisfy them in bed. So much for the subversive content and sexually liberating power of post-1968 vampire cinema from a female perspective.

NOTES

1. It is possible that the casting of Gianna Maria Canale as the villainess of *I vampiri* was meant to exploit the actress's real-life reputation of homewrecker and concubine, just like her iconic role as man-eater Sabina did in proto-peplum *Spartaco* (Riccardo Freda, 1953). Born in 1927, Canale had in fact been Freda's lover since the late 1940s and the fact that the director, almost twenty years her senior, left his wealthy, upper-class wife Angiola Dondina for her caused a stir in the Italian press, especially when the newly formed couple flew to Brazil in September 1948 to shoot some movies (Curti 2017a: 17–18, 65–83).
2. The treatment of *La maschera del demonio* is much more graphic than the finished film as far as female disfigurement is concerned. In the treatment (Unknown 1959–1960), Gorobec beats Asa with 'a wooden bar' until 'her body goes to pieces', leaving 'only a screaming head'. Then, 'Gorobec grabs the witch's head by the hair

while the Gorgon-like creature tries to bite him', and an Orthodox priest 'sprinkles the monstrous head with holy water', opening 'wounds and cracks as if the skin is attacked by a corrosive acid'. Finally, the head melts down to reveal the skull and 'falls to dust'.

3. Together with *La cripta e l'incubo*, *Il sangue e la rosa*, *Danza macabra* and *Il mostro dell'Opera* are generally considered the earliest examples of lesbian-themed Italian vampire cinema. In the latter three films, however, lesbianism is a very marginal element, basically a 'hook for voyeurs' (Pezzotta 1997: 30). In *Il sangue e la rosa* – a loose adaptation of *Carmilla* set in 1960s Italy – there is a scene in which young lady Carmilla Karnstein briefly kisses Miss Giorgia Monteverdi on the mouth, but the plot actually revolves around Carmilla's attempts to seduce her male object of desire, cousin Leopoldo Karnstein, engaged to Giorgia. In *Danza macabra*, lesbianism is summarily dismissed as the most unnatural perversion: lesbian Julia tries to force herself on adulteress Elisabeth lying in shock on the conjugal bed next to the dead bodies of her husband William and her lover Herbert; Elisabeth screams 'I like men, do you understand? [. . .] I would rather die than do this!' and stabs Julia to death (in the afterlife, Elisabeth would go on rejecting Julia with lines like 'I am a woman, do you understand? A real woman! [. . .] I despise you! I hate you!'). In *Il mostro dell'Opera* there is an openly lesbian character, 'Yvette, born in the city of Lesbo, in the Sappho province', and some girl-on-girl caressing and biting takes place due to the sexual vibes emanated by the male vampire, but the story always remains focused on heterosexual couples.

4. *Il mulino delle donne di pietra*'s starlet Scilla Gabel, whose stage name evokes Homer's man-eating monster Scylla, started her career as a body double for Sophia Loren, the *maggiorata* ('busty woman') par excellence. In *La strage dei vampiri*, Graziella Granata runs down a staircase wearing a flimsy, very low-necked negligee in order to show her large breasts bouncing. Gastaldi (1991: 179) states that Maria Luisa Rolando was cast as the villainess in *L'amante del vampiro* because she had 'two tits [sic] on which you could study geography', and it is precisely this part of her body that a male vampire grabs in the risqué promotional material for the movie reproduced in Gifford (1969: 77). The lure of the breasts, though, is not restricted to evil women: in both *L'amante del vampiro* and *La maschera del demonio*, the diegetic need to show a crucifix hanging from the damsel in distress' neck offers the occasion for a 'close-up of a florid, pulsating female cleavage' (Curti 2015: 64), whose titillating allure supposedly is sanitised by the religious symbol.

5. Among the thirty-three vampire films studied in the monograph, only *La maschera del demonio* and *Dracula cerca sangue di vergine . . . e morì di sete!!!* had a female contribution at the writing stage. The former was rewritten, among others, by Fede Arnaud, Lucia Torelli and Maria Nota according to the documents submitted by the producers to the Italian Show Business Bureau, while much of the latter's dialogue was made up day by day by production secretary Pat Hackett (Morrissey 1974: 20–1). Such contributions went uncredited in the film prints.

6. First submitted to the Italian Film Censorship Office in 1950 under the title *Dies Irae* (Nullaosta 7425 1950), Dreyer's film was re-released in Italian theatres in 1958 (in Danish with Italian subtitles) and again in 1959 (dubbed), possibly in an

attempt to cash in on Hammer's Gothic revival. Miller's *The Crucible* premiered in Italy in November 1955 as *Il crogiuolo*, for Luchino Visconti's direction, to a good public and critical success.

7. In *La cripta e l'incubo*'s screenplay Sheena is crucified upside-down like Saint Peter and her hands are mangled by the spikes in close-up (Gastaldi and Valerii 1963), but the government officials enacting preventive censorship marked the passage in blue and both the upside-down crucifixion and the gory details did not make it in the finished film. Among the unfilmed bits of the screenplay there also are a shot in which Laura moves her lips close to Sheena's and a dream sequence in which Laura and Sheena enjoy pleasure and pain by taking turns in whipping each other while pushing a small carriage with no clothes on.

8. In a May 1980 interview for Parisian newspaper *Libération*, Bava stated that Asa is sentenced to death for committing incest with Javutich (quoted in Leutrat 1994: 158), although the incest subplot is nowhere to be found in *La maschera del demonio*'s existing treatments (Unknown 1959–1960; Gomarasca et al. 2004: 20) and shooting script (Unknown 1960).

9. As testified by the preventive-censorship report, *I tre volti della paura*'s screenplay envisaged a radically different ending for *I Wurdalak*, with vampirised Sdenka choosing to die by impalement in order not to infect her beloved Count Vladimiro d'Urfé. In Aleksey Tolstoy's novella *La famille du Vourdalak*, Marquis d'Urfé is mocked by vampirised Sdenka for his earlier attempts at gallant courtship, but ultimately escapes unharmed from the clutches of the peasant wurdalaks.

10. In *La maschera del demonio*'s shooting script, Katia voices her dislike for her condition more energetically than resignedly: she complains to her father that her younger brother Costantino can go out hunting in the forest, while she is shut into the castle with nothing to do (Unknown 1960). It is worth recalling that, in both the shooting script and the finished movie, Katia has just turned twenty-one, which was the age of majority in Italy until March 1975.

11. Lesbian vampires were already a selling point in 1960s ballyhoo, although much more timidly in both texts and accompanying pictures. This is shown by *Il sangue e la rosa*'s launch article *Vampiri e sesso nel film di Vadim* ('Vampires and sex in Vadim's film'), which fraudulently states that, following 'Vadim's favourite formula of non-stop sex', the movie revolves around 'a girl attracted to the fiancée of her cousin' (Anonymous 1960b: 43). A decade later, equally mendacious is a promotional article for *Nella stretta morsa del ragno*, stating that 'Elisabeth is married to William but she is the lover of both Herbert and Julia' (Anonymous 1971: 76): just like in *Danza macabra*, *Nella stretta morsa del ragno*'s female protagonist Elisabeth feels only disgust towards lesbian Julia.

12. The full slogan reads 'Tremate, tremate, le streghe son tornate! Non più puttane, non più Madonne, finalmente siamo donne' ('Tremble with fear, the witches are back! Neither whores nor Madonnas any more, finally we are women') (Crainz 2005b: 517).

4. MALE VAMPIRES

POST-WAR ITALY'S MASCULINITY IN REAL LIFE AND ON FILM

The previous chapter has shown that, in the early phase of the Gothic horror *filone*, misogynistic repression coexisted with more ambivalent narrative dynamics highlighting the hardships women have to face in a man's world. At closer inspection, *Il mulino delle donne di pietra*'s titular museum-mill is a perfect metaphor for Wood's (1979a, [1970] 1979b and [1979] 1985), Williams's (1984) and Berenstein's (1996: 9–10) idea that horror is a highly contradictory genre in which the enforcement of the political, socio-economic, racial and gender status quo goes hand in hand with a subterranean critique of dominant ideology. First, the museum-mill does not only showcase sculptures of infamous serial murderesses and stereotypically evil women like Salomé, as it is often misreported in plot synopses, but features a problematic hybrid between femme fatale and tragic lover (Cleopatra), a queen beheaded for court machinations (Anne Boleyn or, less likely, Mary Stuart) and a martyrised national heroine (Joan of Arc) too. Second, all these statues – whether representing so-called 'good' or 'bad' female archetypes – contain the corpses of innocent girls bled dry by two middle-aged men obsessing over young and beautiful Elfi due to borderline-incestuous attachment (her father, professor Wahl) and sheer lust (her suitor, doctor Bohlem), which certainly begs the question of who the actual vampire of the narrative is. Such a question, however, has rarely, if ever, been asked in the academia. After Clarens's (1968: 190–4) and Mora's (1978: 289–342) seminal analyses of the Gothic horror *filone*, there has been a tendency to see 'the Italian horror film' as 'concentrat[ing] almost entirely on the devastating effects of a sexually provocative witch/vampire woman on hapless masculinity' (Newman 1986a: 22), to the point that the male vampires appearing in Italian cinema have never been studied in depth.

Contrary to their female homologues, who remained confined to horror/thriller hybrids, supernatural horrors and pepla, in the aftermath of the Hammer *Dracula*'s worldwide box-office success male vampires started appearing in almost every genre of Italian cinema, extending their domain from chillers and sword-and-sandal adventures to comedy, and even popping up for a cameo in Mario Amendola's 1963 *Sexy proibitissimo*, one of the last striptease compilations attempting to exploit the extraordinary box-office success of Alessandro Blasetti's 1959 *Europa di notte* (see Chapter 1). Although displaying more variety in terms of film-genre appearances, Italian male vampires are far less nuanced characters than female ones, and therefore rather univocal and uniform figures if subjected to gender readings. In fact, whatever the genre context and the production year, Italian male vampires basically act as hyper-sexed demon lovers that women young and old, nubile and married, either secretly desire (the woman-as-willing-victim stereotype) or are unable to turn down (the woman-as-powerless-victim stereotype). The will to piggy-back on Hammer's smash hit *Dracula* and ensuing Dracula cycle – which revolved around 'this very charming, handsome man' (Terence Fisher, quoted in Eyles et al. 1973: 14) by whom 'women were eager to be nipped' (Hammer executive Michael Carreras, quoted in Frayling 2011: 126) – is a plausible yet only partial explanation for Italian male vampires' one-dimensionality over the next sixteen years. Useful insights for an investigation into Italian makeshift Draculas from 1959 *Tempi duri per i vampiri* to 1975 *Il cav. Costante Nicosia demoniaco, ovvero: Dracula in Brianza* can be found by revisiting the zeitgeist of post-war Italy.

As made explicit by Christian Democrat Angela Maria Guidi Cingolani in her 1 October 1945 speech as a newly elected Consultative Assembly member ('we [women politicians] certainly could not do any worse than you men have done!') (quoted in Tambor 2014: 3), and by 1950s Italian-language domestic manuals ascribing 'feminine progress [. . .] to the recent crisis of the masculine world' (quoted in West 2006: 26), Second World War tore down a long-standing patriarchal bulwark that was particularly cultivated by the Fascist regime: 'the myth of male infallibility' (Garofalo 1956: 4). Moreover, with the advent of TV around the mid-1950s, and the inception of the economic miracle and consumer culture in the late 1950s, the traditional balance of power between genders slowly began to shift in Italy:

> In a rigidly patriarchal culture, gender hierarchy greatly hinders the expansion of consumer-goods consumption because, by imposing themselves as mediators between the women and the marketplace, men grant

housewives a very limited autonomy of choice, one that is basically restricted to the purchase of food and a few household goods. [However,] the booming consumer-goods market [of late-1950s and 1960s Italy] demanded more and more interlocutors [...] in possession of a certain degree of autonomy: when this superior need of the market found an obstacle in masculine demands for a total submission of females to males, the market removed the obstacle by bypassing men and addressing women directly. (Bellassai 2011: 106)

Thus, due to the influence of mass-media advertising, during the so-called 'boom' of 1958–1963 women progressively took centre stage and became the ideal citizens of modern, neocapitalist Italy as both housewives responsibly managing consumption in the private sphere of the home and married or unmarried spendthrift purchasers of non-essential goods. Coinciding with the abolition of state-run brothels, the 'harem' of the wannabe 'sultan' that is the Italian male (Parca [1965] 1977: 48–91, 215–35), the emergence of a consumerist female power was perceived by many Italian commentators from the early 1960s in terms of a weakening – if not a downright feminisation/devirilisation – of the *bel paese* as a whole (Alberoni 1967: 170–82; Bellassai 2011: 104–5). At the same time, consumer culture's reparative attempts to reassure Italian males of their virility and gender leadership seemed to somewhat add insult to injury, because advertising agencies started linking traditional masculine values like authority, strength, determination, pragmatism and self-reliance to the stereotypically feminine spheres of the care of the self and housekeeping. This is shown by the 1963 press advertisements for cosmetic products for 'modern', 'successful', 'sober and virile', 'essentially manly', 'definitely masculine' males quoted in Bellassai (2011: 116), and by the hugely popular 1961–1965 Moplen commercials aired on Italian State TV's advertising show *Carosello*, in which 'Milanese comedian Gino Bramieri' played a 'househusband' moving with the times and efficiently running the house in place of his careerist 'architect wife' (Manzoli 2012: 109).

In spite of the fact that in Italy what Bourdieu ([1998] 2001) terms 'masculine domination' managed to keep gender equality at bay until the late 1970s and early 1980s (as seen in Chapter 3, the parity between spouses in family law was established in 1975, and the dispositions about honour killing contained in article 587 of Codice Penale were maintained as far as 1981), Italian cinema started bringing to the screen flawed, vulnerable, passive, ineffectual male protagonists from the earliest days of the newly founded Republic, especially focusing on the depiction of 'male prowess and sexual vigour, previously celebrated by [Fascism] and so central to the representation of masculinity in Hollywood cinema, [...] as untenable for Italian men' (Rigoletto 2014: 4–5). The examples discussed by film scholars usually come from auteur cinema, for instance the humiliated father of *Ladri di biciclette / Bicycle Thieves* (Vittorio

De Sica, 1948), the lovelorn wanderer of *Il grido* (Michelangelo Antonioni, 1957), the countless *inetti* played by Marcello Mastroianni from *La dolce vita* (Federico Fellini, 1960) and *Il bell'Antonio* (Mauro Bolognini, 1960) up until *La città delle donne / City of Women* (Federico Fellini, 1980), and Marco Ferreri's men on the verge of extinction (Chatman 1985; Marcus 1986; Rohdie 1990; Bondanella 2001; Reich 2004; Rigoletto 2014: 14–44). Yet, Italian genre cinema abounds with weak, disoriented, inadequate male characters ever since the end of Second World War too. For instance, in the comedy *Come persi la guerra* (Carlo Borghesio, 1947), vaudeville star Erminio Macario plays a little man who, with his timidity, naivety, ineptitude and fundamental kindness, demolishes the Fascist mystique of virility as military and sexual voracity (Ben-Ghiat 2005), while in early-1950s comedies like *Il seduttore* (Franco Rossi, 1954), *L'arte di arrangiarsi / The Art of Getting Along* (Luigi Zampa, 1954) and *Un eroe dei nostri tempi* (Mario Monicelli, 1955) actor Alberto Sordi incarnates a far more dislikeable version of the man-child, one that combines Macario's simple-mindedness and lack of physical prowess with laziness, vainglory, cowardice, selfishness and deceitfulness. And it is exactly by virtue of films like *Il seduttore*, *L'arte di arrangiarsi* and *Un eroe dei nostri tempi*, together with more high-profile pictures like *Lo sceicco bianco / The White Sheik* (Federico Fellini, 1952) and *I vitelloni* (Federico Fellini, 1953), that Sordi will become one of the *mostri* ('monsters') of the scathingly satirical comedy of manners known as *commedia all'italiana*, which, in the aftermath of the success of *I soliti ignoti / Big Deal on Madonna Street* (Mario Monicelli, 1958) and throughout the 1960s and 1970s, represented not only how low the average Italian man can sink to get ahead during and after the economic miracle, but also the many sexual failures of self-proclaimed Latin lovers (Gili 1980; Laura 1981; D'Amico 1985: 98–103, 108–32, 151–63; Aprà and Pistagnesi 1986; Giacovelli 1995 and 1999; Canova 2004; Fournier-Lanzoni 2008; Comand 2010; Bini 2011b; Manzoli 2012: 143–91; Fullwood 2015).

For reasons of space and thematic pertinence, however, only early Gothic horrors and horror-tinged adventures will now be analysed to outline the masculinity-in-crisis background against which the representation of male vampires as powerful, irresistible demon lovers developed from the late 1950s onwards. As implied in Chapter 3 when bloodthirsty dominatrices were discussed, there seems to be no peace for males in the Gothic horror *filone*. In *La maschera del demonio*, Javutich and doctor Kruvajan become undead slaves for the love of a woman, and so does Count Vladimiro d'Urfé in *I tre volti della paura*'s episode *I Wurdalak*. In Massimo Pupillo's 1965 *Il boia scarlatto*, former peplum star Mickey Hargitay plays a psychotic bodybuilder 'who is presumably impotent', a 'dishonour' (Curti 2011: 148) he shares with paraplegic doctor John Hichcock from *Lo spettro / The Ghost* (Riccardo Freda as Robert Hampton, 1963). Doctor Bernard Hichcock from *L'orribile segreto del Dr. Hichcock*, on the other hand, is a necrophile who dreams 'to be capable of absolute subjugation [of women], without possibility of resistance' (von Krafft-Ebing [1886] 1991: 393) while actually being totally dominated by his corpse bride Margaretha and her chambermaid Martha. Another sexually deranged leading man is doctor Stephen Arrowsmith from *Amanti d'oltretomba*, who prefers scientific research to female company (his wife Muriel consequently lusts after the all-brawn-and-no-brains gardener David) and can only reach orgasm by torturing living beings.[1] Villains are belittled *qua* males in horror-tinged adventures as well, most notably in *Roma contro Roma*, where the much-feared Roman consul oppressing the people of Armenia is a mere puppet in the hands of his ruthlessly ambitious wife Tullia (played by Maria Antonietta Golgi, already employed in the role of irresistible peasant bloodsucker Sdenka in *I Wurdalak*). By the same token, *Roma contro Roma*'s seemingly invincible villain Aderbale – a high priest who is invulnerable to human weapons and able to perform wonders such as resurrecting the dead, controlling the mind of the living and teleporting – is ridiculed by a finale showing that all his powers actually derive from his mistress goddess Oro: once she is blinded by hero Gaio, Aderbale loses his sight too and quickly meets an undignified end.

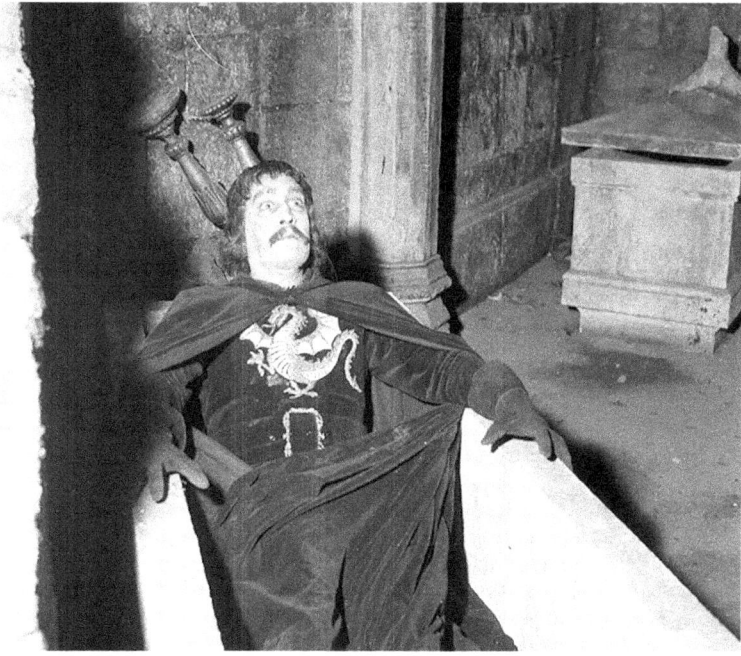

Figure 4.1 Arturo Dominici as makeshift Dracula Javutich on the set of *La maschera del demonio* (photo by Osvaldo Civirani available at Archivio Centrale dello Stato – Archivio fotografico Civirani (film) – 098 Maschera del demonio La – 098–0232).

The heroes of the early Gothic horror *filone* do not fare much better, as best exemplified by young medical student Andrej Gorobec from *La maschera del demonio*, Austrian nobleman Wolfgang from *La strage dei vampiri* and English journalist Alan Foster from *Danza macabra*. Like the aforementioned Javutich and Kruvajan, Gorobec also loses himself in vampire-witch Asa's spellbinding eyes, but is saved at the eleventh hour, and rather fortuitously, by the irruption of a lynch mob of angry villagers who do the killing for him. Wolfgang, on the other hand, is bled dry by both his vampirised wife Luise and his vampirised servant Corinne, and spends most of the denouement confined to bed in an unmanly 'satin nightie with a ruffled collar' (Rigby 2016: 108), acting as a bait to ensnare the vampires. Finally, Alan is a 'subject of inaction' (Di Chiara 2009: 190) who, from the fearless macho he boasts to be in front of his fellow males in the tavern-set prologue, quickly turns into a frightened, powerless witness to supernatural events. Not only is Alan taunted by lady of the house Elisabeth at the beginning of his adventure in the haunted Blackwood mansion ('Is it possible that it is up to me, a woman, to give you courage?'), but

> in the end – in a curious reversal of narrative roles – [he] assumes the position normally reserved to the damsel in distress: it is up to Elisabeth to [try and] save him from the [. . .] bloodthirsty undead, in a plot twist later recycled verbatim in [. . .] *La vendetta di Lady Morgan*. (Curti 2015: 112)

The same contempt for men with a big mouth and little courage is displayed in *L'ultima preda del vampiro*, where vampirised ballerina Katia shows up naked in her bossy, loudmouth employer's bedroom as he is leafing through pin-up magazine *Frolic*: 'Why do you look at me like that, Lukas? Did you not always say that you like me? I am in your room now. [. . .] Tell me that you want me!', she says baring her fangs, to which he replies by babbling like a baby and fainting – a blatant demonstration that flesh-and-blood women are too much for him. As for the rest, heroic figures are unflatteringly depicted as business-like, asexual professionals along the lines of Hammer's doctor Van Helsing (reporter Pierre Lantin junior in *I vampiri*, the Orthodox priest in *La maschera del demonio*, doctor Nitch in *La strage dei vampiri*, doctor Low in *L'orribile segreto del Dr. Hichcock* and doctor Joyce in *Amanti d'oltretomba*), as sexually opportunistic and cowardly petty-bourgeois stock characters (Hans in *Il mulino delle donne di pietra*, an ideal brother of *Danza macabra*'s man on the verge of a nervous breakdown Alan), or as clueless *innamorati* who arrive too late to save the day but just in time to get themselves killed (Vladimiro in *I Wurdalak* and Pierre in *La vendetta di Lady Morgan*).

Man is a Hunter: The Male Vampires of 1959–1975

In such a desolate scenario for masculinity, vampire villains might have paradoxically stood out as a positive model of identification for the very many Italian males mourning the death of traditional virility and the feminisation/devirilisation of the *bel paese* after Second World War. Indeed, behind Italian makeshift Draculas lurks the figure of the *gallo* ('cock, rooster'), that is to say the hypersexed, hyper-virile, aggressively predatory Latin lover of the Casanova or Don Juan kind, who gets all the women he desires by one means or the other and 'accumulates female conquests in a way that could be defined paratactic, [. . .] without any emotional involvement or distinction [among his conquests]. He finds every woman irresistibly attractive, therefore for him all women are attractive in the same way' (Manzoli 2012: 174). These words, originally referring to Giacomo Casanova as brought to the screen in auteur kolossal *Il Casanova di Federico Fellini / Fellini's Casanova* (Federico Fellini, 1976), perfectly fit the 1959–1975 Italian male vampire in that he basically is a lady killer for whom all women are but necks to be penetrated for nourishment. However, contrary to Fellini, who – like the less highbrow directors of 1950s Italian comedies and the post-1958 *commedia all'italiana* – genuinely despised the myth of the Italian womaniser and mercilessly ridiculed it (Reich 2004: 78–104; Manzoli 2012: 172–84; Rigoletto 2014: 34–44), the filmmakers involved in Italian vampire cinema did not show a strong dislike towards the undead *gallo* running after nubile, engaged and married women of all ages.[2]

Obviously, given the Catholicism-influenced moral restrictions to filmmaking outlined in the previous chapters, the bloodsucker seeking the unlimited satisfaction of carnal desires ends up negatively sanctioned (*L'amante del vampiro, L'ultima preda del vampiro, Ercole al centro della Terra, Maciste contro il vampiro, La strage dei vampiri, Ercole contro Moloch, Il mostro dell'Opera, Il Conte Dracula, Riti, magie nere e segrete orge nel Trecento*. . . and *Dracula cerca sangue di vergine . . . e morì di sete!!!*) or somewhat reformed (*Tempi duri per i vampiri* and *Il cav. Costante Nicosia demoniaco, ovvero: Dracula in Brianza*) more often than not (*I tre volti della paura*, whose triumphant male vampire Gorka from the episode *I Wurdalak* is discussed further below). Yet, much like the last-minute punishment of the Gothic horror *filone*'s monstrous females, the happy ending exacting justice on Italian Draculas might be considered a mere token to be paid for slipping sex past state censors, as the movies' main attraction lies in the sexual escapades of the fanged Casanova rather than in the struggle of the good guys to protect womankind. Under this light, although consistently and unmistakably bearing the stigma of evil to be eradicated, the Italian male vampire can be seen as a champion of traditional machismo within ideologically charged narratives bent, among other things, on the virile compensation of disgruntled masculinity – an uncanny, sleazy fellow traveller to the spotless Ercoles and Macistes of 1958–1964, whose hypertrophic muscles 'reflected [the] need for reassurance over the value of the strong male body in uncertain times' (O'Brien 2013: 193).

A survey of 1959–1975 vampire cinema made in Italy confirms that cautionary appeals to sexual restraint and compensatory male empowerment lived side by side. This is evident in vampire horrors and vampire-themed pepla, where male bloodsuckers are allowed their fair share of female necks before bringing about their own destruction by asking too much – too many women (*L'amante del vampiro*, *Ercole contro Moloch*, *Il mostro dell'Opera*, *Il Conte Dracula*, *Riti, magie nere e segrete orge nel Trecento*... and *Dracula cerca sangue di vergine... e morì di sete!!!*), women who belong to somebody stronger (*L'ultima preda del vampiro*, *Ercole al centro della Terra* and *Maciste contro il vampiro*), a child bride (*La strage dei vampiri*). The most interesting attempts to find a balance between indulgence and punishment, though, are horror parodies *Tempi duri per i vampiri* and *Il cav. Costante Nicosia demoniaco, ovvero: Dracula in Brianza*.

Tempi duri per i vampiri presents the hyper-sexed, predatory masculinity of the Hammer Dracula as easily attainable for Italian males, who seemingly have it in their genes, but ultimately labels the *gallo*'s way of life as not preferable. The film opens by contrasting dignified, Eastern-European vampire Baron Roderico of Bramfürten (English actor of Italian descent Christopher Lee), a tall, dark stranger whom women simply cannot resist, with clownish, short and chubby, impoverished Italian Baron Osvaldo Lambertenghi (thoroughbred Roman Renato Rascel, a specialist in the role of *il piccoletto*, 'the small guy', ever since the 1930s), hopelessly in love with Lilla, a twenty-something servant who is as pure as the lilac blossoms whose name she bears. Based on these premises, one would expect the comedic substance of the film to arise from the clash between self-confident vampire Roderico and his clumsy human nephew Osvaldo. Yet, it is not so: accommodating the economic needs to keep Lee's shooting schedule as brief as possible and to exploit the enormous domestic popularity of Rascel's slapstick antics, the conflict entirely takes place within Osvaldo's personality, Jekyll-and-Hyde-style. In fact, a bite from Roderico and a second-hand black cape with red lining awake the dormant *gallo* inside timid, ineffectual suitor Osvaldo, who subsequently spends his days as an awkward bellboy and his nights as a tireless stud able to bite forty-two women in a few hours, making no distinction between Italian and foreign, virgin and non-virgin, married and unmarried, young and old preys. The only woman Osvaldo does not bite is of course Lilla, whose pure kiss of love cures him of the inextinguishable vampiric thirst. Eventually, in the Christian-Democrat-approved happy ending, Osvaldo leaves sexual excesses to his aristocratic uncle (who is last seen walking away arm-in-arm with two Scandinavian models) and embraces a life of middle-class monogamy by taking on a managerial job and marrying his virgin dream girl.³

Some sixteen years after the release of *Tempi duri per i vampiri*, *Il cav. Costante Nicosia demoniaco, ovvero: Dracula in Brianza* brought to the screen the very same master narrative: a hapless Italian male meets a foreign vampire whose libertine lifestyle he tries out for a while but ultimately rejects in favour of marital sexuality, by which it is meant a procreation-bent union that, as seen in Chapter 3, allows for occasional infidelities on the part of the husband. In *Il cav. Costante Nicosia demoniaco, ovvero: Dracula in Brianza* only a few, superficial details changed from 1959 blueprint *Tempi duri per i vampiri*, namely the protagonist's socio-economic status and the vampire's sexual preferences. As for the former, Costante Nicosia (Sicilian actor Lando Buzzanca, who spent most of the late 1960s and the 1970s playing the Mediterranean macho with a voracious sexual appetite) is a prosperous industrialist in the toothpaste sector. As for the latter, Romanian Count Dragulesku (Englishman John Steiner mimicking the aplomb of Lee's 1958–1973 Dracula) is a bisexual vampire who presides over a harem of three young, constantly horny women and an older, effeminate gay man. Indeed Count Dragulesku – absent in the film's screenplay, where the protagonist is bitten by a Romanian hotel manager (Fulci and Avati 1975) – is the only case in 1956–1975 Italian vampire cinema of a male bloodsucker explicitly involved in homosexual activities: until *Il cav. Costante Nicosia demoniaco, ovvero: Dracula in Brianza*, even the possible homosexual implications of showing a male vampire biting, or attempting to bite, a human male were neutralised by narrative ellipsis (*La maschera del demonio*, *I Wurdalak* and *Il Conte Dracula*), or justified as either a means for survival (*Danza macabra*, *La vendetta di Lady Morgan*, *Nella stretta morsa del ragno* and *La notte dei diavoli*) or a key to reach the hyper-virile, aggressively predatory, heterosexual ideal of *gallo* masculinity (*Tempi duri per i vampiri*).⁴

'He is not a man – he is something more, much more!', raves a married woman in *Tempi duri per i vampiri*, sporting the same dreamy expression and naughty smile that Mina Holmwood gives her husband Arthur in the Hammer *Dracula* upon her return home after spending the night with the Count at the mortician's store. The married woman of *Tempi duri per i vampiri*, though, is not referring to Lee's tall and handsome demon lover Roderico, but to stumpy, big-nosed Osvaldo, who bit her overnight while her lawful husband was, in her own words, 'sleeping like a baby'. This is a crucial point all the following Italian movies featuring male vampires insist on: contrary to their female homologues, whose power – as we have seen in Chapter 3 – tends to be directly proportional to their beauty, Italian Draculas do not have to be good-looking to get what they want. The key to their success is behaving like so-called 'real men', with manliness consisting in a mix of sexual magnetism and brute strength. The prevalence of one component over the other allows for a broad classification of

Italian male vampires, who can be divided into seducers (more sex appeal than brute strength) and rapists (little or no sex appeal, plenty of brute strength).

In the two aforementioned horror parodies and in Italian vampire horrors, the male vampire generally seduces women into letting themselves be bitten. His attractive power, however, lies less in elegant clothes, aristocratic demeanour and Lugosi-like mesmerising gaze than in the fact that he is more masculine – that is to say more willing to get involved in sexual activities and more skilled in carrying them out – than his human competitors. Indeed, just like in the Hammer *Dracula* (Waller 1985: 119; Auerbach 1995: 124–5; Hutchings 2003: 60–78; Pirie 2008: 66–8, 100), Italian Draculas conquest females by preying upon women's latent/unconfessed desires, loneliness and dissatisfaction with human partners. *La strage dei vampiri* is a case in point. Female protagonist Luise has just married well-off aristocrat Wolfgang and moved in with him in a luxurious, newly refurbished castle for the honeymoon. There, during a party, Luise's romantic temperament (symbolised by her musical talent and love for ancient buildings and Italian Renaissance gardens) is contrasted with Wolfgang's matter-of-fact nature (symbolised by his concern for money, food and wine). As soon as the spectre of character incompatibility between spouses is evoked, the vampire shows up: while Wolfgang neglects his wife to entertain guests and play the master of the house, the undead seducer makes Luise feel like she is the centre of the world and a real woman by staring at her and holding her tight during a dance until she faints. Soon after the fainting spell, as guests start gossiping and Wolfgang rather abruptly tells them that he is 'more than certain' that his wife is not pregnant,[5] Luise locks herself alone in the nuptial bedroom and loosens her hair (a symbol of unleashed female passion in Italian cinema ever since the diva films of the 1910s), implicitly inviting the vampire in. At this point, 'the director does not dwell on poeticisms' like Fisher did in the highly elliptic scene of Lucy's seduction in the Hammer *Dracula*, but shows a villain more eager to kiss Luise's breasts than biting her neck (Curti 2011: 73). Finally, once Wolfgang's wife is sucked dry, the vampire dedicates his attentions to the slightly younger, nubile servant Corinne, whose vampirisation follows the same procedure: after Corinne loosens her hair, the vampire enters her bedroom through the window, makes her lie on the bed and starts fondling her breasts.

In *L'amante del vampiro*, *L'ultima preda del vampiro*, *Il mostro dell'Opera*, *Il Conte Dracula* and *Riti, magie nere e segrete orge nel Trecento* . . . the male vampire similarly exploits the sexually connoted curiosity of young, unmarried women wandering around spooky, forbidden places at night, away from the sight of their fathers, boyfriends, employers and doctors. First he gives the wayward girls a taste of the pleasures of the flesh, then sits back waiting for the initiated to start craving for more. Echoing a line uttered in the Hammer *Dracula* ('Victims consciously detest being dominated by vampirism, but are unable to relinquish the practice, similar to addiction to drugs'), *L'amante del vampiro* in fact connects vampire sex to drug use twice:

> The vampire especially targets young women. Once they are bitten, it is like they fall victim to a drug that lures them to the monster again and again. They look for him because, from that moment on, they can love him only. [. . .] It is like being drunk!

'Vampires! What a wonderful theme for a new ballet. Sensuality, warmth, terror . . . and yearning eyes, more exasperated than those of a person poisoned by cocaine!'. The former line of *L'amante del vampiro* is repeated verbatim in *Malìa* issue 1 (February 1961), an original *fotoromanzo* titled *L'urlo del vampiro*, and appears more or less paraphrased in both the *KKK* and the *I racconti di Dracula* pulp-novel series, for instance in *KKK* issues 1 (June 1959), 44 (December 1961), 116 (April 1969) and *I racconti di Dracula* issues 4 (1960), 6 (1960), 57 (1964), 68 (1974). Finally, the association between vampire sex and intoxication is reprised in adults-only Italian comic-book *Zora la vampira* issue 1 (September 1972): 'The bite of the vampire is a drug that makes you drunk', states a caption to a sequence in which the newly vampirised heroine masturbates, fellates and rides her 'master' Dracula.

The implications of the vampirism-drug equivalence are clear: not only sexual pleasure is addictive but, most importantly, the female victims of the vampire Casanova are consciously or unconsciously asking for it, proving somewhat accomplices to their own doom. Which leads us to the aforementioned *Sexy proibitissimo*, a striptease compilation that – following the misogynistic mentality of an erotic-exotic *filone* that infallibly portrays women of all latitudes and epochs as 'sex-crazed beasts, perpetually lying in ambush, much more clever and perverse than man, the poor fall guy' (Risé 1964: 100) – presents us with a Dracula and a Frankenstein monster who are literally forced to attack young women after being teased with sexy dances ('The woman could quickly undress and be done with it, but no, there is a man in the room, even if he is a monster. Then why not provoking him a little bit? A brief, innocent striptease . . . ', remarks *Sexy proibitissimo*'s voice-over narration). In sum, to quote a 'homage to the Lord of Darkness' Dracula that appeared in Italian illustrated film magazine *King Cinema* as vampire movies became trendy again in the late 1960s, 'the relationship between monster and victim' is subsumed into 'a more intimate one: the relationship between man and woman, that is to say between male sadist and female nymphomaniac' (Farina 1969: 86), with the latter adhering to 'the sexist stereotype of the woman who inevitably feels pleasure after an initial reluctance and resistance' (Pezzotta 2014: 43).

In the wake of the Hammer *Dracula*'s release, Italian newspapers were rife with articles comparing real-life sex crimes to vampire attacks. Take, for instance, the case of the red-headed 'vampire of Mestre', attacking girls in the streets at night with a hammer and never caught (De' Rossignoli 1961: 349), or that of 'the Dracula of Porta Genova', Giuliano Ballerini, a twenty-year-old who knocked several Milanese women unconscious, robbed/molested them and allegedly drank the blood spurting from their wounds (De' Rossignoli 1961: 358–9). Not to mention 'the vampire of Venice' Giovanni Busetto, a manic-depressive painter obsessed with religious principles who, after a romantic setback, bit two female passers-by at the neck (Rossi-Osmida 1978: 120–6). In Italian vampire cinema, though, the rapist's domain is not the horror genre, but the rigidly Manichaean narratives of pepla *Ercole al centro della Terra*, *Maciste contro il vampiro* and *Ercole contro Moloch*, where young, beautiful and virtuous females refuse to give in to the vampire's demand for blood/sex and the villain resorts to physical violence to have his way with them – the subsequent brutalisation of scantily clad girls providing the spectators with brief, possibly titillating moments of transgression before the unfailing, cathartic incineration of the bad guys by the sunlight (*Ercole al centro della Terra*), by a grenade (*Maciste contro il vampiro*) or by a purifying fire (*Ercole contro Moloch*). But who are these vampire brutes, specifically?

In *Ercole al centro della Terra*, Lyco (tall, dark and gruesome Lee minus the usual fangs and sex appeal) is a power-hungry aristocrat who strikes a deal with 'the cruel gods of darkness' to become the immortal vampire king of Ecalia by drinking the blood of his niece Deianira, Ercole's wife, 'on the night the moon is devoured by the great dragon'. Additional ominous notes come from the villain's association with predatory animals: he controls an army of bat-like humanoids and the name 'Lyco' is etymologically related to the Greek word *lukos*, 'wolf'.[6] In *Maciste contro il vampiro* the titular vampire is Kobrak, a giant, fanged-and-clawed, shapeshifting sorcerer whose name recalls the snake, an all-time symbol of evil in Catholicism: he commands a gang of pirates, who provide him with virgin blood by ravaging the coastal villages of the Middle East. In *Ercole contro Moloch* the bloodthirsty villain is Moloch, the horribly disfigured son of a woman called Demetra ('Demeter'), like the vessel that carries Count Dracula to England in Stoker's novel, and of infernal deity Moloch, probably an echo of the evil god who demands children sacrifice in *Cabiria* (Giovanni Pastrone, 1914). As in the previous two cases, vampire Moloch is physically imposing and associated with the animal world, as he is fanged, clawed, and hides his hideous features behind a mask halfway between wolf and bat.

From *Tempi duri per i vampiri* to *Il cav. Costante Nicosia demoniaco, ovvero: Dracula in Brianza*, Italian vampire cinema basically is a procession of 'sexual tyrants' (Rigby 2016: 95) attempting to build a comprehensive harem so that all their whims can be satisfied as far as women's age, hair colour, physique and, more rarely, personality are concerned. Within this machoistic framework, the male vampire figure – whether seducer or rapist, attractive or repellent – inevitably overlaps with that of the patriarch. Indeed, the vampiric *gallo* rules over the aforementioned harem with an iron fist, as shown most blatantly in early Gothic horrors *L'ultima preda del vampiro*, *La strage dei vampiri* and *Il mostro dell'Opera*. In *L'ultima preda del vampiro*, vampire Count Gabor Kernassy satiates his blood lust with airhead ballerina Katia only to unceremoniously dispatch her with an improvised stake when she demands to be his one and only love. The vampire from *La strage dei vampiri* is similarly unscrupulous and strict with his female partners. Not only the prologue shows him abandon his vampire bride to a lynch mob of angry peasants in order to save himself but, throughout the movie, he confirms the patriarchal double morality of post-war Italy outlined in Chapter 3, forbidding his conquests to have contacts with other men while he lusts after all the females who cross his way. Finally, *Il mostro dell'Opera* marks the height of Italian vampire cinema in terms of masculine compensation. In the film, Countess Laura from the Middle Ages has his naive, clingy lover Stefano walled-up alive to get rid of him and go on living with her lawful husband. Over the centuries, the romantic setback and *brutta figura* ('poor figure, humiliation') turn Stefano into a pitchfork-wielding, 'misogynist bloodsucker' (Curti 2017b: 103) who takes delight in torturing seven young women chained to the walls of a foggy extradimensional dungeon and dressed in skimpy, strategically ragged outfits. 'Look at them!', he tells his latest prey Giulia, the twentieth-century reincarnation of Countess Laura, 'These are your victims! I destroyed them as you destroyed me! Now, at every new moon, they wait for the blood of a young woman to resurrect them, so I can kill them once again!'

Dealing with power structures and power struggles within the institution of the family, *L'amante del vampiro* and *I Wurdalak* are particularly interesting from a patriarchal point of view. *L'amante del vampiro* revolves around the vampire marriage between Countess Alda and servant Herman, and the 'crisis in their relationship, perhaps brought on by their long period of cohabitation' (Bini 2011a: 59). In the sixteenth century Herman was bitten by Alda and became her vampire butler, attending to all her needs from serving tea properly to providing her with female blood – a plot point that has won the film the reputation of 'feminist' work in that Herman seemingly is dominated by the Countess, playing the 'slave' who sleeps in the cellar to the vampire 'mistress' occupying the upper floors of the castle (Piselli and Guidotti 1989: 56; Gomarasca et al. 2002: 42). A careful analysis of *L'amante del vampiro*, however, reveals a radically different scenario, more akin to the idea – developed by later Italian Gothic horrors *L'orribile segreto del Dr. Hichcock* and *La frusta e il corpo / The Whip and the Body* (Mario Bava as John M. Old, 1963) as well – that in a sadomasochistic relationship it is always the person in the slave position who is actually in control (Olney 2012).

Far from being a sign of submission, Herman's going out hunting every night, gorging on female blood so that castle-dwelling, idle and unproductive aristocrat Alda can feed by sucking him dry, is the very staple of his masculine domination. Herman himself confirms it, when he puts Alda in her place one night after she snobbishly dismisses him for being an unbearably ugly walking corpse: 'It is I who preserve you alive, young and beautiful, do not forget it! Or I will throw you out in the sun just for the pleasure of seeing you fall to dust!'. In sum, we are in front of the classic patriarchal dynamic in which a woman's survival totally depends on her male partner-protector acting as a mediator between the female and the outside world. More than a dominatrix, Alda should then be considered a character modelled upon the idealised housewife of the late 1940s and early 1950s, who never needs to venture outside the home, while her man Herman, the bloodwinner, is the typical patriarchal husband who not only dominates his bride but is also paranoid about losing his position as, in his own words, 'the one and only master of my world'. This is why he stakes every new, hungry and potentially wayward female vampire he creates to feed Alda, and why, seeing himself doomed by the approaching sunrise, switches allegiance and helps good guys Luca and Giorgio to kill the Countess: there must not be other vampires before and after him. At the same time, and equally importantly, throughout the film Alda plots to kill Herman not to seek emancipation, but to substitute him with gentler, more humane master Luca.

Although shifting from aristocratic to peasant vampires, and from late-1950s Central Italy to early-nineteenth-century Eastern Europe, *I Wurdalak* presents us with a similarly patriarchal world where the life of the farmer protagonists 'revolves around the elderly *pater familias* [Gorka], who is served and revered like a king; his male progeny follows his every word no matter how unreasonable [. . .]; the women are passive and obedient' (Curti 2015: 82). So consolidated is the hierarchy, that the unexpected vampirisation of Gorka by a wurdalak highwayman proves a false turning point, incapable of subverting the patriarchal status quo described above. The film in fact gives an ironic lesson about blood being thicker than water by having Gorka's living relatives (two adult sons, one daughter, one daughter-in-law, one grandson) doom themselves to the vampire contagion for fear of contradicting the undead *pater familias*, who eventually ends up reigning over a submissive vampire family that is virtually indistinguishable from the former human one.

As a matter of fact, the theme of the vampire family submitted to the patriarch survives the earthquake of the 1968 anti-authoritarian protests unscathed. This is true not only for Hammer, whose Dracula easily controls his brides and disciples from the 1958 *Dracula* to *The Satanic Rites of Dracula* (Alan Gibson, 1973), but also for Italian vampire cinema. *Il Conte Dracula*, for instance, brings to the screen the Stokerian scene in which Dracula orders his three daughters-brides away from his man Jonathan Harker but glaringly omits their rebellious retort 'You yourself never loved; you never love!' (Stoker [1897] 1980: 42), while, as we have seen in Chapter 3, what all-powerful widow Countess Dracula really wants in *Il plenilunio delle vergini* is to marry another vampire macho. Even in post-1968, self-proclaimed modern and transgressively revolutionary vampire-themed comic-book series heteronormative patriarchy rules uncontested. In *Jacula* issue 1 (March 1969) and *Zora la vampira* issues 1 and 2 (September–October 1972), the titular heroines are presented as blossoming young women who consider virginity and parental control as a burden to get rid of but, once deflowered by Dracula, simply turn from dominated daughters touching themselves in secret to dominated sex-slave brides of whoever male vampire happens to be the strongest or the most well-endowed (or both) at that particular moment.[7]

True, vampire masculinity becomes less granitic as years go by and starts showing cracks in the early 1970s, after Roman Polanski's *Dance of the Vampires* popularised an irreverent take on vampire mythology in both the European and Anglo-American film market (see Chapter 2). For instance, the ageing, sickly Dracula from *Dracula cerca sangue di vergine ... e morì di sete!!!* needs to apply make-up to be presentable, moves around in a wheelchair and, as the facetious Italian title 'Dracula looks for the blood of a virgin ... and died of thirst!!!' suggests, he ends up killed by his female victims' lack of sexual restraint (in scene 41 of an early draft of the screenplay, the film's weak, starving Dracula even dies impaled by a teenage girl wielding a sharp twig) (Unknown 1973). In the same desecrating vein, *Il cav. Costante Nicosia demoniaco, ovvero: Dracula in Brianza* pokes fun at the vampirised protagonist's unsuccessful attacks on 'a nymphomaniac upper class man-eater who [. . .] recites verses of [Gabriele] D'Annunzio's poems' and on a whip-cracking sadomasochistic dominatrix (Curti 2017b: 141), which is an attempt to capitalise on both the Polanski-style vampire comedy and the Italian comedies of the 1970s where Lando Buzzanca plays a so-called 'real man' facing impotence, sterility and all kinds of sexual complexes (D'Amico 1985: 173–6; Manzoli 2012: 161–91).[8] Yet, in order to really see Italian male vampires in crisis, one has to wait for the last year of intensive film production in Italy. In a seventy-second dream sequence from the episode *La cavallona* in Sergio Martino's 1976 portmanteau comedy *40 gradi all'ombra del lenzuolo*, the titular 'big-ass babe' Emilia Chiapponi – played by Edwige Fenech, the insatiable sex goddess of Italian cinema ever since the late-1960s film-scandal *Top sensation* (Ottavio Alessi, 1969) and early-1970s *decamerotici* like *Quel gran pezzo della Ubalda tutta nuda e tutta calda* (Mariano Laurenti, 1972) – tears Dracula's clothes off, mounts on top of him, steals his punchline 'Let me sink my ravenous teeth in your soft neck' and sets out to bite him. At which point Dracula, defrauded of his role, undignifiedly runs away half-naked and in fear, whining: 'You did not understand anything! I am the vampire!'.

PART II VAMPIRE SEX AND VAMPIRE GENDER

NOTES

1. The treatment of *Amanti d'oltretomba*, originally titled *Orgasmo*, is far bolder than the finished film. In the prologue, Stephen drugs Muriel and David with an aphrodisiac and has sex with his wife 'on the nuptial bed' in front of the gardener, who becomes extremely excited. Stephen then leaves his wife to David and watches them having sex. He finally executes the adulterers via electrocution just before they reach orgasm. Later, upon being strangled by his second wife Jenny (Muriel's sister, possessed by Muriel's spirit), Stephen grows tremendously excited, 'tears her nightgown apart and kisses her passionately, furiously', as Jenny's state of possession allows him to torture his adulterous first wife again. In the end, Muriel's ghost hypnotises Stephen by showing him her 'naked and bouncing breasts', has sex with him and burns him alive (Caiano and De Agostini 1964).
2. Here, a terminological caveat is needed. As noted by Reich (2004: 54), the *gallo* figure should be distinguished from the concept of *gallismo*. The *gallo*, as it has just been explained by referring to the Casanova and Don Juan archetypes, is a man endowed 'with an extraordinary virile force' and 'whose masculinity is determined by his multiple experiences with women', while *gallismo* is an affectionately disparaging term coined by Sicilian writer Vitaliano Brancati to describe the behaviour of unexceptional men who maintain 'a façade of sexual potency' by 'relating the often exaggerated and fabricated details of the conquest to [their male] companions'.
3. *Tempi duri per i vampiri*'s final appeal to moderation convinced the Italian Film Censorship Office (Nullaosta 30310 1959), but not the Vatican censors: 'The satire of vampirism is just an excuse to make a frivolous, superficial film [. . .] weaving together scenes and situations that are equivocal and improper. Forbidden' (Centro Cattolico Cinematografico 1959b).
4. In adults-only Italian comic book *Jacula* issue 16 (October 1969), the editor of the readers' letters column even tried to put an end once and for all to questions about homosexual vampires by authoritatively stating that, if they have a choice, male vampires prefer female victims and female vampires prefer male victims.
5. When, later in the film, vampirised-but-not-yet-dead Luise starts suffering of dizzy spells, Wolfgang once again firmly excludes that she might be pregnant. This, together with the fact that Wolfgang and Luise treat their gardener's little daughter Resi as their own, seems to suggest that they cannot have children.
6. Apropos of animal analogies, the film's treatment – clearly indebted to Fisher's *Dracula* and *The Brides of Dracula* – is worth quoting at length: 'Lyco, the vampire, wreaks havoc everywhere. The flesh of the young women bears the mark of his bestial teeth. The farmers build funeral pyres all over the blood-soaked countryside to burn the corpses of the poor victims, but [. . .] the flames cannot burn the girls, who break free from the chains that tie them to the woodpiles and roam the countryside howling like hungry wolves. It is the death that lives, death that spreads death' (Continenza and Tessari 1961).
7. The heteronormative and ultimately moralistic mentality of 'porno-horror comics' is efficaciously sketched in Barbiani (1980: 50–2), with Jacula and her husband Verdier serving as the most prominent example of 'ministerial vampires' who 'champion conjugal love and would probably vote for abrogating divorce in Italy'.

8. E.g., *Un caso di coscienza* (Giovanni Grimaldi, 1970), *La prima notte del Dottor Danieli, industriale, col complesso del . . . giocattolo / The Lovemarkers* (Giovanni Grimaldi, 1970), *Il vichingo venuto dal sud / No One Will Notice You are Naked* (Stefano Vanzina as Steno, 1971), *Homo eroticus* (Marco Vicario, 1971), *Il merlo maschio / The Naked Cello* (Pasquale Festa Campanile, 1971), *Io e lui* (Luciano Salce, 1973), *L'arbitro / Football Crazy* (Luigi Filippo D'Amico, 1974) and *Il gatto mammone* (Nando Cicero, 1975).

PART III

SANGUINE ECONOMY, BLOODY POLITIC

5. VAMPIRES OF THE LATE 1950S AND EARLY 1960S

From reconstruction to the 'boom'

In this chapter and the next one, the 'unmasking of cultural artifacts as socially symbolic acts' (Jameson [1981] 2002: 5) that constitutes the aim of the monograph proceeds with an analysis of the socio-economic and political implications of 1956–1975 Italian vampire cinema. Here, the theoretical points of reference are the scholars of literature and film mentioned in the Introduction, who – reworking Marx's ([1867] 1954: 224–85) indictment of the nineteenth-century European bourgeoisie as vampiric – have investigated the dynamics of class and imperialistic struggle in the vampire narratives of the Anglo-American tradition and in Murnau's *Nosferatu*, exposing vampires as socio-economic leeches and/or political oppressors. As we shall see, many Italian vampire movies also identify bloodsucking figures with enemies within (a specific group of people in the nation-state's social body) and/or enemies without (scheming foreigners), essentially adapting Marxian and Marxist invectives to the post-war Italian zeitgeist, from the dawn of the economic miracle in the late 1950s to mid-1970s austerity. However, direct references to the oeuvres of Marx and Marxist thinkers are absent from the Italian vampire movies of the late 1950s and early 1960s, and extremely rare in Italian cinema as a whole until the second half of the 1960s, when the Christian Democrats' anti-Communism began to loosen up, at least in the Italian Show Business Bureau (the Italian Socialist Party officially entered the government coalition in December 1963) and in the Italian Film Censorship Office (whose jurisdiction was limited exclusively to matters of public decency by law 161 of 21 April 1962). The distinction between this chapter and the next one is thus chronological: the former is devoted to the somewhat oblique vampire metaphors of the late 1950s and early 1960s, while the latter concerns itself with the explicitly politicised vampires of the first half of the 1970s.

Putting forward political and socio-economic readings of the vampire film output of the late 1950s and early 1960s first of all requires a work of contextual analysis detailing the causes and consequences of the 1958–1963 economic miracle. As in the previous two chapters' exploration of gender issues, the starting point is the reconstruction period. From the immediate post-war until well into the second half of the 1950s, Italy was an underdeveloped country. According to the 1951 census, 42 per cent of the Italian working population made a living in the primary sector, with the percentage rising dramatically in the South (Ginsborg 1990: 210). Such agricultural activities were mostly labour-intensive and technologically backward by twentieth-century Western standards, and productivity was generally low, based as it was on the landowners' pure and simple exploitation of destitute seasonal workers struggling for bare survival. Facing dropping profit margins due to war damages, impoverished soil, managerial ineptitude, natural disasters, occasional peasant unrest and the advent of international competitors following the end of Fascist protectionism, the big landowners (many of them aristocrats whose titles ceased to be legally recognised with the Italian Constitution of 1948) started selling part of their land to their sharecroppers – a move also encouraged by the 1948–1950 agrarian laws approved by the newly elected Italian Parliament. This fragmentation of property, combined with limited state and private investments in infrastructural modernisation, made only subsistence farming possible in large parts of the countryside (Ginsborg 1990: 210–11). As a result, in 1951 and for a few more years, Italian standards of living remained abysmal, with no more than 'five kilograms of beef per capita consumed yearly' (Crainz 2005a: 88) and 'the elementary combination of electricity, drinking water and an inside lavatory' to be found in less than 10 per cent of households (Ginsborg 1990: 210). Yet, the overall economic situation was not completely bleak: contrary to the primary sector, the 'industrial sector could boast of some advanced elements in the production of steel, cars, electrical energy and artificial fibres'. True, from the mid-1940s to the late 1950s cutting-edge factories 'were limited both geographically, being confined mainly to the North-West, and in their weight in the national economy as a whole' (Ginsborg 1990: 210), but it is on these foundations that the economic miracle would be built.

The names with which Italian economy's great leap forward in the secondary and tertiary sectors was dubbed by politicians and the press from the spring of 1959 onwards suggest the idea of a sudden, unexpected event ('boom'), a gift from God ('miracle'). This is because the Christian Democrat, Socialist and Communist leaders of the time publicly hailed 1958 as a year of economic crisis due to some negative backlashes connected to the inception of the European Economic Community (Crainz 2005a: 58–60). However, historians have convincingly argued that Italy's economic miracle was not random at all. Its bases were laid in 1953, mainly due to the work of top managers Oscar Sinigaglia and Enrico Mattei, who used the funds from the Marshall Aid to reorganise and modernise the state-owned metallurgical industry and the domestic extraction of methane gas and hydrocarbons, thereby providing Italian entrepreneurs with cheap materials and energy sources for their factories. In the same year, private industries like vehicle manufacturer FIAT began massive investments in new plants in Northern Italy, while the Parliament approved laws granting easy access to credit and tax benefits for Northern-Italy industries delocalising production in the South (Ginsborg 1990: 212–17; Crainz 2005a: 117–30). Clearly, '[m]onetary stability, the non-taxation of business interests, the maintenance of favourable lending rates by the Bank of Italy [. . .] served to create the correct conditions for the accumulation of capital and its subsequent investment in industry' (Ginsborg 1990: 214). The most decisive factor for the late-1950s 'boom', though, was the extremely low cost of Italian labour. In fact, the post-war mass unemployment and the aforementioned crisis in agriculture 'ensured that demand for work far exceeded supply, with predictable consequences in terms of wage rates' (Ginsborg 1990: 214). Moreover, not only most Italians were desperate to work for no matter how little the salary; during the authoritarian, fiercely anti-Communist, Christian Democrat governments of the late 1940s and 1950s, the police and the army also reduced union activities almost to zero, effectively increasing productivity via exploitation (Crainz 2005a: 1–42).

The economic miracle is summed up by the following figures provided by Ginsborg (1990: 214–16) and Crainz (2005a: 87–130; 2005b: 13–18). Net national income went from the 17,000 billion lire of 1954 to the 30,000 billion of 1964, while over the same period per-capita income rose from 350,000 to 571,000 lire. The 8 million Italians working in agriculture in 1954 fell to fewer than 5 million ten years later. Most of them moved from the impoverished rural South and North-East to city areas to take up jobs in factories, and since the 1939 law designed to prevent the inurbation of farmers was repealed only in 1961, throughout the 1950s internal migrants basically were at the mercy of their new employers, who could easily enact all sorts of labour abuse by threatening a denunciation for the crime of illegal migration.[1] It is thus that, in the early 1960s, Italy ceased to be a prevalently agricultural country (by 1964, 40 per cent of the working population was employed in the secondary sector, 35 per cent in the tertiary). Specific data on what, and how much, Italian industries produced between the mid-1950s and 1963 reveal a crucial aspect of the 'boom', namely its export-driven nature: as vehicle manufacturing skyrocketed from 148,000 to 760,000 units, fridge manufacturing from 370,000 to 1.5 million units, TV-set manufacturing from 88,000 to 634,000 units, the production of 'textiles and food products gave way to those consumer goods which were much in demand in the advanced industrial countries, and which reflected per capita incomes far higher than Italy's own' (Ginsborg 1990: 214–15). Indeed, although Italian standards of living were improving by the early 1960s, with the combination of electricity, drinking water and an inside lavatory to be found in almost 30 per cent of households according to the 1961 census (contrary to the less than 8 per cent of 1951), Italy was still too poor a country for the majority of its citizens to enter the age of *benessere* ('affluence') and be able to afford the cars and home appliances they were beginning to see advertised everywhere around them.

Official data show that, in Italy, the ownership of consumer durables expanded greatly in a very short turn of years:

> Whereas in 1958 only 12% of Italian families owned a television, by 1965 the number had risen to 49%. In the same period the number owning fridges increased from 13% to 55%, and washing machines from 3% to 23%. Between 1950 and 1964 the number of private cars in Italy rose from 342,000 to 4.67 million. (Ginsborg 1990: 239)

While in the Italian left-wing press of the early 1960s there was much talk of the television-in-the-shack paradox, the booming access to the *nuovi consumi* ('new consumer goods') concerned Italian society almost exclusively from the lower middle class upwards, above all in the North and Centre (Crainz 2005a: 138–62). Apart from the traditional *haute-bourgeoisie* elite, that is to say the owners and top managers of the heavy industry, two professional groups within the middle class were particularly benefited by the economic miracle: white-collar workers from a lower-middle-class background holding a secondary-school or university diploma, and small-firm-level industrialists. The former were the better-paid echelon of the fastest-growing section of the Italian workforce in the late 1950s, absorbed *en masse* by the industrial sector, the tertiary sector and the ever-growing bureaucratic apparatus of the state. The latter were a 'new generation of Italian businessmen', men 'of limited culture and education, but determined and audacious, [. . .] prepared to travel all over the world in order to build up markets for their products', mainly clothes, footwear, office supplies, electric appliances or parts thereof, all manufactured in small (often clandestine) but constantly expanding workshops. They were

> the *nouveaux riches* not only of the major cities, but perhaps above all of the provinces [of Lombardy, Emilia Romagna and Tuscany]. In Vigevano, to take just one example of a smallish town near Milan, [. . .] there were 900 workshops and factories making shoes; one quarter of all Italy's shoe exports came from Vigevano. (Ginsborg 1990: 236–7)

These two professional groups were also responsible for the skyrocketing number of Italian people enjoying holidays in the country over the summer and during the weekends, with hotel and camping reservations more than doubled from 1956 to 1965 (Ginsborg 1990: 242–3; Crainz 2005a: 143–6). Together with luxury goods like cars, fridges, TV sets and washing machines, for white-collar petty bourgeois and small-firm-level industrialists, holiday breaks became a 'status symbol' charged with a 'demonstration effect': by shedding their traditional accumulation-bent stinginess in favour of a new lifestyle characterised by expenditure, the rising lower strata of the bourgeoisie 'explicitly or implicitly show[ed] off, manifest[ed], symbolise[d] and strengthen[ed] their social position', confirming 'to both social peers and social inferiors the distance from everything that is work, necessity, industriousness' in the attempt to resemble as much as possible the highest class of them all, aristocracy, unproductive par excellence (Alberoni 1967: 262). Appropriating the concept of conspicuous consumption from Thorstein Veblen's 1899 study *The Theory of the Leisure Class: An Economic Study of Institutions*, the leading sociologist of post-war Italy thus efficaciously portrays the whole of the rampant Italian bourgeoisie as involved in a symbolic struggle for social distinction/promotion in which the clerical lower-middle class imitates the small-firm-level industrialists, the small-firm-level industrialists the top managers and captains of industry of the *haute bourgeoisie*, the *hauts bourgeois* the twentieth-century remnants of the feudal, landowning aristocracy (deprived of legally recognised titles by the Italian Constitution of 1948, but still endowed with abundant economic and symbolic capital).

As the middle class was busy with conspicuous consumption, working-class people, and especially the inurbated peasants who had become blue-collar factory workers in the second half of the 1950s and the early 1960s, managed to access the *beni di cittadinanza* ('citizenship goods') for the first time in their lives, that is to say to fulfil very basic needs of nourishment, clothing and hygiene, meet the standard of what is 'perceived as right, proper and dutiful for any civilised man', and be considered citizens of the Italian nation-state (Alberoni 1967: 119). For instance, while mostly living in self-built shacks in the outskirts of the cities or in overcrowded city attics/basements, and working like slaves in factories and building sites, the migrant workers from the South and the North-East were finally able to afford daily meals, proper shoes and warm clothing for the bad season. Not coincidentally, a wellbeing indicator such as the yearly per-capita consumption of beef in Italy rose from the less than 5 kilograms of the mid-1940s to the 9 kilograms of the mid-1950s ('matching the level of the poor and autarchic, pre-war Fascist period'), and reached 13 kilograms in 1960 and 20 kilograms in 1966, all this combined with other types of meat, dairy products, fruit and vegetables (Crainz 2005a: 88) – an increased consumption that enriched town-dwelling, petty-bourgeois shop owners, who immediately joined their white-collar homologues in the symbolic struggle for social distinction/ promotion. Evidently, for the late-1950s and early-1960s blue-collar working class, the *nuovi consumi* largely remained a deluxe mirage, even if the opportunity of payment by instalments was widely available. Italian blue-collar workers' expenses not strictly related to basic needs were absorbed by motor vehicles cheaper than cars (between 1950 and 1964 'the number of owned motorcycles went from 700,000 to 4.3 million') (Ginsborg, 1990: 239) and entertainment, perhaps playing a part in the boom of the discographic market, whose sales went from 'the five million records sold in 1953' to 'the eighteen, twenty-two and thirty million records sold in 1958, 1962 and 1965 respectively' (Crainz 2005a: 82).

If the inception of the 'boom' caught Christian Democracy and the Left by surprise in 1958, the *rivoluzione dei consumi* ('consumer-goods revolution') that followed revealed the Italian politicians' absolute unpreparedness to seriously engage with consumer capitalism, and to correct its downsides and distortions. Such unpreparedness was due to the fact that Italian politicians, whether militant Catholics or Socialists/Communists, shared a simplistic view of 'capitalism as incapable of producing development and progress', and a strong dislike for modernisation, seen as the harbinger of the catastrophic erasure of the ancient 'world of the poor' that traditionally constituted the stronghold of the secular power of both Catholics and Marxists (Crainz 2005a: 43). As a result, all major parties first and foremost concerned themselves with exploiting the booming economy for propaganda purposes in view of electoral competitions at municipal, provincial, regional and national level. On the one hand, the Christian Democrats willy-nilly embraced the 'miracle' euphoria: they judged that putting forward the idea of an upcoming era of prosperity within capitalism – whose possible excesses had of course to be mitigated by the Christian values of frugality, renunciation and solidarity – was after all the best antidote to the so-called 'red threat', and used media events like the 1956–1964 construction of the Milan–Naples motorway, the *Financial Times*'s awarding of a monetary Oscar to the Italian lira as the most stable currency of 1959, the 1960 Rome Olympics and the inauguration of the Fiumicino airport in Rome in 1961 as occasions to increase the party's national and international prestige. On the other hand, the Left, and especially the Communist Party, denounced the very same events as a way to mask the huge imbalances the 'boom' was introducing in the already-unequal Italian society. Ultimately, though, party politics did very little to govern the *grande trasformazione* ('big transformation').

It is not possible, here, to provide a detailed account of the actions taken by post-1958 Italian governments in socio-economic matters. The main point is that from 1958 onwards Christian Democracy and its left-wing allies (the Socialist Party first granted a centrist government the vote of confidence in early 1962, then joined the governing coalition from December 1963 to June 1968) overwhelmingly privileged private interests over public ones, even more so after the growth of Italian economy came to a halt in the summer of 1963, when the increase in workers' salaries – brought about by a reprisal in union activities against a by-then unbearable exploitation – significantly exceeded the increase in productivity. Four examples, taken from Crainz (2005b: 21–94), would suffice. First, while dutifully involved in a crackdown on unreported employment (*caporalato*, the so-called 'the gangmaster system', was outlawed in 1961), Italian governments always sided with captains of industry in seeing unions and worker protests as the main cause for recession, and left workers at the mercy of their employers, the police and the army. Second, any draft law about urban planning, much needed in times of massive internal migrations, was systematically sabotaged during parliamentary discussions to protect the interests of private speculators. Third, electric energy was nationalised in 1962, but this was done by having the state pay huge indemnities to the private-firm owners rather than to shareholders, with the former also left free to use state money as they wished. Fourth, in recession year 1964, in order to give confidence to investors after the negative *congiuntura* ('conjuncture') of 1963, the existing fiscal laws were modified to grant high-income earners complete anonymity, thereby legalising tax evasion. Within this framework of deregulated 'export-led growth' emphasising 'private consumer goods, often of a luxury nature, without any corresponding development in public consumption', the 'boom' assumed the character of a wild, spasmodic, unchecked search for 'individual' and/or 'familial' gain at the expense of the collectivity (Ginsborg 1990: 216). The mottos 'Mors tua vita mea' ('Your death is my life') and 'Ognun per sé e Dio per tutti' ('Each one provides for himself and God provides for all') indeed became the guiding principles for the conduct of many Italians, from the *haute bourgeoisie* and small-firm-level industrialists profiting on the exploitation of destitute migrant workforce down to the destitute migrant workers themselves, largely abandoned by the state and therefore forced to fend for themselves through more or less amoral forms of familism (Alberoni 1967: 319–30; Crainz 2005a: 87–162; 2005b: 13–21).

Eat or be eaten: vampires of the economic miracle

A topical film of the 'boom', horror parody *Tempi duri per i vampiri* opens with an explosion wiping out the old world of the *ancien régime*. It is the late spring or the summer of 1959, somewhere in the Carpathian countryside: Baron Roderico of Bramfürten – whose Poeian first name sounds to Italian ears as a crasis of *rodere* ('gnaw') and *ricco* ('rich') – is a vampire who has been living in his ancestral castle for 400 years, ruling as an absolute master over the region. The days of the bloodsucking feudal lord, though, seem to be numbered, as Roderico's castle is about to be blown up by a group of civil engineers in order to make room for a nuclear power plant. Therefore, a hearse drawn by two black horses and carrying a white coffin (a blatant nod to the Hammer *Dracula*) hastily leaves the manor headed for Frankfurt train station, where Roderico's old butler mails his master to Italian Baron Osvaldo Lambertenghi, Roderico's nephew and last living descendant. We will be back to this servant who, in spite of being a very minor character in terms of screen time, is a crucial figure in the sociological design of the film.

As the setting moves from Central-Eastern Europe to the *bel paese*, it is immediately made clear that the Italian Baron is facing a major crisis of his own: just as Roderico is evicted from his Carpathian domain by the march of progress, in the Italy of the economic miracle Osvaldo has to sell the family manor to a business company and use all the proceeds to pay off his debt with tax collectors. Aiming to take advantage of the booming economy and consequent increase in consumption, the company's board of directors promptly turns the historical place into a commodity – a luxury hotel for foreign tourists, for the traditional Italian *haute bourgeoisie* and, above all, for the Italian *nouveaux riches* created by the economic miracle, who are particularly anxious to convert the newly acquired economic capital into social capital, showing off their distance from necessity in hopes of cleansing the stigma of their miserly, petty-bourgeois past, and join the dominant group of the *hauts bourgeois*. As demonstrated by Alberoni's (1967) and Bourdieu's ([1979] 2010) social inquiries into the judgement of taste, money is the next best thing to blood for those who seek social distinction but were not born into an upper-class family.

The word Osvaldo uses in one of his first lines to describe his personal situation is 'tragedy', and he is not exaggerating. Contrary to the aristocrat protagonist of Giuseppe Tomasi di Lampedusa's 1958 best-selling historical novel *Il Gattopardo*, who is granted a slow, golden twilight after the end of the Kingdom of the Two Sicilies, Osvaldo suddenly loses his ancestral home and wealth, that is to say his past, class and status, and finds himself in a sink-or-swim situation, a battle for survival in a hostile environment. True, forced to start a new life from scratch, he is immediately hired as a hotel bellboy in his former manor, but the offer of shelter and salary in exchange for work is nothing but a bourgeois vengeance against the nobleman. In fact, as a bellboy, Osvaldo is constantly bossed around and humiliated not only by the big businessmen who bought him out of his castle, but also by their clerical, petty-bourgeois subordinates such as hotel manager Vassalli ('Vassals') and the concierge. An exchange between the latter and Osvaldo is particularly revealing. Having addressed the concierge with the informal expression 'Young man', bellboy Osvaldo is harshly reminded that 'When talking to a superior, you must call him *cavaliere* and use the courtesy form!' Not to mention the film's stereotypical Milanese *commendatore* – an old, bald, fat, uneducated, arrogant *nouveau riche* who drives the latest Fiat 2100: adding insult to injury, the *parvenu* calls the castle 'an authentic antiquity' and invades it to acquire nobility by osmosis, while titled Osvaldo slaves moving the *commendatore*'s heavy luggage around.

However, no matter how humiliated by the verbal (and sometimes also physical) abuse of the bourgeoisie, Osvaldo sticks to his noble principles and tries to maintain aristocratic behaviour and dignity. For instance, when a young female guest of the hotel sends him on an errand, he refuses to accept her generous tip as a display of both chivalry and nobility's disinterest in money. Such *beau geste* does not impress anybody except Osvaldo's love interest Lilla, a twenty-something poor gardener who has worked for Osvaldo all her life, like all her relatives before her. Lilla loves Osvaldo as much as he loves her, but the two do not give in to passion: Osvaldo does not because as a disgraced Baron he cannot afford, in his own words, to 'cover [her] with gold and jewels'; Lilla does not because she thinks of herself as a mere servant, unworthy of an aristocrat's love (until the very end of the film, she keeps calling Osvaldo 'Signor Barone' even if, after the Italian Constitution of 1948 and the 1959 sale of his estate, he holds the title only formally). Evidently, the main obstacle to the interclass romance is that both lovers refuse to let go of the past. It is in this stalemate situation that transnational vampire Baron Roderico arrives to Italy as a *deus ex machina*, to teach Osvaldo to forget about aristocracy, move on with the times and become a ruthless bourgeois. As a matter of fact, in *Tempi duri per i vampiri*, there is no trace of the xenophobia-tinged, reverse-colonialism paranoia that literature and film scholars traditionally consider the cornerstone of vampire narratives from the novel *Dracula* onwards (Hatlen [1980] 1988; Garnett 1990; Dingley 1991; Zanger 1991; Gelder 1994: 65–107; Halberstam 1995: 86–105; Malchow 1996: 124–66; Arata [1990] 1997; Senf [1979] 1997; Valdez Moses 1997; Hendershot 2001: 50–1; McKee 2002; Valente 2002; Warren 2002; Davison 2004: 87–157; Phillips 2005: 11–33; Gibson 2006: 15–95; Abbott 2007: 61–72; Kaes 2009: 108–12; Mulvey-Roberts 2016: 129–78; Hudson 2017: 21–114, 163–91). Rather than as an alien vermin, a polluting foreign body migrating West to subjugate the host nation's body politic, Roderico acts as a benign, if creepy, magical helper from whom human characters must learn how to adapt to the rapidly changing socio-economic reality of the 'boom' years in order to avoid extinction.

According to Stoker ([1897] 1980: 33), Dracula is a descendant of some of the noblest, strongest, bravest and proudest warrior 'races' in history. If life is a Darwinian struggle in which only the fittest can make it, the undead Count certainly possesses the willpower and the skills to crush his competitors: he is a fighter, a survivor, and so is Roderico in *Tempi duri per i vampiri*. Abruptly evicted from his Carpathian castle, Roderico wastes no time in melancholic brooding and relocates himself in a new habitat, Italy, which he assumes to be backwards enough to allow him to keep on living as a feudal landlord.

Unfortunately for him, the country has just had a late industrial revolution and aristocrat landowners are bound to extinction. However, the transnational vampire has no intention of lying down and dying: as the family crypt in Osvaldo's castle has been desecrated and turned into an American bar, Roderico simply sleeps under the barman's counter; with no female peasants in sight, he feasts on Scandinavian models. His capacity to adapt seems almost limitless, just like that of Stoker's Dracula, who is a boyar warlord, a *haut bourgeois* dealing in London estates, a qualified petty-bourgeois solicitor, a working-class handyman helping out carriers, and even a servant, making the bed and cooking for his unsuspecting guest Jonathan Harker.

Osvaldo, on the other hand, does not seem to be able to adjust to his new life as a bellboy. He tells Roderico 'You must adapt, uncle!', but for Osvaldo adapting means passively accepting circumstances – that is why he ends up at the mercy of rampant bourgeois who wish him dead. Drastic measures need to be taken to save Osvaldo, and Roderico chooses the most drastic of them all, passing on the curse of vampirism to his nephew. The shock treatment works: once vampirised, Osvaldo overcomes his mild, romantic nature, and becomes aggressive, willing to fight for living space and privilege in the Italian social arena ('During the day you are a stupid dummy, this is why you lost the castle!', he contemptuously snarls to his human self in front of the mirror). First of all, Osvaldo puts his (tooth)mark on forty-two female guests of the hotel in one night, claiming a *droit du seigneur* over the daughters and wives of the wealthy bourgeoisie and making them experience a pleasure they have never reached before with their human partners (see Chapter 4). Second, Osvaldo proceeds to scare the wits out of the businessmen, the hotel manager Vassalli and the *commendatore*, thus taking vengeance on those who dared to belittle him earlier in the film. It is only after having proved his manhood to his social superiors that the now-confident Osvaldo regains his ancestral castle. He cannot buy it back because he has no money, but with some cunning and Roderico's help, he has Vassalli fired and is appointed as the new hotel manager. Finally, Osvaldo gets his dream girl Lilla, rescuing her at the last minute from a half-hearted assault by Roderico.

In the end, Osvaldo feels too grateful to stake his vampire uncle, so Roderico is left free to go his way with two Scandinavian models. As for Osvaldo, he falls from the heights of nobility and lands on his feet because he successfully adapts into a bourgeois clerk. He might not own the castle like in the old days, but he is the man in charge, he runs the place. Borrowing from Hutchings's (2003: 58–9) analysis of class relations in the Hammer *Dracula* and 1950s England, the parable of the Italian vampire can be conceived of as the transformation of a self-pitying, disgraced aristocrat into a 'Carnivore' bourgeois whose ruthlessness is an affirmation of his 'inalienable right to lead'. The aristocracy, however, is not the only class in need to renegotiate its ancestral identity in late-1950s Italy.

Osvaldo marries Lilla, whom marriage elevates from feudal slavery to bourgeois status, allowing her to survive the disappearance of the class that traditionally offered servants protection in exchange for total submission. In sum, it seems that in the grimly titled *Tempi duri per i vampiri* ('Hard times for vampires') there is a happy ending for everybody, to the point that, just before the end credits, Osvaldo asks himself and the spectators if these can really be considered hard times for vampires. Indeed, even in the case of the bossy hotel manager whose place is taken by Osvaldo, it is difficult to speak of dark future prospects: Vassalli may have lost his job, but the ruthlessness in command he has displayed throughout the movie leaves no doubt that he can survive any adversity. The only character who meets a tragic destiny is Baron Roderico's old servant, who commits suicide at Frankfurt train station after mailing his master to Italy, but this is the proverbial exception that confirms the rule. 'May I kill myself?', asks the butler to his master, submissive until the very end. After having been granted permission to take leave, he melancholically adds 'What kind of life is left for me anyway?', and throws himself under an off-screen passing train. Contrary to Baron Roderico, Baron Osvaldo and serf Lilla, the old servant cannot face the downfall of aristocracy and goes extinct like every being that does not possess the will and the skills to adapt to a changing environment.

The opening credits feature the disclaimer 'The characters of this film are absolutely imaginary'. Of course they are not, because *Tempi duri per i vampiri* is a work of satire meant to comment on actual social dynamics in the early years of the economic miracle. The effects of the 'boom' on the working class are not explored at all: 1959 was perhaps too early to assess how the booming economy, new affluence and consumerism impacted factory workers and peasants, plus the business-minded film producers most certainly wanted to steer clear from any social commentary on backwardness and exploitation that might upset Christian Democracy, at that time in firm control of the Italian Show Business Bureau and the Italian Film Censorship Office. The movie focuses on the middle class instead, by thematising the downfall of aristocracy and the upward mobility of both servants and the new rich from the *petite bourgeoisie*. As we have seen, when the traditional socio-economic order is broken, characters must renegotiate their ancestral identity or die. The example for them to follow is that of the transnational vampire, who for once is shown to be a positive model instead of being portrayed as a scapegoat, an alien evil to be hated, disowned and purged for the greater good of society. Consequently, in *Tempi duri per i vampiri* there is no Van-Helsing-like character to re-establish law and order: in the Italy of the 'boom', however frightening, uncertainty of identity, social fluidity and downright chaos are harbingers of new possibilities for self-fulfilment and social promotion – everything is up for grabs and one needs a set of strong, sharp canines to survive, since it is dog eat dog and the so-called 'herbivores' get eaten first.

Perfectly attuned to 'the aggressive and pragmatic spirit of "booming" Italy' (Curti 2011: 88–9), the film at the same time pays heed to Christian Democracy's will to make Italy's great leap forward into modernity less traumatic as possible. As a matter of fact, *Tempi duri per i vampiri* advocates for the necessity of restraint and moderation, the triumphant bourgeois of the happy ending being a *via media*, a midway compromise, literally a marriage, between the fading highest class (feudal aristocracy) and the lowest (serfdom). Therefore, Osvaldo embraces certain predatory aspects of his vampire uncle like determination, cunning, self-confidence, but rejects others, for instance preferring middle-class monogamy and work ethics to the sexual excesses and unproductivity of Baron Roderico. As stated in the first treatment of the film, whose screenplay and final cut were approved without reservations by government officials, '[Osvaldo] remains [Osvaldo], but a new [Osvaldo], who did not undergo so many transformations in vain. He will maintain the purity of his soul, but a new strength will allow him to contrast other people's prevarications' (Anton 1959).[2]

Adopting a dichotomy popularised by Umberto Eco's 1964 collection of essays *Apocalittici e integrati: comunicazioni di massa e teorie della cultura di massa*, it could be broadly said that the Italian screenwriters and filmmakers of the 1950s and 1960s displayed two different attitudes towards the economic miracle: genre cinema, which had neither interest nor advantage in openly contesting the status quo, generally was *integrato* ('integrated') and mediated between good and bad aspects of the 'boom', trying to negotiate an imaginary path for Italian people's survival in times of radical changes, whereas auteur cinema, often fuelled by left-wing ideology, was downright *apocalittico* ('apocalyptic') in its aprioristic refusal and indictment of capitalist modernisation. Comedy of terrors *Tempi duri per i vampiri*, with its midway-compromise happy ending, seems to belong to integrated cinema. Yet, in spite of its bright Ultrascope-Ferraniacolor-Technicolor photography and upbeat tone, the film strikes some pretty sombre notes that resonate with the critique of the *grande trasformazione* as alienating, dehumanising, liberticidal and culturally genocidal to be found in coeval Italian auteur cinema efforts like *Rocco e i suoi fratelli / Rocco and his Brothers* (Luchino Visconti, 1960), *Accattone* (Pier Paolo Pasolini, 1961) and *Mamma Roma* (Pier Paolo Pasolini, 1962). Director Steno and the screenwriters of *Tempi duri per i vampiri* were no Marxists as far as it is known (Ventavoli 1999), but their representation of the bloodthirsty, carnivorous middle class' power to incorporate all other classes, including its traditional antagonist the aristocracy, possibly alludes to the rise of what Marx and Lenin would have called the dictatorship of the bourgeoisie. Moreover, and perhaps more topically as far as cinematic references are concerned, by casting comedy star Renato Rascel as a literal monster taking no prisoners in his struggle for survival in the social arena of late-1950s Italy, *Tempi duri per i vampiri* resonates with the branch of the 1958–1980 *commedia all'italiana* informally known as *commedia dei mostri*, that is to say the scathingly satirical, and often tragedy-tinged, Italian comedies featuring *mattatori* ('star performers') like Alberto Sordi, Vittorio Gassman and Ugo Tognazzi incarnating the cynicism, recklessness and ultimate moral monstrosity of the Italian everyman in the rat race to *benessere*.[3] All in all, then, Steno's self-proclaimed escapist horror parody is less innocuous than appears at first glance. *Tempi duri per i vampiri* suggests that vampires live among us and, as written in the summer-holiday-themed short story *Dracula ai bagni* ('Dracula at the beach club') from the late 1950s, they tend to bite on the left side of the chest, near the heart, where Italians keep the wallet (Buzzati 1959). Such bloodsuckers are not only the profit-bent businessmen of the hotel company and the tax collectors who suck Osvaldo's finances dry[4] at the beginning of the film: as we have seen, in the Italy of the economic miracle, where the law of the jungle is in place, everyone must become a vampire, preying on weaker/dumber creatures, or be eaten.

If Riccardo Freda's 1956–1957 *I vampiri* rehearses the traditional Gothic narrative concerned with feudalism's death (Tudor 1974: 209–10; Baldick 1987: 148; Punter 1996a: 104–5, 1996b: 16–19), the vampire horrors of the 'boom' years would rather follow the path opened by *Tempi duri per i vampiri* and locate vampire figures also outside the nobility of *ancien régime*. Of course, given Italian horror's commercially driven tendency to blur its national origins (Pitassio 2005; Pezzotta 2014; Baschiera 2016; Di Chiara 2016b), it is mostly the middle and lower classes of nineteenth-century and early-twentieth-century Great Britain and Mitteleuropa to be accused of vampirism, so that social parables about the *bel paese* become much more covert than in *Tempi duri per i vampiri*. Yet, the coincidence between the beginning of the Gothic horror *filone* in 1959–1960 and Italy's 1958–1963 economic miracle did not go unnoticed to a contemporary Marxist critic, who saw the budding Italian horror as confirming the nineteenth-century dictum that 'ghosts, monsters and a taste for horror appear when a society enters the industrial age, and becomes prosperous and modern' (Fofi 1963: 80). Crucially, the opening shot of *L'amante del vampiro* – the first Italian attempt at a straightforwardly horror rip-off of the Hammer *Dracula* – is a 'panning over the placid Lazio countryside', amidst newly built, towering 'apartment buildings and television antennas', two symbols of Italy's late yet sweeping modernisation (Curti 2015: 62). Within this framework, regardless of their setting in time and space, the vampire narratives of early Italian Gothic horror can be said to reflect the spasmodic, cynical search for personal financial gain and social promotion that characterised most of the Italian society during, and immediately after, the 'boom'.

The overarching themes allowing us to group together various Italian vampire horrors of the early 1960s are two: the fading out of the aristocracy, and the mutation affecting both the bourgeoisie and the aristocrats' servants, who literally become vampires in their struggle for social promotion at the expense of enervated noblemen. As for the former idea, following the Le Fanu–Stoker–Browning–Freda–Fisher template, the aristocratic vampire is generally killed off in the end (*L'amante del vampiro*, *La maschera del demonio*, *L'ultima preda del vampiro*, *La strage dei vampiri*, *La cripta e l'incubo* and *Il mostro dell'Opera*) or, like Osvaldo in *Tempi duri per i vampiri*, is forced to turn into a bourgeois to survive in late-1950s and early-1960s Italy (*Il sangue e la rosa*). Similarly, non-vampiric aristocrats see little future in their own class, preferring to marry into the wealthy bourgeoisie as Prince Tancredi Falconeri does in the aforementioned 1958 best-seller *Il Gattopardo*, be it a doctor (*La maschera del demonio* and *Amanti d'oltretomba*), a scholar (*La cripta e l'incubo*), an architect (*La vendetta di Lady Morgan*), the daughter of a high-ranking magistrate (*Il sangue e la rosa*). Even a penniless danseuse (*L'ultima preda del vampiro*) or a peasant girl (*I tre volti della paura*'s segment *I Wurdalak*) would do, as long as the bride-to-be is beautiful. These narrative dynamics can be connected to the perceived disintegration of the Italian old world of landed estate in a period of booming economy based on the secondary and tertiary sectors.

As for the attempts at upward social mobility enacted by the classes below aristocracy, a good starting point may be *Amanti d'oltretomba* and *La vendetta di Lady Morgan*, which, made in 1965, are 'a summation of situations, characters and narrative patterns that are commonplace in Italian Gothic horror films of the decade' (Curti 2015: 145). In *Amanti d'oltretomba*, bourgeois physician Stephen Arrowsmith and decrepit servant Solange conspire against their social superiors and act as vampires as part of a plot to appropriate the wealth belonging to Stephen's aristocratic wives Muriel and Jenny: with the complicity of Solange, Stephen kills Muriel and draws her blood; then, Solange is injected the purloined blood to reacquire youth and become beautiful enough for her co-conspirator to marry (the plan is to be repeated with Jenny, Muriel's sister/heir and Stephen's second wife, but fails). Likewise, in *La vendetta di Lady Morgan*, the Blackhouse aristocrat family is sucked dry of its wealth and lifeblood by a gang including rival aristocrat Lord Morgan, a petty-bourgeois governess and two servants, all greedy crooks who become vampires after death. The differences with pre-'boom' *I vampiri*, where the bourgeois are the good guys and the servants mere automata in the hands of the aristocratic villain, are macroscopic: in post-'boom' horrors, starting with *L'amante del vampiro* and continuing (only to cite vampire-themed ones) with *L'orribile segreto del Dr. Hichcock*, *I tre volti della paura*, *Danza macabra*, *La cripta e l'incubo*, *Amanti d'oltretomba* and *La vendetta di Lady Morgan*, cunning, money-, sex- and power-hungry servants take on an active role and pursue an agenda of their own, often in league/competition with reckless, social-climbing bourgeois aiming to supersede aristocrats at the top of the food pyramid. Indeed, the haunted houses of *Danza macabra* and *La vendetta di Lady Morgan* – both movies co-written by Giovanni Grimaldi and released after the 1963 *congiuntura* – host vampire aristocrats, vampire bourgeois and vampire servants, in what could be read as an apocalyptic statement: in the attempt to take advantage of the five-year 'boom', all classes have become self-interested to the point of literal bloodsucking.

Sic semper tyrannis: nazi-fascist and neofascist vampires

While horror parody *Tempi duri per i vampiri* and the early-1960s vampire horrors more or less covertly allude to some socio-economic dynamics of the 'boom' years, 1961–1964 vampire-themed pepla *Ercole al centro della Terra*, *Maciste contro il vampiro*, *Ercole contro Moloch*, *Roma contro Roma* and *Maciste e la regina di Samar* tap into political issues relating to post-war Italy's 'divided memory' (Foot 2009: 97–182) of, and problematic coming to terms with, the events following the 8 September 1943 armistice: German occupation, the creation of the Fascist Repubblica Sociale Italiana in the Centre-North under the aegis of the Nazis, and the partisan struggle that, in synergy with the Allies' Italian Campaign, led to Liberation in April 1945. As was usual for the Italian genre cinema practitioners of the 1950s and early 1960s – always careful not to give the Italian Show Business Bureau and the Italian Film Censorship Office the impression of being too politicised – the writers and directors of vampire-themed pepla approached the 1943–1945 events symbolically, by adopting an allegorical register in which the troubles of Classical Antiquity stand for those of Second World War Italy. Yet, apart from a few in-depth Italian-language articles (Spinazzola 1963, 1965a and 1965b; Ghigi 1977) and a French-language essay by an Italian adventure cinema veteran (Paolella 1965), the cultural instrumentality of pepla has been neglected in Italy until very recently, when Anglophone studies like Lagny (1992), Dyer (1997), Günsberg (2005: 97–132), Burke (2011) and O'Brien (2013 and 2014) prompted a new interest in the economic history and textual and contextual analysis of late-1950s and early-1960s musclemen adventures (Marchena 2009; Della Casa and Giusti 2013; Di Chiara 2016a).

As demonstrated by the diatribe over the adventure cinema of Vittorio Cottafavi between Italian and French critics (Di Giammatteo 1960), and by Marxist film magazine *Cinema nuovo*'s 'kind disagreement' with Spinazzola's (1965a: 270) taking the peplum *filone* as a serious object of study, the aforementioned neglect was due to the reasons of cultural legitimacy outlined in the Introduction and at the end of Chapter 2 – an intellectualist prejudice that ultimately proved to be counterproductive because, in dismissing and ignoring pepla, the neorealism-revering Italian intelligentsia of the time missed out on a culturally and commercially significant instance of neorealist heritage. In fact, in spite of major stylistic differences, the neorealist war movies of the immediate post-war and many a peplum share the same sanitised, Manichaean vision of 1943–1945 Italy, one in which poor, peace-loving, hardworking *brava gente* (the silent majority of Italian 'good people') are victimised by a cruel foreign tyrant (Nazi Germany) aided by a few local *mele marce* (a minority of Fascist collaborators, the proverbial 'rotten apples in the basket') until the arrival of an all-powerful saviour (the US, embodied by the Anglo-American army in neorealist features and by an American or American-seeming bodybuilder in pepla). Let us now focus on *Ercole al centro della Terra*, *Maciste contro il vampiro*, *Ercole contro Moloch*, *Roma contro Roma* and *Maciste e la regina di Samar*, whose vampire characters make the references to the Second World War past unmistakable.

The four main characteristics of the vampires threatening the happiness of Ancient Greece (*Ercole al centro della Terra* and *Ercole contro Moloch*), Ancient Rome (*Roma contro Roma* and *Maciste e la regina di Samar*) and the Middle-East (*Maciste contro il vampiro*) mark the bloodsuckers as a metaphor for the Nazi invader. Like the German soldiers who occupied Centre-North Italy after the September 1943 armistice, the vampire is first of all a foreigner to the local population, either because he/she is from abroad (*Roma contro Roma*'s cyclops-goddess Oro is the daughter of Osiris and therefore comes from Egypt) or does not belong to the human race (*Maciste e la regina di Samar*'s female vampire Selene is an alien from the Moon, while *Maciste contro il vampiro*, *Ercole al centro della Terra* and *Ercole contro Moloch*'s bloodthirsty male villains are evil spawns from the depths of Hell). Second, vampires are defined by their inhuman, literally beastly nature, as best exemplified by *Maciste contro il vampiro*'s snake-born, fanged and clawed Kobrak ('the cobra'), *Ercole al centro della Terra*'s Lyco ('the wolf'), and *Ercole contro Moloch*'s Moloch, who is fanged, clawed and wears a mask halfway between a wolf and a bat (see Chapter 4). The wolf imagery is crucial here: Hitler's German Shepherds often appeared in Nazi propaganda and wolf–dog hybrids henceforth became a stereotypical feature of the Nazi army in non-German war movies (Hitler's very own first name meant 'noble wolf', as widely publicised by the Third Reich). Third, in a clear allusion to the Nazi-backed Repubblica Sociale Italiana, pepla's vampires generally rule over the population through a puppet government composed of local, power- and money-hungry collaborationists. In particular, the military raids carried out on civilians by the vampire's minions – filled as they are of burned-down villages, screaming mothers holding crying children, and martyrised corpses hanged as macabre warnings to the rebels – resemble the house-to-house searches carried out by the Nazi-Fascists in Centre-North Italy to appropriate resources for the continuation of the war effort, eradicate partisan cells, and enforce reprisals, conscription and racial laws.[5] Fourth, borrowing from a commonplace of anti-Nazi propaganda, pepla's vampires are shown to use brainwashing either to co-opt single individuals (*Ercole al centro della Terra* and *Roma contro Roma*) or to create an army of 'perfect warrior[s], alive but with no will of [their] own' (*Roma contro Roma*), 'automatons made of flesh and bones, soulless and faceless slaves' (*Maciste contro il vampiro*), soldiers with a heart of stone that execute orders like robots (hence the stone golems from *Maciste e la regina di Samar*, obeying a high priest whose skull face recalls the *Totenkopf* insignia on SS uniforms and the *testa di morto* adorning the berets of the Brigate Nere paramilitary groups during the Repubblica Sociale Italiana).

Of paramount importance to understand the representational strategies of 1961–1964 vampire-themed pepla is the Italo–Swiss propaganda documentary *Giorni di gloria* (Mario Serandrei, Luchino Visconti, Giuseppe De Santis, Marcello Pagliero, 1945), whom the opening credits dedicate 'to all those who, in Italy, have endured and fought the Nazi-Fascist oppression'. Formally produced by Titanus (actually involved in distribution only), *Giorni di gloria* was the result of the joined efforts of the Anglo-American Psychological Warfare Branch Film Division and of the cross-party National Association of Italian Partisans, and sought to facilitate a nationwide, collective self-absolution from the Fascist past through the portrayal of Italian people's spontaneous, dignified, cohesive opposition to Nazi invaders after the 1943 armistice and the power void caused by the escape from Rome of King Vittorio Emanuele III and the Italian Army's high ranks (Eisenschitz 2014). Obviously for an Anglo-American-sponsored work, the words 'Communism' and 'Socialism' are never mentioned in the voice-over commentary, while Communist filmmakers Mario Serandrei, Luchino Visconti and Giuseppe De Santis strategically ignore the years of Fascism's mass consensus to focus on the 1943–1945 decline under Nazi patronage, which allows the film to present Italy as a victim of 'foreign infiltrators' and 'Barbarians' (1943–1944 statements by Benedetto Croce, quoted in Ben-Ghiat 1999: 89) – a 'poor lamb, offered in holocaust, fighting to defend itself', in Alvaro's ([1944] 1986: 40) famous words – and to imply that the whole Fascist *ventennio* had been but a 'parenthesis' in the life of an intrinsically humane, democratic country, the pathological deviation of a minimal part of the Italian population, the most fanatical and violent in its search for power and wealth (Croce, quoted in Ben-Ghiat 1999: 89).

Giorni di gloria's rhetoric, based on the externalisation of guilt and the dismissal of the Repubblica-Sociale-Italiana adherents as mere collaborationists rather than as real combatants, would also imbue Roberto Rossellini's 1945 *Roma città aperta*, *Paisà* (Roberto Rossellini, 1946), *Avanti a lui tremava tutta Roma / Before Him All Rome Trembled* (Carmine Gallone, 1946), *Vivere in pace* (Luigi Zampa, 1947) and the other Italian war movies of the immediate post-war that, for reasons of ideological pacification, national unity and moral uplifting in view of the reconstruction, were similarly keen on denying both the mass appeal of Fascism and the civil-war aspects of the Resistance (Pesce 2008:

27–86; Lichtner 2013: 45–62, 97–9). What really makes *Giorni di gloria* a seminal work in relation to the five pepla discussed here is the fact that it explicitly compares the Nazi-Fascists to vampires: 'Who are the authors of these massacres? [Kurt] Mälzer, [Eugen] Dollmann, [Pietro] Caruso and many other vampires . . . ', states the voice-over commenting on the Nazi-Fascists' 1943–1945 war crimes on Italian soil, always taking extreme care in distinguishing between the numerically overwhelming Nazi 'hordes' and the few 'reactionary gangs' of 'Fascist slaves' acting like 'puppets in a mad carnival of blood'. The political declination of the vampire metaphor is further strengthened by emphasising the occupants' foreignness (the use of the word 'hordes' to describe the German army encourages spectators to make an association with Barbarian invasions), and by highlighting the beast-like nature of the Nazi-Fascists (the Brigate Nere are said to go around in 'packs' like wolves; the SS exacting a 'beastly vengeance' on the Italian people are called 'the German Moloch', a reference to the 1914 *Cabiria*'s child-eating god of evil to be reprised in *Ercole contro Moloch*, where the titular villain is called 'the symbol of a cruel regime').[6]

Ostensibly, the screenwriters and directors of vampire-themed pepla referenced Nazi-Fascism for reasons of narrative economy, to create with a few broad strokes a series of unredeemable, universally despicable supervillains for Manichaean narratives financed by Italian, French, West German and North American distributors (see Chapters 1 and 2). At the same time, writers and filmmakers might have also been encouraged to deal with 1943–1945 national history by their producers, who perhaps sought to piggy-back on the late-1950s and early-1960s 'anti-Fascist and partisan *filone*' (Spinazzola 1962: 73–4) consisting of *Il generale Della Rovere / General Della Rovere* (Roberto Rossellini, 1959), *Estate violenta / Violent Summer* (Valerio Zurlini, 1959), *La lunga notte del '43 / It Happened in 1943* (Florestano Vancini, 1960), *La ciociara / Two Women* (Vittorio De Sica, 1960), *Il carro armato dell'8 settembre* (Gianni Puccini, 1960), *Il gobbo / The Hunchback* (Carlo Lizzani, 1960), *Tutti a casa / Everybody Go Home!* (Luigi Comencini, 1960), *Il federale / The Fascist* (Luciano Salce, 1961), and many others. These were Italian auteur cinema efforts and *commedie all'italiana* that found critical and/or commercial success by bringing to the screen Benito Mussolini's deposition on 25 July 1943, the September 1943 armistice, German occupation, the Repubblica Sociale Italiana and the Resistance after a decade of almost complete silence following *Giorni di gloria* and the already-mentioned Italian war movies of 1945–1947 (Pesce 2008: 87–165). Industrial analysis, though, provides only part of the picture – the one relating to vampire-themed pepla as concerned with the historical past. To fully expose the cultural instrumentality of *Ercole al centro della Terra*, *Maciste contro il vampiro*, *Ercole contro Moloch*, *Roma contro Roma* and *Maciste e la regina di Samar*, the political situation in early-1960s Italy needs to be outlined.

In the Italy of the immediate post-war, many former Fascist Party members kept their position of responsibility as public servants in the name of the continuity of state institutions, and similarly untouched were the formerly Fascist big landowners and leading businessmen, because the Allies did not want the country's political, judicial, military and economic powers to fall into the hands of the Left. Moreover, many Fascists convicted for the war crimes committed in the name of the Repubblica Sociale Italiana benefited from the amnesty promulgated for reasons of national pacification by the last Ministry of Justice of the Kingdom of Italy, Communist leader Palmiro Togliatti, on 22 June 1946 (Ginsborg 1990: 72–120). The outlawed Fascist Party could thus be recreated in late 1946 under the name of Movimento Sociale Italiano, which immediately obtained a handful of seats at the general election of 1948. From then on, the Movimento Sociale Italiano started building up electoral consensus by playing the cards of anti-Communism and patriarchal traditionalism, until it became a key ally of Christian Democracy in early 1960, when appointed Prime Minister Fernando Tambroni, a Christian Democrat, gained a narrow parliamentary approval for his centrist government thanks to the votes of extreme-right representatives (Ginsborg 1990: 143–5, 254–8). In order to give a further demonstration of strength, in June 1960 the Movimento Sociale Italiano organised a congress in Genova, 'a city which had been awarded a gold medal for its part in the Resistance', and invited as a guest of honour 'the last prefect of Genova during the [Repubblica Sociale Italiana], who had been responsible for the deaths and deportations of many Genoese workers and anti-Fascists' (Ginsborg 1990: 256). Violent mass protests involving former partisans as well as common people followed in Genova and in other Italian cities (where anti-Fascist riots intertwined with worker protests), and the police and the army opened fire on the crowds upon governmental order, killing several demonstrators. According to Crainz (2005a: 169–79), Tambroni was trying to create civil-war-like chaos and pass it off as a Communist coup in order to implement strong measures against the Left. Whatever the case, the tense situation was solved by the moderate currents of Christian Democracy, which forced Tambroni to resign and, seeing that a large part of public opinion identified with the values of Resistance and opposed the participation of the neofascists to the government, started building the centre-left alliance that would rule the country from December 1963 to June 1968.

The crumbling of Tambroni's government in late July 1960 and the subsequent opening to the Left by Christian Democracy brought to an end the fiercest period of the Cold War in Italy, as signalled by the fact that the Resistance ceased to be a taboo subject: 'a climate of anti-Fascist revival' began in late 1960, with 'a ministerial circular extend[ing] the teaching of history in upper schools as far as the Resistance' (previous curricula stopped at the end of First World War), and with official Second World War commemorations like state ceremonies and Italian State Radio and Italian State TV broadcasts finally including Socialist and Communist speakers (Crainz 1999: 127). Yet, reactionary forces still held a considerable influence. For example, in March 1961, the neofascist protests against a TV sketch parodying the Blackshirts and the Fascist colonial dreams of the 1930s and 1940s prompted Christian Democrat Prime Minister Amintore Fanfani to publicly admonish the management of Italian State TV for mocking the homeland (Crainz 1999: 127–8). As a result, as late as 1968–1969, state-sponsored broadcasts about the 1943–1945 period put 'the full responsibility for the evils of the era [. . .] on the Nazis', and obscured 'such important matters as the hopes of the Resistance for a radical social transformation, as well as the basic nature of the conflict between Fascism and anti-Fascism' (Crainz 1999: 129).

If this is the political climate in which Italian producers, screenwriters and directors set out to exploit the commercial success of both Pietro Francisci's *Le fatiche di Ercole* and the Hammer *Dracula* by making vampire-themed pepla, it is possible to read the 'popular historical lesson' (Lagny 1992: 174) of *Ercole al centro della Terra*, *Maciste contro il vampiro*, *Ercole contro Moloch*, *Roma contro Roma* and *Maciste e la regina di Samar* also as a warning about the resurgence of Fascism in early-1960s Italy, with the vampires lurking in the dark caves of the faraway lands of 'fanta-antiquity' (Salotti 1986: 151) acting as a stand-in for the Movimento Sociale Italiano and, more in general, for the former Fascists who maintained their position of power in the democratic institutions of the Italian Republic. Unfortunately, none of the people involved in making these films ever went on record commenting upon their politics. For instance, when asked about *Ercole al centro della Terra* – in which the threatened kingdom is called Ecalia (Italia?) and the doors of scheming usurper Lyco's palace are adorned with swastika-like decorations – director Mario Bava kept his usual low profile by stealing the bet anecdote from his colleague Riccardo Freda. This allowed Bava to talk about craft rather than about message:

> I made a bet that I could make a feature film only by using a modular wall with a door and a window, and four mobile columns, without any other scenery. Therefore, I shot *Ercole al centro della Terra* by continuously moving these few elements around, in an endless series of shot-countershot. No spectator ever noticed. (Quoted in Cozzi 1970–1971: 101)

The most attentive genre-cinema scholar of 1960s Italy further problematises anti-Fascist readings when he advises against 'dilating beyond measure the libertarian and Spartacist potential' of historical-mythological movies (Spinazzola 1963: 106), for after all their Manichaean narratives pitting an unlawful usurper/oppressor against a people's hero are an expression of a dangerously reactionary 'populist paternalism' (Spinazzola 1964: 52–3). To limit ourselves to examples taken from vampire-themed pepla, the oppressed masses are always shown to be totally ineffectual, most blatantly in *Maciste e la regina di Samar*, where, after a lengthy subplot about the setting up of an underground resistance movement, Maciste has to save the day alone because a storm prevents the insurgents from showing up on the battlefield. Moreover, after the vampire rulers are killed by the muscleman heroes, the newly liberated people, whose motto until that moment had been 'Freedom or death!' or variations thereof, simply call for more humane masters to obey, as monarchy (*Ercole al centro della Terra, Maciste contro il vampiro, Ercole contro Moloch* and *Maciste e la regina di Samar*) and colonialism (*Roma contro Roma*) are never contested as tyrannical per se. In sum, we are in front of a twofold paradox: not only the pepla's musclemen overthrowing fascistoid regimes physically and ideologically embody the clerico-Fascist ideal of the strong, Messiah-like Man of Providence able to enforce the law, order and tradition that the impotent masses crave (Dyer 1997: 169–77), but also the revolution ultimately serves the preservation of the authoritarian status quo (Marchena 2009: 31–6; Burke 2011). Lacking precise information about the political convictions of the almost totality of the producers, screenwriters and directors of vampire-themed pepla, it is not possible to establish if the films were intentionally conceived as vehicles for a specific left-wing or right-wing ideology. What is certain is that vampire-themed pepla appeared politically innocuous enough to state censorship and were left free to make money at the box office, which was probably the main concern for most of the people involved in their making.[7]

NOTES

1. The migration of Italian peasants to the mining and industrial districts of West Germany and Belgium was equally massive, although the Italians moving abroad 'regarded their stay as temporary' and 'rarely remained more than a year at a time, and even more rarely did their families leave to join them' (Ginsborg 1990: 228).
2. There are substantial discrepancies between the first treatment (Anton 1959), the screenplay submitted by the producers to the Italian Show Business Bureau and the finished film. The main difference is that in both the treatment and the screenplay submitted to government officials Osvaldo is not a fallen aristocrat forced to take on a menial job, but a poor bellboy all along, meeting the vampire by chance.
3. Not coincidentally the quintessential *commedia dei mostri* – the aptly titled *I mostri* (Dino Risi, 1963) – was produced by Mario Cecchi Gori and co-written by Agenore Incrocci and Furio Scarpelli, respectively the producer and the uncredited screenwriters of *Tempi duri per i vampiri*.
4. *Tempi duri per i vampiri*'s demagogical equivalence between tax authorities and vampirism was deemed harmless enough by the Italian Film Censorship Office, and reprised in the vampire skit of Mario Amendola's 1963 striptease compilation *Sexy proibitissimo*, where it is stated that 'since vampires never die [. . .] the state gave

them all a lifelong working position at the tax office'. Incidentally, the film Cecchi Gori and CEI-Incom co-produced immediately before *Tempi duri per i vampiri* was Totò star vehicle *I tartassati / The Overtaxed* (Stefano Vanzina as Steno, 1959), a comedy that revolves around a wealthy bourgeois' clumsy attempts at tax evasion and ultimate surrender to the rightful punishment.

5. The most graphic of such sequences, in the opening of *Maciste contro il vampiro*, was conceived and directed by Triestinian Jew Giacomo Gentilomo, who survived real-life raids in Nazi-occupied Rome by hiding in a convent (Lughi [1991] 2008: 130). In Gentilomo's other vampire-themed peplum, *Maciste e la regina di Samar*, the word 'holocaust' is used to describe the human sacrifices for vampire Selene organised by the puppet-government.
6. The 'symbol of a ferocious dictatorship', according to *Ercole contro Moloch*'s screenplay (Unknown 1963).
7. According to Della Casa and Giusti (2014: 62), Lionello Santi, the head of Galatea – the production company of many horrors and pepla, including the hybrid *Roma contro Roma* – was a Communist, but of course, as a businessman, his main allegiance was to moneymaking, as shown by the fact that, throughout his career, he exploited his ties to the Italian Communist Party to strike production/distribution deals with Soviet countries while collaborating with US companies such as Embassy Pictures and American International Pictures.

6. POST-1968 VAMPIRES

FROM THE 'BOOM' TO AUSTERITY

If horror parody *Tempi duri per i vampiri* and the early-1960s vampire horrors and vampire-themed pepla were at best timidly politicised, bringing to the fore 'a desperation related to the present but often expressed through the disguise of the past' (Curti 2011: 8), Italian vampire cinema from the 1970s tackled then-current political and socio-economic issues more directly, adopting a prevalently contemporary setting, and openly and abundantly referencing Marx and trendy Marxist thinkers of the day. As for the latter characteristic, the main sources of inspiration were the writings of world-renowned foreign intellectuals like critical theorist Herbert Marcuse, although post-war Italy had its very own Marxist tradition of ferocious critique of consumer capitalism (as we shall see further below, the most famous representative of such tradition, Pier Paolo Pasolini, made use of the vampire metaphor in a 1968 article indicting the infectiousness of bourgeois conformism). The 1970s politicisation of Italian vampire cinema is the result of two factors. On the one hand, we have the end of the most acute phase of the Cold War in Italy, sanctioned by Prime Minister Fernando Tambroni's resignation in summer 1960 and by the official alliance between Christian Democrats and Socialists in late 1963, which led, among other things, to the appointment of Socialist Achille Corona as the Minister of Tourism and Cultural Activities after more than fifteen years of Christian Democrat rule over the Italian Show Business Bureau. On the other hand, we have a new political conscience developed by students and workers facing the inequalities and distortions brought about by the ungoverned 'boom' of 1958–1963 and the post-1963 failure of the reformist program of the centre-left coalition. The second factor deserves in-depth contextualisation, as the six vampire movies analysed in this chapter – . . . *Hanno cambiato faccia, La corta notte delle bambole di vetro, Il prato macchiato di rosso, L'uomo che uccideva a sangue freddo, Dracula cerca sangue di vergine . . . e morì di sete!!!* and *Il cav. Costante Nicosia demoniaco, ovvero: Dracula in Brianza* – were all made in the aftermath of the anti-establishment student protests of 1968 and the *autunno caldo* ('hot autumn') of 1969–1970, when the student movement joined forces with exploited factory workers, leading to an unprecedented mass revolt against the capitalist class and the parties of parliamentary politics that would last until the late 1970s.

Nineteen-sixty-eight is unanimously considered a crucial year for anti-authoritarian protests all over the world. In Italy – just as in the US, in France, in West Germany and in many other countries outside the Western bloc such as Czechoslovakia, Poland and Yugoslavia – the rebellion was initiated and led by the urban youth, and especially involved a mass movement of students in their mid-to-late teens and early twenties. Indeed, even before the Italian Parliament extended compulsory education to fourteen years of age with law 1859 of 31 December 1962, the youth of the *bel paese* was accessing secondary education *en masse*. According to official data, junior high-school students went from the 500,000 people of 1947 to the 900,000 people of 1955 and the 1.6 million people of early 1962, while university students went from the 268,000 people of 1960 to the over 450,000 people of 1968 (Ginsborg 1990: 298–302; Crainz 2005a: 77–8).

As it has been remarked by many historians, the mass protests of the Italian youth did not come out of the blue. Rather, they were the virulent radicalisation of a generational clash and discontent with the status quo that first became apparent in 1958, when tiny groups of university students occupied some faculties in Naples to demonstrate against state examinations, overcrowded classrooms and the professors' lack of commitment to their educational mission (Crainz 2005a: 76–7). The small-scale Naples uprising was easily repressed by the local authorities, but it provided the blueprint for students of other cities to follow: from 1962 onwards, high-school and university students would periodically occupy public buildings all over the country, mainly to ask for a reform of the Italian school system. In fact, together with the post-war baby boom, the extension of compulsory education to fourteen years of age had greatly increased the number of students undertaking, or wishing to undertake, secondary and tertiary education, but nothing was done to modernise curricula, hire more teaching personnel and improve infrastructures (Crainz 2005b: 201–15). Moreover, it is not to be forgotten that many high-school and university students (most of them of middle-class extraction) had already played a major role in the violent anti-Tambroni/pro-workers protests of summer 1960: so much for Alfassio-Grimaldi and Bertoni's (1964: 377–85) idea that the consumerist ideology of the economic miracle made young Italians into self-centred, atomised, docile individuals interested only in achieving the 'Car-Marriage-Job' status symbols.

From the anti-Fascist revival of the early 1960s to the anti-US-imperialism demonstrations of the mid-1960s, Italian students and, more in general, young Italians contesting the capitalist status quo from a variety of ideological stances – from traditional Marxism to libertarian anarchism – were given a series of nicknames by the national press: *giovani dalle magliette a strisce* ('striped-shirt youngsters'), beatniks, *capelloni* ('long-haired'), hippies, provos, and so on. As shown by Crainz's (2005a: 180–8; 2005b: 187–200) archival research, the tone of most newspaper articles dealing with the rebellious youth of the early-to-mid-1960s oscillated between paternalism (the parliamentary left-wing) and the certainty that the protests were just a subcultural phenomenon involving small groups of anti-social misfits, a passing fad that, like worker protests, could easily be brought to an end by the police and the army (the centre and the extreme right wing). It is with the beginning of academic year 1967–1968 that fear started spreading among the older generations.

The now-famous Italian *Sessantotto* ('1968 rebellion') actually started in November 1967, with about 1,000 students occupying the Università Cattolica in Milan. As happened in Naples in 1958, the Milanese students adopted the weapon of occupation to attract media attention, and put forward very basic, practical demands relating to the reduction in economic, class and bureaucratic barriers preventing access to higher education (*in primis*, the reduction of university fees), the opening of new facilities, more up-to-date curricula, more commitment on the part of the professors and right of student assembly. In autumn 1967, the Italian Parliament was indeed discussing a reform of the university system, but the debate basically focused on the single issue of allowing the 'university barons' to keep on being lavishly paid, absentee employees – a privilege that was of course granted, since many members of the Chamber of Deputies and Senate had a parallel career as university professors (Crainz 2005b: 222–3). Given the indifference of state institutions, the student revolt grew bigger and bigger, expanding from the Università Cattolica in Milan to the universities and high schools of Turin, Trento, Rome, Naples, Florence, Pisa, Pavia, Bologna, Genova, Cagliari, Palermo and many more. Most crucially, it took on more general connotations, becoming a protest against the whole of Italian post-war society, a sort of public trial against the political caste, the police, the army, the magistrature, state- or party-controlled media, the institution of the family and the Catholic church, all perceived as 'fascist', that is to say old, self-interested and repressively authoritarian.

Contextually, as the government decided to ignore the students' demands and treat protests as a problem of public order requiring firm military interventions and exemplary convictions by judges, the Italian youth abandoned the non-violent forms of dissent of the early 1960s, as demonstrated by the battle of Valle Giulia on 1 March 1968, after which crash helmets, stones, bats and Molotov cocktails became fundamental instruments of so-called 'self-defence' for protesters during public demonstrations (Ginsborg 1990: 302–4; Crainz 2005b: 260–71). Following the idealistic thrust of both the Parisian student protests of May 1968 and the US countercultural movement of the mid-1960s (as codified and somewhat rationalised by Marcuse), the main slogans of the *Sessantotto* became 'Vietato vietare' ('It is forbidden to forbid') and 'L'immaginazione al potere' ('Power to the imagination'). The most immediate result of the ideological and physical battles that took place in 1968 Italy was the approval of law 910 of 11 December 1969, granting all students in possession of a high-school degree access to university education. Yet, the biggest achievement of the student movement was the creation of a united front with the urban working class (especially the unskilled and semi-skilled migrant workers living in Turin, Milan and respective suburbs), a host of young and middle-aged factory workers exasperated by exploitation and the unfulfilled promises of the 1963–1968 centre-left governments.

As we have seen in Chapter 5, the economic miracle came to a halt with the *congiuntura* of summer 1963, when the increase in workers' salaries significantly exceeded the increase in productivity. Ever since the immediate postwar, workers' unrest was rife in Italian cities and countryside, but the Christian Democrats – committed to protecting the interests of big landlords and industrialists against the so-called 'red threat' – always managed to repress it, in blood more often than not, to the point that even the most moderate Catholic unionists of the 1950s and early 1960s were forced to admit that, in matters of employment and class relations, the Christian-Democracy-run Republic had until then been 'more a state of police than a state of law' (Crainz 2005b: 181). It was only with the fall of Tambroni's government and the first talks of a centre-left alliance that union activities could gain momentum and become effective, leading to the aforementioned wage rises. The monetisation of exploitation and hazardous working conditions, however, was not enough for the workers: having grown exponentially from the mid-1950s to the mid-1960s, the urban working class was becoming more and more conscious of its strength and bargaining power, and less and less prone to be ruled by the traditional Catholic or left-wing unions, which were increasingly deemed to be too lax and aligned with the conservative powers. In particular, the thousands of young, unskilled or semi-skilled workers who had recently migrated from impoverished rural areas of the South to the big cities of the Centre-North showed signs of extreme radicalisation, violently clashing with the representatives of the status quo, be it the police, the army, union officials and even left-wing politicians, as best exemplified by the events of Piazza Statuto in Turin in July 1962 (Ginsborg 1990: 250–3). After the end of the 'boom', the emergency deflationist policies and the investment strike enacted by the capitalist class produced the usual consequences ('Unemployment rose, with women being the first to lose their jobs') (Ginsborg 1990: 275), but the formation of the first centre-left government in late 1963 blocked the workers' struggles, as the 1961–1962 negotiations between the Christian Democrats and the Left had led to the formulation of an 'ambitious program' of 'structural reforms' – an uncanny embrace of capitalism and Socialism for 'the economic and political integration of the lower classes into the nation-state' (Ginsborg 1990: 266) that galvanised the hopes of both the blue-collar proletariat and the white-collar lower-middle class.

The season of reformism under the aegis of Christian Democrats and Socialists soon proved to be utopia: as mentioned in Chapter 5, no significant action was ever taken to increase public spending, fight tax evasion and protect the workforce from labour abuses. Basically, by July 1964, when anti-Communist army general Giovanni De Lorenzo might or might not have threatened the republican institutions with a military coup, any project of serious reform in favour of the working class and the underprivileged was shelved indefinitely, as in the post-*congiuntura* period of economic crisis the government's priority became bringing the capitalist class's profits back to the levels of the 'boom' years. The centre-left, then, survived as a mere instrument for the involved political parties to maintain power, and the centrist-Socialist governments that ruled Italy until June 1968 were characterised by 'sterile immobilism and irresponsibly wasted time' (Silvio Lanaro, quoted in Crainz 2005a: 240).

In the second half of the 1960s, state organs largely limited themselves to lamenting the critical state of the country. For instance, according to the Ministry of Labour, in 1966 'the average net salary received by industry workers is 70,000 lire per month', while the Italian Institute of Statistics calculated that, in the same period, 'the minimum expenses for the basic survival of the average nuclear family reach 100,000 lire per month'. Indeed, ever since late 1964, Doxa polls had been revealing that – having to face the 'working-hour curtailments' (read: faster working rhythms for a lower salary) and the 'layoffs' enforced by industrialists all over the country to compensate for the increased cost of labour – '22.7% of Italian families' were in debt (Crainz 2005b: 17). Meanwhile, the Bank of Italy estimated that the legal exportation of capital from Italy to foreign countries went 'from the US$336 million of 1963 to the US$3.4 billion of 1969' (as for the illegal exportation of Italian currency to Switzerland, the figures are unofficial, but 'far superior') (Crainz 2005b: 38). In such a situation, with rampant inflation rapidly eroding the salary rises of 1960–1963, it was the fear of relapsing into pre-'boom' poverty that prevented the working class from reprising the early-1960s class struggle, as noted in

1965 by the prefect of Turin, who wrote with some satisfaction to the Ministry of the Interior that strikes generally tended to fail after 1964 because 'workers are in fear of losing their job in this moment of economic crisis' (quoted in Crainz 2005b: 48). From the opposite side of the ideological spectrum, at the inception of the *Sessantotto*, Marxist intellectual Pasolini ([1968] 1979: 39) provided the same diagnosis and used the vampire metaphor to warn against the post-*congiuntura* season of proletarian conformism and retreat into the private sphere, indicting it as an embourgeoisement of the working class:

> When I say 'bourgeoisie' I mean [. . .] a veritable disease, [. . .] so contagious that it has infected all those who try to fight it: Northern workers, migrant workers from the South, the bourgeois of the opposition, the lone opposers like myself. The bourgeois – this is said in wit – is a vampire who cannot rest until he has bitten his victim on the neck, for the sheer satisfaction of seeing people become pale, sad, ugly, devitalised, twisted, corrupted, anxious, guilt-ridden, calculating, aggressive, terroristic, like himself. How many workers, intellectuals, students have been bitten overnight by the vampire and, without knowing, are becoming vampires themselves!

It took the anti-establishment youth rebellion of 1968 to rekindle the students–workers alliance first established during the anti-Tambroni revolts of summer 1960, and to re-ignite the mass protests of the exploited working class.

Students would occasionally join factory workers' strikes throughout the early 1960s, but it was during the big strike at Turin's FIAT factories in spring 1968 that the slogan 'Studenti e operai uniti nella lotta' ('Students and workers united in the struggle') first appeared (Crainz 2005b: 235–59, 321–42). The Italian youth's demystification of the university system as an unproductive storage of reserve labour had in fact been so radical that the students did not see academic institutions as central any more for the future of the country and preferred to go to the people in order to revolutionise capitalist society as a whole, starting from factories and urban peripheries (Righi 2011: 103–35). To do so, the student movement fragmented into several factions and the first extraparliamentary left-wing groups were formed in 1968–1969 (Potere Operaio, Lotta Continua and so on), aiming to take the class struggle out of the hands of the Italian Socialist Party, the Italian Communist Party and the unions, which were accused of being traitors happily integrated in the 'bourgeois power-machine' of parliamentary politics, yet another counter-revolutionary weapon of repression in the 'capitalist arsenal' (Lotta Continua collective 1970: 1). When, in 1968–1969, employment and productivity figures began to rise again in the automobile and electric-appliances factories of Northern Italy, prompting the press to speak of another upcoming 'boom' after the 1963 *congiuntura*, the worker–student front did not simply ask for salary raises. Instead, it demanded the thorough subversion of class relations: the long, grinding hours of labour at the assembly line were denounced as alienating; the distinction between white- and blue-collar workers was indicted as the most effective instrument for capitalists to dilute class struggle from the inside; the needs for forming grass-roots factory soviets and disengaging salary increases from productivity levels were stressed. Here, a rhetoric mixing Marx, Lenin, Che Guevara and Mao was accompanied by unannounced mass strikes, absenteeism, occupations, acts of sabotage, violent picketing against scabs, foremen and managers, blockings of motorways and train stations, and guerrilla-warfare-like clashes with the police. Southern Italy quickly became a battleground as well, in both rural areas and urban centres, as shown most blatantly by the massacre of Avola (2 December 1969) and the popular revolts of Battipaglia (9 April 1969) and Reggio Calabria (July 1970–February 1971) (Ginsborg 1990: 337–47; Crainz 2005b: 277–81, 336–46, 470–9).

Nationwide disorders were accelerated by the Turinese and Milanese factories' *autunno caldo* of 1969–1970, which coincided with the beginning of a period of state-colluded right-wing terrorism falsely attributed to the extraparliamentary left-wing (the so-called *strategia della tensione*, or 'strategy of tension', inaugurated by the bombing of Piazza Fontana in Milan on 12 December 1969). Social unrest lasted until the end of the 1970s, because any salary rise was to be immediately nullified by an inflation left largely unchallenged by the post-1968 governments, especially following the devaluation of the lira, the rampant growth in public debt and the 1973–1974 austerity connected to the 1971 international monetary crisis and the 1973 oil crisis (Ginsborg 1990: 351–4; Crainz 2005b: 416–9; 424–43). It is in this situation of permanent conflict – further exacerbated by the anti-state/anti-capitalist terrorist activities of ultra-left-wing groups – that the production of Italian vampire cinema reprised after an almost five-year hiatus, more politicised than ever, with the indictment of the status quo going hand-in-hand with an apocalyptic stance that sees true, revolutionary change as unachievable.

Resistance is futile: the vampire conspiracy

A hotbed for worker and student protests from the 1962 events of Piazza Statuto to the 1968 university occupations and the 1969–1970 *autunno caldo*, Turin was also the city in which . . . *Hanno cambiato faccia* – the first explicitly political declination of the vampire in 1970s Italian cinema – was conceived, as detailed in Farina (2016: 123–8) and Guarneri (2019a). Born in 1939 in Turin, where he got his university diploma in law in the early 1960s, . . . *Hanno cambiato faccia*'s writer and director Corrado Farina was too old to be involved with the 1968 student movement, while his wealthy-bourgeois background estranged him from 1960s-1970s workers' struggles and left-wing political militancy. The genesis of his vampire-themed feature-film debut is therefore to be linked to his post-graduation working experience in the tertiary sector. In 1963, Farina started working for one of the biggest advertising agencies in Italy, Armando Testa's, writing and directing commercials aired on Italian State TV or screened in cinemas. In the second half of the 1960s, the movie *I'll Never Forget What's'isname* (Michael Winner, 1967) and the reading of by-then countercultural classics like Vance Packard's 1957 *The Hidden Persuaders* and Marcuse's 1955 *Eros and Civilisation: A Philosophical Inquiry into Freud* and 1964 *One-Dimensional Man* (first translated in Italian in 1958, 1964 and 1967 respectively) precipitated an existential crisis for Farina, who increasingly felt uneasy about his daily work concerned with the profit-bent manipulation of consumers' conscience. As a result, in 1967–1968, while he was still living in Turin and considering to quit his job in advertising and move with his wife and children to Rome to make a name for himself in the film industry, Farina authored a comic-strip titled *Il Grande Persuasore* ('The Great Persuader'), which satirised his own profession and bosses, and drafted the treatment for a modern-Italy-set retelling of Stoker's novel *Dracula* that was to become . . . *Hanno cambiato faccia*.[1] The shoestring-budget nature of . . . *Hanno cambiato faccia*, financed by some members of the artistic and technical cast united in the cooperative Filmsettanta, has been described in Chapter 2. What is crucial, here, is to investigate how the film conjugates the Gothic paraphernalia of Hammer's period pieces *Dracula, The Brides of Dracula, Dracula: Prince of Darkness, Dracula Has Risen from the Grave, Taste the Blood of Dracula* and *Scars of Dracula* with a countercultural stance on post-war consumer capitalism, thereby adapting mostly Anglophone narrative and theoretical traditions to the post-*Sessantotto* Italian situation as filtered through Farina's own personal experiences.

Written, shot and released during a period in which the Italian working class reached its numerical apogee (42 per cent of the working population, according to the 1971 census) (Crainz 2005b: 434) and its highest level of radicalisation (in 1969 the unprecedented and hitherto-unsurpassed number of 232 million hours of strike was recorded) (Crainz 2005b: 452), . . . *Hanno cambiato faccia* focuses on the trials and tribulations of white-collar rather than blue-collar labour, thematising the anti-authoritarian revolt of Alberto Valle, a thirty-something university-degree-holder with an expertise in advertising, like Farina himself. One day Valle, a low-rank employee of heavy-industry colossus Auto Avio Motors, is sent by his bosses on a business trip to a remote villa in the Piedmontese countryside, in order to meet the owner of Auto Avio Motors, Ingegnere Giovanni Nosferatu. The trip to Ingegnere Nosferatu's villa is clearly meant to mirror Jonathan Harker's trip to castle Dracula from the 1897 novel (not coincidentally, Valle's direct superior at the factory is called Harker), but the vampire of ... *Hanno cambiato faccia* shares more similarities with the owner of FIAT, Avvocato Giovanni Agnelli, than with Stoker's Count: both Giovanni Nosferatu and Giovanni Agnelli are white-haired captains of industry who are formally outside the world of parliamentary politics and yet they control it via economic pressures and the mass media they own. 'The leaders act under my control' and 'I own the newspapers, I own the police', says Ingegnere Nosferatu to Valle – an innuendo to Agnelli's ownership of newspaper *La Stampa* and ties with the various post-war governments, whose pro-capitalist-class measures in matters of state financing to private industry, taxation of high incomes and repression of worker protests have been previously outlined.[2] This basic equivalence tinges the film with paranoidly conspiratorial connotations:

> Ingegnere Giovanni Nosferatu is not simply a master, a man who has power. Rather, he is [. . .] the master of the masters. He sucks the blood of everybody, to keep alive [. . .] a structure of power, a system, an organism that is not made of flesh. Ingegnere Nosferatu is [. . .] the master of all the villains, and it is not by chance that actor Adolfo Celi was cast in the role, since he had already played a supervillain in *Thunderball* (Terence Young, 1965) and *Diabolik / Danger: Diabolik* (Mario Bava, 1967). (Farina, quoted in Guarneri 2019a)

Secluded in an isolated villa, his existence ignored by the vast majority of his employees, 170-year-old Ingegnere Nosferatu incarnates 'a secret power' (Farina, quoted in Guarneri 2019a), a great puppeteer that allows Farina to update Stoker's Victorian-era classic with Marcuse's ([1964] 1968: 7) indictment of 'the destructive power and repressive function of the [post-war] affluent society', which

> exact[s] the overwhelming need for the production and consumption of waste; the need for stupefying work where it is no longer a real necessity; the need for modes of relaxation which soothe and prolong this stupefication; the need for maintaining such deceptive liberties as free competition at administered prices, a free press which censors itself, free choice between brands and gadgets.

While writing that the 'totalitarian tendencies of the one-dimensional society render the traditional ways and means of protest ineffective – perhaps even dangerous because they preserve the illusion of popular sovereignty' (Marcuse [1964] 1968: 256), the German-American critical theorist still provides a glimmer of hope in that he believes in the existence of truly revolutionary forces able to 'explode the society' (Marcuse [1964] 1968: xv), namely 'the outcasts and outsiders, the exploited and the persecuted of other races and other colors, the unemployed and the unemployable' (Marcuse [1964] 1968: 256). In appropriating and reworking Marcuse's thought, however, Farina focused on the apocalyptic side only. In particular, the Italian screenwriter and director seized upon one concept – 'beat ways of life [. . .] are no longer contradictory to the status quo [. . .]. They are rather [. . .] its harmless negation, [. . .] quickly digested by the status quo as part of its healthy diet' (Marcuse [1964] 1968: 14) – and made it the narrative backbone of his film. Indeed, through two intertwined plotlines, . . . *Hanno cambiato faccia* revolves around the idea of a system of power so strong and all-pervasive that it is able to co-opt and reabsorb even the most violent, visceral, genuine forms of youthful rebellion.

In the main plotline, Valle visits Ingegnere Nosferatu's lair and, upon discovering that his host is using the sexual commodification of the human body, hallucinogenic drugs and the most modern, psychoanalysis-derived techniques of mind conditioning on a mass scale to control people's life from cradle to casket, shoots the capitalist vampire and runs away from the villa.[3] In the downbeat ending, though, Valle realises that waging war against somebody who owns the whole of society (the government, the opposition, state bureaucracy, the police, the army, the banks, the means of production and circulation of goods, the high-ranks of the Catholic church, the media, left-wing, right-wing and even feminist intellectuals) is futile, so he returns prodigal-son-like to Ingegnere Nosferatu and accepts becoming one of his henchmen: the last shot of the film is a freeze frame of Valle shaking the vampire's hand, superimposed with the caption 'il terrore, oggi, si chiama tecnologia – h. marcuse' ('nowadays terror is called technology – h. marcuse') in blood-red letters.[4] In the secondary plotline, we follow the destiny of Laura, a free-spirited hippy girl who aimlessly roams the countryside bare-breasted in order to scandalise repressed petty bourgeois like Valle. In her case, too, the encounter with Ingegnere Nosferatu spells the end of her youthful rebellion and quest for freedom: bitten on the neck by the vampire and offered a job as the head secretary of a big company, she sells out her ideals for what she calls 'a quiet, serene life, maybe a husband, children, economic security'. It is precisely upon meeting the newly vampirised Laura – brainwashed into bourgeois conformism and sporting tied hair, a black formal dress with matching gloves and an elegant green coat instead of her usual free-waving hair, red trousers and hippy-style jacket – that Valle abandons all hopes and resigns to serve Ingegnere Nosferatu.[5]

A few months before bleak tale of blue-collar alienation *La classe operaia va in paradiso / Lulu the Tool* (Elio Petri, 1971) won the Grand Prix for Best Film at Cannes Film Festival 1972 and the most important film-related Italian prizes, white-collar parable . . . *Hanno cambiato faccia* was awarded the Golden Leopard for Best Debut Film at Locarno Film Festival 1971. However, in its country of production, Farina's movie had little circulation, made no money at the box office and was bashed by critics, except for a couple of laudatory reviews (Laura 1971; Carnazzi 1972; Giacci 1973). Left-wing intellectuals were particularly harsh with . . . *Hanno cambiato faccia*, labelling it as 'reactionary' because the film's analysis of 'the complex structure of capitalism and the consumer society' is reduced to a 'schematically narrow' and 'exasperated Manichaeism [. . .] typical of those people who do not intend to denounce a situation in order to transform it, but simply to contemplate it, consciously or unconsciously, in its immobility' and immutability (Peruzzi 1972: 216–18).[6] Notwithstanding calls from the Italian left-wing film press for works promoting an optimistic determination to fight the system, the impotent resignation to the ruling capitalist class' *trasformismo* – that is to say the ability of those in power to adjust to political, socio-economic and cultural changes, co-opt revolutionary ferments and preserve the status quo – soon proved to be the dominant political mood of 1970s Italian vampire cinema, as shown by another debut film released in 1971, *La corta notte delle bambole di vetro*, and by the 1973 releases *Il prato macchiato di rosso* and *L'uomo che uccideva a sangue freddo*.

'We make no distinction between the past and the present . . . ', a vampire's minion tells Valle, who then quickly realises that 'Myths do not die, they mutate. You have changed your faces, but you keep sucking the blood of the people!'. *La corta notte delle bambole di vetro* shares this very premise, merely transposing it from post-*Sessantotto* Italy to post-1968 Prague, where decrepit aristocrats from the Austro-Hungarian-empire era and the Communist regime's middle-aged politicians, bureaucrats, artists and esteemed professionals from science and academia join forces to perpetuate their existence through orgiastic satanic rituals culminating in blood sacrifices of young people: 'We are the force of the past . . . ', *La corta notte delle bambole di vetro*'s vampires explain,

> We will hold the reins of power in the world as long as there are people willing to be killed, to shed their blood, and nothing must ever change. Our only enemies are people with a free-thinking mind and an awakened consciousness, so we do not tolerate any rebellion . . . We need the young to keep ourselves alive. They must become like us. They must think like us. And those who refuse are put to sleep!

Evidently, *La corta notte delle bambole di vetro*'s climate of conspiratorial paranoia – a must for auteur and genre cinema in Italy after the beginning of the *strategia della tensione* in December 1969 (O'Leary 2011: 79–104; Bisoni 2014: 89–90) – is the same one that pervades . . . *Hanno cambiato faccia*, as both films thematise the secret power of vampires pulling the strings of common people's existence from behind the scenes, unseen. However, contrary to Farina, *La corta notte delle bambole di vetro*'s screenwriter and director Aldo Lado privileged the narrative tropes of the newly discovered giallo *filone* over

Stoker's Gothic classic, as attested by the fact that, for the sake of verisimilitude, the screenplay's supernatural scene in which old dignitaries rejuvenate during the blood sacrifice of a girl (Lado and von Spiehs 1971) never made it into the final film.

La corta notte delle bambole di vetro opens with the mysterious disappearance of twenty-year-old Mira Sherkova, the Czechoslovakian girlfriend of Gregory Moore, an American journalist in his late thirties temporarily working in Prague as a foreign correspondent. Following the Dario Argento template, the stranger in a strange land starts his own private investigation, which leads him to link the disappearance of Mira and several other Czechoslovakian girls to a cultural association called Klub 99, where 'a toothless nobility, some politicians, some rich guys with nothing to do and a bunch of tedious, illustrious professionals' (Lado and von Spiehs 1971) gather to share their passion for chamber music, stamps, entomology and chess. Behind this apparently harmless, respectable façade lurks the vampire conspiracy described above, and when Gregory discovers the truth, the Klub 99 members – 'the greatest personalities in Europe' in the protagonist's own words – use their socio-economic and political influence to prevent him from blowing the whistle. Gregory is first reduced to a cataleptic state, then stabbed to death, and the vampire villains, who in the screenplay boast to be undefeatable since they are 'as old as the world itself' (Lado and von Spiehs 1971), triumph: yet another downbeat ending after . . . *Hanno cambiato faccia*, all the more defeatist in that Gregory's catalepsy is meant to convey the ultimate impotence of the new generations and the futility of resistance against 'the force of the past'.

As in the case of Farina, Lado felt very much disconnected from the political and generational struggles of 1960s Italy: born in Venice in 1934, he spent most of the 1960s in Paris, studying at the Sorbonne and working as an assistant director in Italo–French co-productions. Moreover, upon his return to Italy in 1967, he 'was not that young any more', which prevented him from taking an active part in the youthful rebellion building up at that time. Yet, the student years in the Paris of 'Jean-Paul Sartre, the great *chansonniers* and the avant-garde painters' made it easier for him to understand, if only as an outsider, 'the political situation and the generational clashes' of the end of the decade (Lado, quoted in Švábenický 2014: 21). With the aim to make money but at the same time 'imbued with left-wing ideology' (Lado, quoted in Švábenický 2014: 27), Lado teamed up with Italian producer Enzo Doria (a supporter of young auteur cinema, as explained in Chapter 2) to make a film indicting not this or that specific regime of the Eastern or Western bloc, 'but, more widely, the power system that ruled, and still rules, the whole world [. . .] us[ing] the blood of the young, like a vampire' (Lado, quoted in Švábenický 2014: 37). Indeed, in *La corta notte delle bambole di vetro*, the Klub 99 is said to 'have branches in Paris, London, New York, Tokyo, everywhere' – a planetary perspective that cleverly blends the countercultural indictment of technocracy as a form of totalitarianism encompassing Left/Right dichotomies (Marcuse [1964] 1968 and [1958] 1969; Roszak 1969: 8–9) with the necessity of crafting a universally understandable, internationally sellable product.

The result is a pessimism that takes no prisoners: those in power are evil, corrupted and corrupting, with no ideology/interest other than their self-preservation/self-perpetuation; the youths either capitulate to the ruling class' blandishments (promises of 'wealth and sex', it is specified in the film) and are assimilated, or rebel only to be easily 'put to sleep' like Mira. The narrative design, as the Italian left-wing film critics of the time would have had it, is strictly Manichaean, with invincible villains to be impotently hated and powerless victims to be pitied. Pity is also the feeling inspired by the third category of characters, that of the foreigners who hang around the Czechoslovakian capital as tourists of the revolution after the Prague Spring of 1968. This category is twofold. First, it includes young American hippies using their wealthy families' money to live a bohemian life behind the Iron Curtain and shock the so-called 'square people' back home. Second, external observers include older men and women who, to quote a monologue of Gregory's edited out from the finished film, 'would like to become protagonists' and therefore 'fight a little bit to understand the courage [. . .] of the younger generation', but then find out it is 'too late' for them and must settle for the role of admiring 'spectators' of anti-authoritarian struggles or, at worst, 'accomplices' of the status quo (Lado and von Spiehs 1971). Here, Gregory is talking about himself in a moment of mid-life crisis, but the discourse can be extended to his fellow bourgeois, middle-aged friends and successful professionals Jacques, Jessica and Ivan, whose cynical, often self-mocking sense of humour barely manages to mask their mourning for having lost their youthful energy, rage and ideals, and having become useless to the revolution (like Gregory, Jacques ends up killed for discovering too much, while Jessica and Ivan go on being unaware pawns in the hands of the vampire rulers).

Il prato macchiato di rosso and *L'uomo che uccideva a sangue freddo* essentially follow the path opened up by . . . *Hanno cambiato faccia* and *La corta notte delle bambole di vetro*, introducing, as a surplus attraction, the mad-scientist stereotype, in a mix of vampiric and Frankensteinian mythologies already seen in the previous decade in Italian vampire horrors *I vampiri*, *Il mulino delle donne di pietra*, *L'orribile segreto del Dr. Hichcock* and *Amanti d'oltretomba*. *Il prato macchiato di rosso*, whose screenplay bore the provisional title *Vampiro 2000* (Ghione 1972), is the third and last feature directed by Riccardo Ghione, who started his career in the late 1940s working on independent newsreel projects with left-leaning filmmakers and screenwriters like Luchino Visconti, Giuseppe De Santis, Michelangelo Antonioni, Carlo Lizzani, Francesco Maselli, Marco Ferreri and Cesare Zavattini (Curti 2018: 64–72). As in Ghione's two previous features – the Wilhelm-Reich-inspired erotic drama *La rivoluzione sessuale* (1968) and the hippy-go-lucky thriller *A cuore freddo* (1971) – the central theme of *Il prato macchiato di rosso* is the tension between the *haute bourgeoisie*'s reactionary traditionalism and the anti-authoritarian instances from both the academia and the various liberation movements of the 1960s. Specifically, Ghione's vampire story starts from Marx's ([1867] 1954: 224–85) indictment of the capitalist bourgeoisie as vampiric to build a counter-cultural hodgepodge of anti-Nazism/anti-Fascism, anti-imperialism and technophobia: the Genoveses, a money-hungry upper-class family from Northern Italy convinced of belonging to the *Übermensch* master race, use a black-caped robot to bleed dry social outcasts ('worthless beings like prostitutes, tramps, gipsies, vagabonds, [. . .] those who have no job, no family, no roots . . . those whom nobody mourns when they die') and then sell the purloined blood in war-ravaged countries 'like Vietnam', to people who can afford to pay 'a price higher than that of oil and gold'. The vampire family consists of Antonio Genovese, a raving-mad scientist who likes to play God, and of his attractive wife Nina, whose lameness is meant to be a physical mark of sexual perversion, indulging as she is in an incestuous relationship with her brother Alfiero, a man who likes to dress in Nazi uniform and joke about the body cremations taking place in the Genoveses' bread oven.[7]

Similarly, Alain Jessua's Italo–French co-production *L'uomo che uccideva a sangue freddo* is centred around mad scientist Doctor Devilers, a social Darwinist who, in exchange for money, keeps French industrialists, bankers, magistrates, politicians and intellectuals young, thanks to the blood and organs of destitute migrants from the clerico-Fascist dictatorships of Portugal and Spain (the *bel paese* is never mentioned as a blood reserve but, as noted by a contemporary Italian reviewer, given Italy's huge internal and external migratory fluxes throughout the 1950s, 1960s and 1970s, the Italian connection is at the very least implied) (Lucato 1973). In Doctor Devilers's own words, his clinic-cum-seaside-resort is 'a miniature of our society', where solidarity is based only on power affinities and the stronger ones who have fought and won for themselves a 'privileged' position in life have the right to be selfish and 'take advantage' of the weaker. Consequently, in the film's climax, Doctor Devilers urges one of his guilt-ridden wealthy patients (and, by extension, the spectator) to abandon all hypocrisies and have the guts to contemplate a dead Portuguese boy hanging from a meat-hook in the cold-store of a hyper-technological laboratory, the poor migrant's torso slashed open and devoid of organs.

For all the above vitriolic socio-political critique often bordering class-hate, *Il prato macchiato di rosso* and *L'uomo che uccideva a sangue freddo* once again end on a downbeat note, just like Farina's and Lado's engagé takes on vampirism. In *L'uomo che uccideva a sangue freddo*, Doctor Devilers is stabbed to death by a middle-aged businesswoman who refuses to rejuvenate at the expense of destitute migrant labourers, but a twist-ending has the soft-hearted bourgeois charged with voluntary manslaughter and the clinic's bloody business go on as usual, under the direction of another doctor. 'Foreign workers are useful ... We will always need them!', the police commissioner concludes while driving the heroine to her imprisonment, thereby revealing that the upper-class vampires' conspiracy is so rooted into the control rooms of society that it is ultimately undefeatable. Then, the samba *Paraíso de pobre* ('Paradise of the poor') accompanies the final helicopter shot, which shows a new cargo of migrant workers, full of hopes for a better future, being carried by truck to the slaughterhouse-clinic.

Although in a far less apocalyptic mood, *Il prato macchiato di rosso*'s ostensibly happy ending also exudes bitter irony, impotence and defeatism. First, the ultimate triumph of the reactionary, capitalist villains is prevented only by the police force that the outcasts of society victimised by the Genoveses have always hated so much. Second, upon being rescued at the very last minute by the authorities, the two young protagonists – a hippy couple of bourgeois extraction (he an American university student; she the daughter of a wealthy Italian goldsmith) – hit the road and disappear into a meadow lush with flowers, suggesting that their dreams of freedom are a utopia for which there is no space in the industrial society of today. Such an ending, combined with the film's characterisation of the two hippies as sympathetic but passive, perpetually stupefied simpletons, childish pleasure-seekers unprepared to face the threats of the real world, definitely resonates with Roszak's (1969: 32–9) indictment of the progressive '"adolescentization" of dissenting thought and culture' over the course of the 1960s, that is to say the transformation of youthful rebellion against the authoritarian, technocratic society into a fashionable lifestyle based on the pursuit of 'unrestricted joy', a 'carefree drifting' that is 'much more a flight *from* than *toward*'.[8]

History repeats itself: first as tragedy ... then as farce

Within the framework of politicised Italian vampire cinema from the early 1970s, dominated as we have so far seen by feelings of impotence and defeatism in the face of the ruling/capitalist class's *trasformismo*, Paul Morrissey's comedy/horror hybrid *Dracula cerca sangue di vergine ... e morì di sete!!!* seemingly stands out as an exception. This is because its plot, by all appearances set in the 1930s,[9] revolves around Count Dracula's failure to move on with the times and consequent gory demise at the hands of a Marxist peasant 'who eventually makes a revolution and becomes the new master of the house' (Curti 2017b: 118). Having run out of female virgins in his ancestral Transylvanian domain, an ageing, sickly Count Dracula is convinced by his servant Anton to move to Italy, where, given the age-long influence of the Catholic church on the population, there should be no shortage of virgin girls of marriageable age to feed on. Moreover, Anton adds, Italians are the kind of people who are 'impressed' by nobility titles and, by implication, deferential to social superiors. The *bel paese*'s reality, though, soon proves to be different from the villains' expectations: the Catholic prohibition of premarital sex is not observed that scrupulously by the Italian youth any more, and an egalitarian, anti-aristocratic ideology has begun to spread among the lower classes. Enter Mario Balato, a young peasant employed as a handyman by the impoverished, debt-ridden Marquises Di Fiore. Living in a cottage adorned with a red hammer-and-sickle graffiti and calling himself a 'worker', not a 'servant', Mario spends his free time reading left-wing pamphlets, waiting for another revolution 'just like Russia' that would wipe out 'the rich scum' and bring about a classless society in which toil and wealth are equally distributed among citizens. At the same time, the radicalised handyman offers sexual services to twenty-year-old Safiria and Rubinia, two of the four daughters of the Marquises, and vainly tries to convince the girls during coitus that 'the only hope is in Socialism'. Upon realising that the Transylvanian Count seeking a virgin bride among the Marquises' daughters is a vampire, Mario wastes no time and, obeying the insurrectionary Marxist slogan inviting proletarians to use their working tools as weapons, grabs his axe, chops off Dracula's limbs one by one, and finally executes him. 'He lives off the blood of other people!', Mario states right before plunging his axe's handle into the vampire's heart, 'He never was, and never will be, of any use to anybody!'. The film ends with a shot of Mario and Perla, the Marquises' fourteen-year-old daughter whom Mario had previously raped to prevent her from raising Dracula's appetite: the young Communist seizes upon the teenage aristocrat, leads her into the family manor and shuts the door – the death of the Marquise (stabbed by Anton) and the absence of the Marquis (an inveterate gambler spending most of his time in London casinos) turning Mario from employee into first-in-command.

If *Dracula cerca sangue di vergine . . . e morì di sete!!!*'s peasant revolution only seemingly constitutes an exception to 1970s Italian vampire cinema's pessimism about the possibility of subverting the status quo, it is because – contrary to Farina, Lado, Ghione and Jessua – Morrissey is unsympathetic to left-wing ideology, famously labelling the post-war Italian filmmakers 'talk[ing] very seriously about how wonderful Communism will be' as 'silly' (Morrissey 1974: 27). As a matter of fact, at closer inspection, the film does not only ridicule the hypocrisy and moral bankruptcy of the withering aristocratic class desperately thirsting for new blood (Dracula, using his socio-economic capital to buy himself nourishment and calling it a marriage) and new money (the Marquises Di Fiore, willing to sell their own daughters no-questions-asked, if the price is reasonable and the buyer has the right social background), but also indicts the revolutionary ideals incarnated by the working-class hero. That Mario's Marxist promise of freedom is nothing but tyranny in disguise, and no less hypocritical than its historical predecessor feudalism, is made clear on numerous occasions. First, peasant Mario's sexual behaviour is just as predatory as Count Dracula's, as shown by the brutality with which the young man treats his sexual partners. For instance, in one scene, 'under his vaunted hammer and sickle, [Mario] slaps Rubinia and forces her to fellate him', his pleasure evidently coming from the slave-becoming-master erotic scenario. Not coincidentally, in an earlier scene, 'Mario withdraws from raping [Safiria]' because her unexpected 'confession of love' and request for an egalitarian relationship based on mutual affection kills his erection fuelled by fantasies of socio-sexual payback (Yacowar 1993: 86). Second, Mario's selfless justification that he raped Perla because the loss of virginity would protect her from Dracula's attacks is satirised as 'self-indulgent [. . .] rationalising': on the one hand, Mario expresses the desire to violate Perla well before the vampire's arrival to Italy; on the other, the deflowering of the teenage girl takes place under 'a large tapestry' depicting a defenceless deer assaulted by a nobleman and his hounds, thereby 'suggest[ing] that the Marxist is simply replacing one predatory politic with another' (Yacowar 1993: 86).

Shot in spring 1975 and domestically released in summer 1975, a couple of weeks after *Dracula cerca sangue di vergine . . . e morì di sete!!!* finally had its Italian premiere after a two-year shelving, Lucio Fulci's horror parody *Il cav. Costante Nicosia demoniaco, ovvero: Dracula in Brianza* also brings to the screen a migrant's struggle for survival away from his ancestral homeland, and expresses scepticism about the coming of a true, revolutionary change in the order of things. As announced by its title, Fulci's movie revolves around a wealthy industrialist of Sicilian origins living in the Northern Italian region of Lombardy – an extraneous, hostile environment to which he has to adapt in order to obtain a dominant position within the social arena. Given the narrative premises, it is not surprising that Palermo-born actor Lando Buzzanca was cast in the titular role. The character of the Sicilian who moves from his native island northward across the Italian peninsula to climb the social ladder is in fact the *pièce de résistance* of Buzzanca's late-1960s and early-1970s repertoire, as testified by commercially successful comedies like *Don Giovanni in Sicilia / Don Juan in Sicily* (Alberto Lattuada, 1967), *Homo eroticus* (Marco Vicario, 1971), *Nonostante le apparenze . . . e purché la nazione non lo sappia . . . all'Onorevole piacciono le donne / The Eroticist* (Lucio Fulci, 1972), *Il sindacalista* (Luciano Salce, 1972), *L'uccello migratore* (Stefano Vanzina as Steno, 1972), *Jus primae noctis* (Pasquale Festa Campanile, 1972) and *Il magnate* (Giovanni Grimaldi, 1973).[10] Specifically, just like Giovanni Percolla from 'boom'-years-set *Don Giovanni in Sicilia*, Ariberto da Ficulle from Middle-Ages-set *Jus primae noctis* and Furio Cicerone from austerity-years-set *Il magnate*, Costante Nicosia obtains an economic and social promotion through marriage. As explained at the beginning of the movie, in the mid-1960s petty bourgeois Nicosia moved from Sicily to Cantù, in the highly industrialised Brianza zone of Lombardy, in search for speculation opportunities, and solved his economic problems by marrying Mariù Bosisio, the daughter of *commendatore* Bosisio, a local industrialist. A 'smart, swift guy' according to his fellow businessmen, in exchange for the woman Nicosia built his father-in-law a toothpaste factory and, by the late 1960s, he became the new owner. *Il cav. Costante Nicosia demoniaco, ovvero: Dracula in Brianza* opens in 1975, about five years after the title character's successful geographical and socio-economic rise, and thematises the protagonist's adaptation anxieties triggered by the traumatic change of habitat.

As Fulci and his screenwriters take pains to establish, for Nicosia becoming a captain of industry has been less difficult a task than continuously having to carry out the duties connected to the newly acquired social position. In fact, after taking over ageing *commendatore* Bosisio's place, the Sicilian entrepreneur has to fight on 'foreign soil' to be socially recognised not only as a *haut bourgeois*, but also as a thoroughbred Northerner. As for the first objective, the rules of the game are rather straightforward. In order to join the long-established elite, the new rich must show his distance from necessity by acquiring all the luxury goods that are considered part of the *haute bourgeoisie*'s standard package: a variety of automobiles ranging from sport car to economy car, city apartments and countryside villas, house servants, artworks, antiques, purebred dogs, fur coats, jewels, club memberships, sport patronage and young mistresses. Not lacking money, *parvenu* Nicosia happily obliges converting his economic capital into social and symbolic capital via conspicuous consumption, particularly distinguishing himself as the wasteful owner of a hopelessly bad basketball team. Troubles arise when he tries to meet the second criterion for accessing the Brianza's upper crust – becoming a Northerner.

The impossibility for Nicosia to leave his Sicilianness behind is attested most blatantly by his uncertain command of the Brianza dialect, which results in a comic linguistic pastiche openly satirising the 'anxious hyper-identification' that characterises 'the "parvenus" who presume to join the group of legitimate, i.e. hereditary, possessors of [a given status], without being the product of the same social conditions' (Bourdieu [1979] 2010: 88). Another major obstacle to Nicosia's adaptation-integration is his morbid superstition connected to the folklore beliefs of his native island: no matter how hard he tries to conform to the demands of the technocratic, increasingly secular high society of Northern Italy and play the role of the twentieth-century rational bourgeois, the Sicilian magnate just cannot help obsessive-compulsively enacting a series of apotropaic magic rituals blending paganism with Christianity. As a result, in spite of a decade of business success 'on the continent', Nicosia still ranks among the dominated. On the one hand, for his Lombard fellow *hauts-bourgeois*, he is nothing but a *terrone* ('soil-eater'), that is to say, an ignorant peasant from

Southern Italy, no matter how rich. On the other hand, and most humiliatingly, he is the plaything of his own superstitious Sicilian relatives who, albeit economically and socially inferior to him, use the threat of *malocchio* ('the evil eye, the jinx') to scare him into hiring them in managerial positions in his factory, even if they are vastly unqualified for the job – a privileging of the symbolic blood ties of pre-capitalist 'domestic economy' over the pragmatic rationalism of capitalism's 'economic economy' (Bourdieu [1994] 1998: 92–112) if there ever was one. It will take a business trip to Romania and the contact with the highest social class of them all for aspiring *haut bourgeois* Nicosia to solve his adaptation problems and find his way to the top of the social pyramid.

Although the Italian heteronormative sexual mentality prevents Nicosia from approving of the Transylvanian nobility's bisexual mores (see Chapter 4), during his trip to castle Dragulesku the Sicilian entrepreneur comes to admire his vampire host and take him as a role model: Count Draguleskku, too, is caught in a tangle of ancestral blood-and-soil bonds but, contrary to Nicosia, he masters them instead of being subjected to them – the aristocrat's social and symbolic capital being so strong that it has survived both the October Revolution and the post-war Soviet occupation of Romania, as best exemplified by the fact that in Communist Transylvania Count Dragulesku still enjoys private property and nobility title, and his name keeps inspiring awe, fear and obedience among the population. Then, consciously or unconsciously, during a moment of drunken stupor aspiring *haut-bourgeois* dominator Nicosia lets himself be bitten on the neck and, upon his return to Italy, develops a thirst for blood to match his appetite for social power. For all his admiration for and desire to emulate the aristocrat, though, Nicosia soon finds out he can never become the Italian Count Dracula: nobility's *privilegia* are a matter of 'nature and essence', that is to say inherited 'by birth' (Bourdieu [1979] 2010: 331). Indeed, all of the industrialist's sexually predatory attacks on unsuspecting victims miserably fail, making him the slave of a dominatrix prostitute and the laughing stock of an upper-class nymphomaniac, a gold-digging girl from the countryside and a rival businessman. Nicosia's attempts to assert his dominance on his employees by prolonging working shifts and increasing working rhythms are also a failure, because the workers grow so disgruntled with his arrogant ways and exploitative demands that they begin to embrace the extraparliamentary left-wing's ideology and to hinder the functioning of the factory. Yet, after this initial crisis, the vampire contagion turns out to be a blessing for the protagonist.

It is precisely the new condition of vampire that suggests Nicosia a way to reconcile the ancestral family ties and the diktats of modern capitalist production: since for the vampirised industrialist blood has become a basic necessity, he can treat it as consumer goods, and apply the rational laws of economic economy to the symbol of pre-capitalist domestic economy. Therefore, he has an *autoemoteca* ('blood bank on wheels') installed in the courtyard of his toothpaste factory, granting his employees a salary bonus for every litre of blood they donate on Sundays. Having diversified his product-line to produce blood for his own private consumption, Nicosia finally obtains a master role in socio-economic and familial relations. The introduction of the *autoemoteca* has in fact allowed him to increase both his socio-economic prestige in Lombardy (the well-rewarded employees-donors adore him and work harder than ever, the toothpaste business is booming, money is pouring, his fellow businessmen envy him) and his symbolic credit within the Sicilian clan (he provides for all his Cefalù relatives, who now see him as a benevolent patriarch and are ready to literally give their blood for him). The bourgeois happy ending par excellence thus closes Nicosia's long and painful journey of adaptation and identity negotiation: contrary to the aristocratic vampire, condemned to sterility and an inexorable, if slow and golden, decline, the bloodsucking captain of industry becomes a father. A guarantor of the continuation of the blood lineage and a heir to an industrial empire, Nicosia and Mariù's male baby Costante junior has the privilege of being born a Northerner *haut bourgeois* already and, as shown in the penultimate shot, endowed with a pair of sharp canines to prey on the weaker – in sum, all it takes to affirm his dominant position in the social arena without incurring in the trials and tribulations endured by Nicosia senior.

In stressing the importance of a halfway mediation between opposites, and in foreshadowing the rise of a bloodthirsty, carnivorous middle class hungry for money and power, the ending of *Il cav. Costante Nicosia demoniaco, ovvero: Dracula in Brianza* – the last vampire film to be made in the golden age of Italian cinema – evidently harks back to Steno's 1959 horror parody *Tempi duri per i vampiri*.[11] Only this time we are not in the economic-miracle period, but in austerity year 1975, the blackest economic year since the end of Second World War, with investments, gross national income and gross domestic product dropping, and inflation increasing more than 20 per cent yearly (Ginsborg 1990: 352; Crainz 2005b: 424). As a consequence, although by 1975 the critical mass of protesting students and workers that formed during the 1969–1970 *autunno caldo* had substantially decreased due to police repression and fear of both the capitalist class's reprisals and right- and left-wing terrorism, thousands of people would still go on strike and flood the streets of the main Italian cities to shout slogans against the 'governo vampiro' ('vampire government') letting the 'sanguisughe del capitale' ('capitalist leeches') feed on the 'sangue degli operai' ('blood of the workers') (Lotta Continua collective 1971, 1972a, 1972b, 1972c, 1972d, 1972e, 1974a, 1974b and 1976). In the first half of the 1970s, Christian Democracy had indeed become so unpopular among the working masses, and was therefore haemorrhaging so many votes to the parliamentary extreme Left, that some currents of the leading centrist party were thinking of accepting the Italian Communist Party's 1973 proposal of *compromesso storico*, a 'historical compromise' to be implemented after the 1976 general election and allowing Communists into the government coalition for the first time since the beginning of the Cold War in 1947 (Ginsborg 1990: 354–8).

Yet, for all its adoption of Marx's ([1867] 1954: 224–85) vampirism-capitalism equation and of Lotta Continua's revolutionary slogans ('Traitor, hypocrite, leech! [. . .] What more do you want from us proletarians? Our blood?', asks a radicalised unionist to Nicosia), *Il cav. Costante Nicosia demoniaco, ovvero: Dracula in Brianza* once again ends by showing that the status quo is immutable: in exchange for a heftier pay cheque, the workers happily agree to serve their employer during the week and to be bled dry in the *autoemoteca* on their day off, while a new vampire capitalist is born in the Nicosia family to ensure that the bloodletting would continue for at least another generation. In this umpteenth restatement of the pessimism and defeatism of 1970s vampire cinema, Fulci and his screenwriters make the *compromesso storico* the main target for their satire. By having triumphant vampire Nicosia call 'compromesso sanguigno' ('blood compromise') the salary raises through which he tricks his employees into accepting a literally blood-draining exploitation, the *compromesso storico* is indicted as yet another *trasformismo* tactic of the reactionary ruling powers. In spite of Fulci's aversion to social commentary in movies and careerist, fundamentally apolitical view of filmmaking as profit-bent entertainment (see Chapter 2), *Il cav. Costante Nicosia demoniaco, ovvero: Dracula in Brianza* can ultimately be said to drive the last nail in the coffin of Italian revolutionary hopes – a surrender to the immutability of the status quo all the more gloomy since the 1927-born director had been a Communist idealist in his youth, even serving jail time in 1948 for protesting against a right-wing attempt to assassinate Italian Communist Party leader Palmiro Togliatti (Albiero and Cacciatore 2004: 19–21).

Notes

1. A fan of horror fiction since his teenage years, in 1960 university student Farina had already made an 8-mm amateur short film parodying Fisher's *Dracula* and titled *Il figlio di Dracula* ('Dracula's son').
2. Like Ingegnere Nosferatu does in the film, between 1955 and 1971 the FIAT management used the Italian police, army and secret services to keep employees under surveillance – a fact that Farina and the whole Italian public opinion discovered thanks to the work of magistrate Raffaele Guariniello in July–August 1971 (Crainz 2005a: 36–9, 2005b: 401), that is to say, at the very same time that . . . *Hanno cambiato faccia* was having its Italian premiere.

3. Valle's stay at Ingegnere Nosferatu's villa allows Farina to quote a few key theorists of consumer capitalism and its discontents: the litanies about mass persuasion and the repression of human instincts echoing in the corridors of the villa come from Packard ([1957] 2007) and Marcuse ([1955] 2015). In ... *Hanno cambiato faccia*'s screenplay, there is even a scene in which Valle finds in Ingegnere Nosferatu's private office a first edition of *Das Kapital* bearing the autograph dedication 'To my great opponent Giovanni Nosferatu. Karl Marx. London, 1868' (Berruti and Farina 1970).
4. The caption refers to the following passage taken from Marcuse's ([1958] 1969: 112–13) study of Soviet Marxism: 'In the Soviet state, the terror is of a twofold nature: technological and political. [...] With the elimination of all organised opposition, and with the continued success of the totalitarian administration, the terror tends to become predominantly technological'. In the screenplay, a montage sequence was to conclude the film after Valle's capitulation: a supermarket full of people buying discounted goods; heaps of trash; workers at the assembly line; automobile carcasses in a junkyard; advertising bills and gadgets; factories regurgitating black smoke in the countryside; dying trees and flowers; a polluted river (Berruti and Farina 1970).
5. The very first idea Farina had for the ending, 'probably inspired by the ending of [Roman Polanski's] *Dance of the Vampires*' (quoted in Guarneri 2019a), was still an unhappy conclusion, but slightly less grim: 'Two lights appear in the distance, it is a taxi. [Valle and his love interest] board the taxi, the driver is told to rush to the nearest police station. The taxi sets off. [Valle and his love interest] kiss in the back seat. The camera tracks back to show the driver, who takes off his sunglasses: he is Ingegnere Nosferatu, a cold smile on his face. The taxi enters Nosferatu's villa and the gate closes behind the car' (Farina 1968).
6. The 1970s Italian film journals' ideological bias against all Italian horrors is sketched in Noto (2016: 215–18), where the author demonstrates that the horror genre was invariably seen by both Marxist and Catholic intellectuals as an escapist form of entertainment 'doomed to reaffirm the existing power relations', no matter how hard the filmmakers tried to infuse the movies 'with the best intentions of societal critique'.
7. Nazi innuendos abound in the film, including the Genoveses' praises of Richard Wagner, whose music 'makes us feel bigger, more important', part of a 'superior race'. In the screenplay, Nina is explicitly said to be of German origin (her surname is von Müller), and the story is set in the Prati neighbourhood of Rome, at that time a bulwark of the Italian extreme right wing (Ghione 1972). For the cliché equation between Nazi-Fascism and sexual perversion in post-war Italian literature and auteur cinema, see Forgacs (1999) and Prono (2001).
8. Theodore Roszak's 1969 critique *The Making of a Counter Culture: Reflections on the Technocratic Society and Its Youthful Opposition* first appeared in Italian translation in 1971, so it might have directly inspired Ghione for *Il prato macchiato di rosso*. It is worth noting that, in the screenplay, the hippy protagonists are not completely helpless victims as in the finished film, but enact poetic justice by having Nina bled dry by the vampire-robot during the final police raid (Ghione 1972).

9. At some point in the film, Pitigrilli's 1931 short-story collection *I vegetariani dell'amore* is mentioned by one of the main characters as being a book that has just come out.
10. By casting Buzzanca as sanguinary captain of industry Nicosia, Fulci's producers most probably wanted to replicate the box-office success of biting anti-capitalist satires *Il sindacalista* and *Il magnate*, in which the Sicilian actor plays a radicalised unionist and a reckless *nouveau riche* respectively. Incidentally, though born and raised in Rome, Fulci was of Sicilian origins himself (Albiero and Cacciatore 2004: 19), and prior to *Il cav. Costante Nicosia demoniaco, ovvero: Dracula in Brianza* he wrote and directed numerous films starring Sicilian comedians, including Buzzanca star vehicle *Nonostante le apparenze ... e purché la nazione non lo sappia ... all'Onorevole piacciono le donne* and countless Franco Franchi and Ciccio Ingrassia star vehicles.
11. Having started his career in the early 1950s as a screenwriter for and an assistant to Steno, Fulci has always been calling him a 'teacher', even a 'father' (Albiero and Cacciatore 2004: 19).

APPENDIX A: THREE ITALIAN VAMPIRE FILMS THAT WERE NEVER MADE

Il teschio del vampiro (1962)

In November 1962 Italian production company CA. PO. MA. Film – co-founded by Alberto Cardone (assistant director on the set of Roger Vadim's *Il sangue e la rosa*) and Marco Masi (perhaps the same 'M. Masi' who wrote a few horror *fotoromanzi* of the 1961–1967 *Malìa* series) – submitted to the Italian Show Business Bureau the screenplay, the estimated budget and the financial plan for a vampire horror titled *Il teschio del vampiro* ('The skull of the vampire'). Based on a screenplay by Cardone and Masi, *Il teschio del vampiro* was to be shot under the direction of Cardone in twenty-four days. The estimated budget was 59.3 million lire, one-third of which consisted of the Italian distributor's *minimo garantito*. The government officials enacting preventive censorship summarised the plot as follows.

> Because of a rainstorm, five young people – Franco, Paola, Riccardo, Antonella and Luciano – take shelter in an old church in the [Italian] countryside. During the night, Luciano falls into a hole full of skulls. Among them, there is the skull of a vampire. Luciano does not say anything to his friends but, when he later goes back to the hole, the skull of the vampire has disappeared. Luciano discovers that he has two marks on his neck and believes that he has been vampirised. Upon their return to the Black Cat Inn, Franco, Paola, Riccardo, Antonella and Luciano talk about the old church and are baffled by the reaction of Rosetta

(a chambermaid) and Maria and Giulio (the owners of the inn). Menica, an old woman from a nearby village, explains why everybody at the inn is afraid of the old church. Luciano is impressed by Menica's explanation and, due to telaesthetic [sic] phenomena, he becomes convinced that he is the perpetrator of the crimes that the actual victim of the vampire is committing. It is only at the end of the film that Antonella tells Luciano the truth. At first, Luciano does not believe her, then he understands everything and destroys the skull of the vampire in order to free Antonella from the monster. However, by destroying the vampire of the old church, Luciano has also put an end to Antonella's life. The young man takes the dying girl in his arms. His other friends [arrive at] the old church and learn the sad truth.

For unknown reasons (most probably economic), the shooting never started.

Dracula terrore d'oltre tomba (1973)

After Luigi Batzella's *Il plenilunio delle vergini*, shot in summer 1972, screenwriter and director Batzella and his business partners Walter Bigari and Ralph Zucker had in mind (or were commissioned) a second vampire horror. Since by late 1972 the production company of *Il plenilunio delle vergini*, Produzioni Cinematografiche Internazionali Virginia, was doomed to bankruptcy, the trio found (or founded) another production company, Grifo International Films. In spring 1973, Grifo International Films submitted to the Italian Show Business Bureau a series of documents relating to the production of a vampire horror titled *Dracula terrore d'oltre tomba* ('Dracula terror from beyond the grave'). The treatment and the screenplay were written by Batzella, who was also to direct and edit the film. The plot summary that follows is based on a copy of the screenplay preserved at the Biblioteca Luigi Chiarini in Rome under the title *Una vergine per Dracula* ('A virgin for Dracula') (Batzella 1973).

One day reporter Steve Laster and his wife Miriam find the corpse of a beautiful young woman inside a car parked in an isolated spot. Laster calls the police, but when police commissioner Morgan and his men arrive, the corpse has disappeared, substituted by a black tulip. The reporter is taken for a madman or a mythomaniac, while Miriam's claims are dismissed as the ravings of someone who has read too many vampire-themed comic books. As the film proceeds, it turns out that there really was a dead body in the car. The murder was committed by the members of a satanic cult led by Sara and Simone, who kill innocent girls to resurrect Dracula and obtain absolute power over mankind. However, for some reason, Dracula resurrects on his own, taking possession of the body of a thief who stole Dracula's magic medallion only to lose it in a car crash. Such magic medallion somehow ends up in the hands of

Miriam, who is therefore abducted by Dracula and his satanic cult. With the help of police commissioner Morgan, Laster saves his wife and kills Sara and Simone (Dracula is also staked, but it is unclear who is responsible for ridding the world of the vampire).

The provisional cast of *Dracula terrore d'oltre tomba* included Gianni Pesola (Steve Laster), Katia Cardinali (Miriam), Dino Strano (police commissioner Morgan), Rosalba Neri (Sara), Ralph Zucker (Simone), Gino Turini (Dracula) and Esmeralda Barros (in a minor role). No estimated budget was provided by Grifo International Films, although the project clearly was to be made on a shoestring budget. The government officials were rather critical of the work upon reading the aforementioned screenplay.

> Over the years poor Dracula has been served in every possible sauce by films of varying quality, and he still cannot find peace. In [*Dracula terrore d'oltre tomba*], he comes back to 'life' (metaphorically speaking) once again, but little or nothing is added to the macabre charm of the character. In fact, this is a small film without any ambition, to be made as quickly as possible, cobbling together the usual clichés in order to scare the most naive and unprepared spectators during a summer release. However, it cannot be denied that the work shows a certain aesthetic care and formal dignity, which can partially mitigate the substantial lack of quality of the project.

For unknown reasons (most probably economic), the shooting never started.

Sangue per il vampiro (Nosferatu story) (1974)

The existence of this film project is testified only by a screenplay preserved at the Biblioteca Luigi Chiarini in Rome. Such screenplay, dated October 1974 and titled *Sangue per il vampiro (Nosferatu story)* ('Blood for the vampire'), was penned by a certain Gianni di Giulio, who was also to direct the film (his directorial debut) under the Spanish-sounding pseudonym Manuel Sartana, for a company called Texana Film. The screenplay opens with a provisional cast list (Christopher Lee, Gordon Mitchell, Richard Conte, Sylva Koscina and Luciana Paluzzi) and a bizarre self-presentation by Di Giulio (who calls himself 'the killer of Satan' and 'the Italian equivalent of Roman Polanski', and states that the character of Dracula 'incredibly penetrates' into his own body 'as if by metempsychosis') (Di Giulio 1974).

According to the screenplay, the story is set in the Old West, in the eighteenth century. A vampire who lives in an isolated, deconsecrated monastery decides that he would not make a distinction between virgin and non-virgin women any more: all he cares about is female blood, to prolong his existence and his pleasures. A series of murders therefore begins, committed by a half-witted, sexually deranged henchman of the vampire (the henchman rapes and kills young women, then brings their blood to his master). The investigators are baffled by the case: they blame a human monster, a ghost, extraterrestrials and even the Soviets. Fatally wounded by the shotgun-wielding father of a brutalised girl, the henchman reveals to the investigators where the vampire can be found. The vampire is staked and his crypt collapses, killing all the good guys.

In the words of Di Giulio (1974),

> for the first time in the history of the film industry, two completely opposed movie genres (horror and western) are sensationally mixed on the set, but [. . .] the most avanguardian [sic] innovation is the 'surprise giallo' technique that has been majestically introduced in the film. This can trigger (nouvelle vague) a new path for cinema worldwide, after the event [sic] of Dario Argento and the Italian-style thriller and horror.

As a matter of fact, the above screenplay abounds with Argento-style point-of-view shots of the killer, although *Sangue per il vampiro (Nosferatu story)* can hardly be defined a 'surprise giallo' as the identity of the killer is revealed in scene 1. The claim about *Sangue per il vampiro (Nosferatu story)* being the first horror/western hybrid is also incorrect. In any case, the shooting never started.

APPENDIX B: FILES FROM THE ITALIAN SHOW BUSINESS BUREAU FONDS AT THE ARCHIVIO CENTRALE DELLO STATO IN ROME

Ministero del turismo e dello spettacolo – direzione generale spettacolo – archivio cinema – lungometraggi – fascicoli per opera, 1946–1965 – concessione certificato di nazionalità (cf 16–5000)

CF 2548 busta 167: *I vampiri*
CF 3098 busta 235: *Caltiki il mostro immortale*
CF 3149 busta 243: *Tempi duri per i vampiri*
CF 3236 busta 256: *Il sangue e la rosa*
CF 3241 busta 256: *Il mulino delle donne di pietra*
CF 3302 busta 265: *La maschera del demonio*
CF 3389 busta 276: *L'ultima preda del vampiro*
CF 3546 busta 295: *Maciste contro il vampiro*
CF 3590 busta 300: *Il mostro dell'Opera*
CF 3611 busta 302: *Ercole al centro della Terra*
CF 3736 busta 317: *La strage dei vampiri*
CF 3923 busta 339: *L'orribile segreto del Dr. Hichcock*
CF 4120 busta 373: *Il teschio del vampiro*
CF 4206 busta 390: *I tre volti della paura*
CF 4215 busta 392: *Danza macabra*
CF 4351 busta 419: *La cripta e l'incubo*
CF 4374 busta 424: *Ercole contro Moloch*
CF 4412 busta 433: *Roma contro Roma*
CF 4548 busta 460: *Maciste e la regina di Samar*

CF 4857 busta 524: *Amanti d'oltretomba*
CF 4960 busta 548: *La vendetta di Lady Morgan*

Ministero del turismo e dello spettacolo – direzione generale spettacolo – archivio cinema – lungometraggi – fascicoli per opera, 1966–1994 – concessione certificato di nazionalità (cf 5001–10000)

CF 6048 busta 723: *La notte dei dannati*
CF 6055 busta 724: *. . . Hanno cambiato faccia*
CF 6266 busta 748: *Riti, magie nere e segrete orge nel Trecento. . .*
CF 6344 busta 757: *Il prato macchiato di rosso*
CF 6404 busta 763: *Il plenilunio delle vergini*
CF 6535 busta 779: *Il mostro è in tavola, barone . . . Frankenstein*
CF 6546 busta 804: *Dracula terrore d'oltre tomba*
CF 6554 busta 785: *Dracula cerca sangue di vergine . . . e morì di sete!!!*
CF 6981 busta 835: *Il cav. Costante Nicosia demoniaco, ovvero: Dracula in Brianza*

Ministero del turismo e dello spettacolo – direzione generale spettacolo – archivio cinema – lungometraggi –- fascicoli per opera, 1966–1994 – coproduzioni (co)

CO 634: *Il Conte Dracula*
CO 840: *Nella stretta morsa del ragno*
CO 956: *La notte dei diavoli*
CO 1056: *Le vergini cavalcano la morte*
CO 1081: *L'uomo che uccideva a sangue freddo*

BIBLIOGRAPHY

Abbott, Stacey (2007), *Celluloid Vampires: Life after Death in the Modern World*, Austin: University of Texas Press.
Abbott, Stacey (2016), *Undead Apocalypse: Vampires and Zombies in the Twenty-First Century*, Edinburgh: Edinburgh University Press.
Alberoni, Francesco (1967), *Consumi e società*, revised edn, Bologna: Il Mulino.
Albiero, Paolo and Cacciatore, Giacomo (2004), *Il terrorista dei generi: tutto il cinema di Lucio Fulci*, Rome: Un mondo a parte.
Alfassio-Grimaldi, Ugoberto and Bertoni, Italo (1964), *I giovani degli anni Sessanta*, Bari: Laterza.
Allum, Percy (1990), 'Uniformity Undone: Aspects of Catholic Culture in Postwar Italy', in Zygmunt Barański and Robert Lumley (eds), *Culture and Conflict in Postwar Italy: Essays on Mass and Popular Culture*, New York: St Martin's Press, pp. 79–96.
Alvaro, Corrado [1944] (1986), *L'Italia rinunzia?*, Palermo: Sellerio.
Anelli, Maria Teresa (1979), *Fotoromanzo: fascino e pregiudizio. Storia, documenti e immagini di un grande fenomeno popolare (1946–1978)*, Rome: Savelli.
Anonymous (1936), 'Il segno del vampiro', *Cinema Illustrazione* 16, April 1936, unnumbered pages.
Anonymous (1948), *'Nosferatu il vampiro' di F. W. Murnau: XXVIII proiezione: domenica 2 maggio 1948*, Rome: Circolo Romano del Cinema.
Anonymous (1957a), 'I vampiri', *Gazzetta del Popolo*, 7 April 1957, unnumbered page.
Anonymous (1957b), 'I vampiri', *Il Giorno*, 15 April 1957, unnumbered page.
Anonymous (1957c), 'I vampiri', *La Notte*, 16–17 April 1957, unnumbered page.
Anonymous (1957d), 'I vampiri', *Il Tempo*, 30 May 1957, unnumbered page.

Anonymous (1958a), '"Films del terrore" per controbattere la televisione?', *Cinematografia d'oggi* 9, September 1958, unnumbered page.
Anonymous (1958b), 'Dracula il vampiro', *L'Unità*, 13 December 1958, p. 5.
Anonymous (1958–1959), 'Dracula il vampiro', *Cinematografia d'oggi* 12–1, December 1958–January 1959, p. 16.
Anonymous (1960a), 'Dracula in gonnella e juke-box', *Mascotte* 1, 10 January 1960, p. 32.
Anonymous (1960b), 'Vampiri e sesso nel film di Vadim', *Mascotte* 6, 30 February 1960, pp. 42–3.
Anonymous (1960c), 'L'orrore fatto in casa', *Mascotte* 8, 20 March 1960, pp. 38–41.
Anonymous (1960d), 'Malati e medici del passato. I vampiri e il medico di Byron', *Progressi di terapia* 1, pp. 28–31.
Anonymous (1960e), 'Campioni d'incassi', *Cinematografia d'oggi* 2–3, February–March 1960, unnumbered page.
Anonymous (1960f), 'I film che vedremo: *La maschera del demonio*', *Mascotte* 14, 20 May 1960, pp. 38–9.
Anonymous (1960g), 'L'amante del vampiro', *ABC* 3, 26 June 1960, p. 42.
Anonymous (1969), '*Il vampiro nudo* di Jean Lavie', *King Cinema* 7, November 1969, pp. 105–7.
Anonymous (1971), 'Il sexy-orror si ispira all'americano Poe', *Cinestop* 1, June–July 1971, pp. 72–6.
Anton, Edoardo (1959), 'Tempi duri per i vampiri', Italian-language unpublished treatment.
Aprà, Adriano and Pistagnesi, Patrizia (1986), *Comedy, Italian Style: 1950–1980*, Turin: ERI.
Arata, Stephen [1990] (1997), 'The Occidental Tourist: *Dracula* and the Anxiety of Reverse Colonization', in David J. Skal and Nina Auerbach (eds), *Dracula: Authoritative Text, Contexts, Reviews and Reactions, Dramatic and Film Variations, Criticism*, New York: W. W. Norton, pp. 462–70.
Argentieri, Mino (1974), *La censura nel cinema italiano*, Rome: Editori riuniti.
Arkoff, Sam (1995), 'Parola di produttore', in Stefano Della Casa and Giulia D'Agnolo Vallan (eds), *Mario Bava: il cineasta che sapeva troppo*, Bellaria: Comune di Bellaria, p. 20.
Astle, Richard (1980), 'Dracula as Totemic Monster: Lacan, Freud, Oedipus and History', *Sub-Stance* 25, pp. 98–105.
Auerbach, Nina (1995), *Our Vampires, Ourselves*, Chicago: University of Chicago Press.
Avondola, Carlo, Calderale, Mario and Garofalo, Marcello (1997), 'Filmografia essenziale (e non) in 200 titoli', *Segnocinema* 85, May–June 1997, pp. 17–33.
Baldick, Chris (1987), *In Frankenstein's Shadow: Myth, Monstrosity, and Nineteenth-Century Writing*, Oxford: Oxford University Press.
Barber, Paul (2010), *Vampires, Burial, and Death: Folklore and Reality*, revised edn, London: Yale University Press.
Barbiani, Laura (1980), 'Coazione del senso e dello sguardo', in Laura Barbiani and Alberto Abruzzese (eds), *Pornograffiti: da Jacula a Oltretomba, da Cappuccetto*

Rotto a Mercenari. Trame e figure del fumetto italiano per adulti, Rome: Napoleone, pp. 9–76.
Baroni, Maurizio (1995), *Platea in piedi 1: 1959–1968: manifesti e dati statistici del cinema italiano*, Sasso Marconi: Bolelli.
Baroni, Maurizio (1996), *Platea in piedi 2: 1969–1978: manifesti e dati statistici del cinema italiano*, Sasso Marconi: Bolelli.
Barra, Luca (2015), *Palinsesto: storia e tecnica della programmazione televisiva*, Bari: Laterza.
Barra, Luca and Scaglioni, Massimo (2016), 'One Story, Two Media: Strategies and Intended Audiences in Italian Productions for Cinema and Television', *Comunicazioni sociali* 3, pp. 412–25.
Barra, Luca and Scaglioni, Massimo (2017), 'Il ruolo della televisione nel sostegno al cinema italiano', in Marco Cucco and Giacomo Manzoli (eds), *Il cinema di Stato: finanziamento pubblico ed economia simbolica nel cinema italiano contemporaneo*, Bologna: Il Mulino, pp. 85–125.
Baschiera, Stefano (2016), 'The 1980s Italian Horror Cinema of Imitation: the Good, the Ugly and the Sequel', in Stefano Baschiera and Russ Hunter (eds), *Italian Horror Cinema*, Edinburgh: Edinburgh University Press, pp. 15–29.
Baschiera, Stefano and Di Chiara, Francesco (2010), 'Once Upon a Time in Italy: Transnational Features of Genre Production 1960s–1970s', *Film International* 8:6, pp. 30–9.
Baschiera, Stefano and Hunter, Russ (2016), 'Introduction', in Stefano Baschiera and Russ Hunter (eds), *Italian Horror Cinema*, Edinburgh: Edinburgh University Press, pp. 1–14.
Batini, Giorgio (1968), *Italia a mezzanotte. Storie di fantasmi, castelli e tesori*, Florence: Vallecchi.
Batzella, Luigi (1972), 'Il plenilunio delle vergini', Italian-language unpublished screenplay.
Batzella, Luigi (1973), 'Una vergine per Dracula', Italian-language unpublished screenplay.
Baviera, Ombretta (1972), 'I misteri della carne', *Cinesex* 59, March 1972, pp. 16–21.
Bayman, Louis (2013), 'Melodrama as Seriousness', in Louis Bayman and Sergio Rigoletto (eds), *Popular Italian Cinema*, Basingstoke: Palgrave, pp. 82–97.
Bayman, Louis (2014), *The Operatic and the Everyday in Post-war Italian Film Melodrama*, Edinburgh: Edinburgh University Press.
Bellassai, Sandro (2000), 'Mascolinità e relazioni di genere nella cultura politica comunista (1947–1956)', in Sandro Bellassai and Maria Malatesta (eds), *Genere e mascolinità: uno sguardo storico*, Rome: Bulzoni, pp. 265–301.
Bellassai, Sandro (2011), *L'invenzione della virilità: politica e immaginario maschile nell'Italia contemporanea*, Rome: Carocci.
Ben-Ghiat, Ruth (1999), 'Liberation: Italian Cinema and the Fascist Past, 1945–1950', in R. J. B. Bosworth and Patrizia Dogliani (eds), *Italian Fascism: History, Memory and Representation*, Basingstoke: Macmillan, pp. 83–101.
Ben-Ghiat, Ruth (2005), 'Unmaking the Fascist Man: Masculinity, Film, and the Transition from Dictatorship', *Journal of Modern Italian Studies* 10:3, pp. 336–65.

Benshoff, Harry (1997), *Monsters in the Closet: Homosexuality and the Horror Film*, Manchester: Manchester University Press.

Bentley, Christopher [1972] (1988), 'The Monster in the Bedroom: Sexual Symbolism in Bram Stoker's *Dracula*', in Margaret Carter (ed.), *Dracula: The Vampire and the Critics*, Ann Arbor, MI: UMI Research Press, pp. 25–34.

Berenstein, Rhona (1995), 'Spectatorship as Drag: The Act of Viewing and Classical Horror Cinema', in Linda Williams (ed.), *Viewing Positions: Ways of Seeing Film*, New Brunswick, NJ: Rutgers University Press, pp. 231–69.

Berenstein, Rhona (1996), *Attack of the Leading Ladies: Gender, Sexuality, and Spectatorship in Classic Horror Cinema*, New York: Columbia University Press.

Bergfelder, Tim (2000), 'The Nation Vanishes: European Co-Productions and Popular Genre Formula in the 1950s and 1960s', in Mette Hjort and Scott MacKenzie (eds), *Cinema and Nation*, London: Routledge, pp. 131–42.

Berlinguer, Enrico (1954), 'Discorso introduttivo alla conferenza nazionale delle ragazze comuniste', in Palmiro Togliatti and Enrico Berlinguer, *Le giovani comuniste per l'emancipazione della donna: discorsi pronunciati alla Conferenza Nazionale delle ragazze comuniste: Roma, 26–28 febbraio 1954*, Rome: Gioventù nuova, pp. 27–47.

Bernardini, Aldo and Martinelli, Vittorio (1993a), *Il cinema muto italiano: i film degli anni d'oro, 1913. Parte prima*, Turin: Nuova ERI and Rome: Centro Sperimentale di Cinematografia.

Bernardini, Aldo and Martinelli, Vittorio (1993b), *Il cinema muto italiano: i film degli anni d'oro, 1913. Parte seconda*, Turin: Nuova ERI and Rome: Centro Sperimentale di Cinematografia.

Bernardini, Aldo and Martinelli, Vittorio (1993c), *Il cinema muto italiano: i film degli anni d'oro, 1914. Parte prima*, Turin: Nuova ERI and Rome: Centro Sperimentale di Cinematografia.

Bernardini, Aldo and Martinelli, Vittorio (1993d), *Il cinema muto italiano: i film degli anni d'oro, 1914. Parte seconda*, Turin: Nuova ERI and Rome: Centro Sperimentale di Cinematografia.

Bernardini, Aldo and Martinelli, Vittorio (1994a), *Il cinema muto italiano: i film degli anni d'oro, 1912. Parte prima*, Turin: Nuova ERI and Rome: Centro Sperimentale di Cinematografia.

Bernardini, Aldo and Martinelli, Vittorio (1994b), *Il cinema muto italiano: i film degli anni d'oro, 1912. Parte seconda*, Turin: Nuova ERI and Rome: Centro Sperimentale di Cinematografia.

Bernardini, Aldo and Martinelli, Vittorio (1995a), *Il cinema muto italiano: i film degli anni d'oro, 1911. Parte prima*, Turin: Nuova ERI and Rome: Centro Sperimentale di Cinematografia.

Bernardini, Aldo and Martinelli, Vittorio (1995b), *Il cinema muto italiano: i film degli anni d'oro, 1911. Parte seconda*, Turin: Nuova ERI and Rome: Centro Sperimentale di Cinematografia.

Bernardini, Aldo and Martinelli, Vittorio (1996a), *Il cinema muto italiano: i film dei primi anni, 1905–1909*, Turin: Nuova ERI and Rome: Centro Sperimentale di Cinematografia.

Bernardini, Aldo and Martinelli, Vittorio (1996b), *Il cinema muto italiano: i film dei primi anni, 1910*, Turin: Nuova ERI and Rome: Centro Sperimentale di Cinematografia.
Berni, Simone (2016), *'Dracula' by Bram Stoker. The Mystery of the Early Editions*, Macerata: Bibliohaus.
Berruti, Giulio and Farina, Corrado (1970), 'Hanno cambiato faccia', Italian-language unpublished screenplay.
Bettetini, Gianfranco (ed.) (1981), *Tra cinema e televisione: materiali sul rapporto tra due mezzi di comunicazione di massa*, Florence: Sansoni.
Bibbò, Antonio (2018), '*Dracula*'s Italian Hosts: The Manipulation of Bram Stoker's Novel in Early Italian Editions', *Perspectives: Studies in Translatology* 26:6, pp. 824–37.
Bierman, Joseph (1972), '*Dracula*: Prolonged Childhood Illness, and the Oral Triad', *American Imago* 29:2, pp. 186–98.
Bierman, Joseph (1998), 'A Crucial Stage in the Writing of *Dracula*', in William Hughes and Andrew Smith (eds), *Bram Stoker: History, Psychoanalysis and the Gothic*, Basingstoke: Macmillan, pp. 151–72.
Bini, Andrea (2011a), 'Horror Cinema: The Emancipation of Women and Urban Anxiety', in Flavia Brizio-Skov (ed.), *Popular Italian Cinema: Culture and Politics in a Postwar Society*, London: I. B. Tauris, pp. 53–82.
Bini, Andrea (2011b), 'The Birth of Comedy Italian Style', in Flavia Brizio-Skov (ed.), *Popular Italian Cinema: Culture and Politics in a Postwar Society*, London: I. B. Tauris, pp. 107–52.
Bisoni, Claudio (2009), *Gli anni affollati: la cultura cinematografica italiana (1970–1979)*, Rome: Carocci.
Bisoni, Claudio (2014), 'Marcuse supera Asimov. Il fantastico distopico nel cinema italiano degli anni Settanta', *Bianco e Nero* 579, April–July 2014, pp. 82–91.
Bizzarri, Libero (1957), 'Cinema senza industria (storia economica di dodici anni)', *Il ponte*, August–September 1957, pp. 1370–88.
Blasetti, Alessandro and Frontoni, Angelo (1976), 'Il "mostro" del cinema', *Playboy* 5, May 1976, pp. 93–7.
Bonaparte, Marie [1934] (1971), *The Life and Works of Edgar Allan Poe: A Psychoanalytic Interpretation*, trans. John Rodker, New York: Humanities Press.
Bondanella, Peter (2001), *Italian Cinema from Neorealism to the Present*, revised edn, New York: Continuum.
Bono, Paola and Kemp, Sandra (1991), 'Introduction: Coming from the South', in Paola Bono and Sandra Kemp (eds), *Italian Feminist Thought: A Reader*, Oxford: Blackwell, pp. 1–29.
Bonsaver, Guido (2014), 'Censorship from the Fascist Period to the Present', in Peter Bondanella (ed.), *The Italian Cinema Book*, London: Palgrave, pp. 66–73.
Boone, Troy (1993), '"He is English and therefore adventurous": Politics, Decadence, and *Dracula*', *Studies in the Novel* 25, pp. 76–91.
Boullet, Jean (1962), 'Terence Fisher et la permanence des mythes', *Midi–Minuit Fantastique* 1, May–June 1962, pp. 1–4.
Bourdieu, Pierre [1994] (1998), *Practical Reason: On the Theory of Action*, trans. Randal Johnson, Stanford, CA: Stanford University Press.

Bourdieu, Pierre [1998] (2001), *Masculine Domination*, trans. Richard Nice, Cambridge: Polity Press.
Bourdieu, Pierre [1979] (2010), *Distinction: A Social Critique of the Judgement of Taste*, trans. Richard Nice, London: Routledge.
Bravo, Anna (2003), *Il fotoromanzo*, Bologna: Il Mulino.
Brega, Gian Piero (1963), 'Film sadici e film sadiani', in Vittorio Spinazzola (ed.), *Film 1963. Il cinema è diventato maggiorenne*, Milan: Feltrinelli, pp. 194–244.
Brennan, Matthew (1992), 'Repression, Knowledge, and Saving Souls: The Role of the "New Woman" in Stoker's *Dracula* and Murnau's *Nosferatu*', *Studies in the Humanities* 19, pp. 1–10.
Brizio-Skov, Flavia (2011), 'Dollars, Bullets and Success: The Spaghetti Western Phenomenon', in Flavia Brizio-Skov (ed.), *Popular Italian Cinema: Culture and Politics in a Postwar Society*, London: I. B. Tauris, pp. 83–106.
Bronfen, Elisabeth (1992), *Over Her Dead Body: Death, Femininity and the Aesthetic*, Manchester: Manchester University Press.
Brooks, Peter [1976] (1995), *The Melodramatic Imagination. Balzac, Henry James, Melodrama, and the Mode of Excess*, London: Yale University Press.
Browning, John and Picart, Caroline (eds) (2009), *Draculas, Vampires, and Other Undead Forms: Essays on Gender, Race, and Culture*, Lanham, MD: Scarecrow Press.
Browning, John and Picart, Caroline (eds) (2010), *Dracula in Visual Media: Film, Television, Comic Book and Electronic Game Appearances, 1921–2010*, Jefferson, NC: McFarland.
Burato, Dorothea (2018), 'Morale comunista, neorealismo e cinema sovietico. La critica cinematografica del PCI nel dopoguerra attraverso le pagine di *Rinascita*', *Immagine* 17, pp. 95–117.
Burke, Frank (2011), 'The Italian Sword-and-Sandal Film from *Fabiola* (1949) to *Hercules and the Captive Women* (1961): Texts and Contexts', in Flavia Brizio-Skov (ed.), *Popular Italian Cinema: Culture and Politics in a Postwar Society*, London: I. B. Tauris, pp. 17–51.
Buzzati, Dino (1959), 'Dracula ai bagni', *Corriere d'informazione*, 21–22 August 1959, p. 3.
Buzzi, Aldo and Lattuada, Bianca (1948), *Vampyr: l'étrange aventure de David Gray*, Milan: Poligono.
Byers, Thomas [1981] (1988), 'Good Men and Monsters: The Defenses of *Dracula*', in Margaret Carter (ed.), *Dracula: The Vampire and the Critics*, Ann Arbor, MI: UMI Research Press, pp. 149–57.
Caen, Michel (1962), 'Erotisme et sadisme dans l'oeuvre de Terence Fisher', *Midi–Minuit Fantastique* 1, May–June 1962, pp. 8–11.
Caiano, Mario and De Agostini, Fabio (1964), 'Orgasmo', Italian-language unpublished treatment.
Caldwell, Lesley (1991), *Italian Family Matters: Women, Politics and Legal Reform*, Basingstoke: Macmillan.
Camilletti, Fabio (2014), '"Timore" e "terrore" nella polemica classico-romantica: l'Italia e il ripudio del gotico', *Italian Studies* 69:2, pp. 231–45.

Camilletti, Fabio (2018), *Italia lunare. Gli anni Sessanta e l'occulto*, New York: Peter Lang.

Cammarota, Domenico (1984), *I vampiri. Arte – Cinema – Folklore – Letteratura – Teatro – Storia e altro*, Rome: Fanucci.

Canova, Gianni (2004), 'Forme, motivi e funzioni della commedia', in Sandro Bernardi (ed.), *Storia del cinema italiano. Volume IX (1954–1959)*, Venice: Marsilio and Rome: Bianco e Nero, pp. 98–110.

Carnazzi, Federico (1972), 'Hanno cambiato faccia', *Cineforum* 118, October–December 1972, pp. 65–73.

Carrano, Patrizia (1977), *Malafemmina: la donna nel cinema italiano*, Rimini: Guaraldi.

Casadio, Gianfranco (1990), *Adultere, fedifraghe, innocenti: la donna del neorealismo popolare nel cinema italiano degli anni Cinquanta*, Ravenna: Longo.

Castelli, Alfredo (1970a), 'Film annunciati', *Horror* 7, June 1970, p. 42.

Castelli, Alfredo (1970b), 'Film annunciati', *Horror* 10, September 1970, pp. 30–1.

Castelli, Alfredo and Monego, Tito (1969), 'La maschera del demonio. Intervista con Mario Bava', *Horror* 1, December 1969, pp. 49–50.

Castoldi, Gian Luca (2005a), *Il pelo nel mondo: i peplum, le suore erotiche e la commedia sexy*, Rome: Profondo Rosso.

Castoldi, Gian Luca (2005b), *Donne in prigione: nazisti, horror e fantascienza, thriller, decameroni e film esotici*, Rome: Profondo Rosso.

Centro Cattolico Cinematografico (1957), 'I vampiri', *Segnalazioni cinematografiche* 41, p. 182.

Centro Cattolico Cinematografico (1959a), 'Dracula il vampiro / Horror of Dracula', *Segnalazioni cinematografiche* 45, p. 103.

Centro Cattolico Cinematografico (1959b), 'Tempi duri per i vampiri', *Segnalazioni cinematografiche* 46, p. 214.

Centro Cattolico Cinematografico (1960a), 'L'amante del vampiro', *Segnalazioni cinematografiche* 48, p. 32.

Centro Cattolico Cinematografico (1960b), 'Il mulino delle donne di pietra', *Segnalazioni cinematografiche* 48, p. 120.

Centro Cattolico Cinematografico (1960c), 'L'ultima preda del vampiro', *Segnalazioni cinematografiche* 48, p. 214.

Centro Cattolico Cinematografico (1961a), 'La maschera del demonio', *Segnalazioni cinematografiche* 49, p. 138.

Centro Cattolico Cinematografico (1961b), 'Maciste contro il vampiro', *Segnalazioni cinematografiche* 50, p. 134.

Centro Cattolico Cinematografico (1961c), 'Il sangue e la rosa / Et mourir de plaisir', *Segnalazioni cinematografiche* 50, p. 175.

Centro Cattolico Cinematografico (1962a), 'La strage dei vampiri', *Segnalazioni cinematografiche* 51, p. 80.

Centro Cattolico Cinematografico (1962b), 'Ercole al centro della Terra', *Segnalazioni cinematografiche* 51, p. 205.

Centro Cattolico Cinematografico (1962c), 'L'orribile segreto del Dr. Hichcock', *Segnalazioni cinematografiche* 52, p. 214.

Centro Cattolico Cinematografico (1963), 'I tre volti della paura', *Segnalazioni cinematografiche* 54, p. 160.
Centro Cattolico Cinematografico (1964a), 'Ercole contro Molock', *Segnalazioni cinematografiche* 55, p. 10.
Centro Cattolico Cinematografico (1964b), 'Roma contro Roma', *Segnalazioni cinematografiche* 55, p. 149.
Centro Cattolico Cinematografico (1964c), 'La cripta e l'incubo', *Segnalazioni cinematografiche* 56, p. 15.
Centro Cattolico Cinematografico (1965a), 'Maciste e la regina di Samar', *Segnalazioni cinematografiche* 57, p. 74.
Centro Cattolico Cinematografico (1965b), 'Danza macabra (Terrore)', *Segnalazioni cinematografiche* 58, p. 175.
Centro Cattolico Cinematografico (1965c), 'Amanti d'oltretomba', *Segnalazioni cinematografiche* 58, p. 328.
Centro Cattolico Cinematografico (1966), 'La vendetta di Lady Morgan', *Segnalazioni cinematografiche* 59, p. 143.
Centro Cattolico Cinematografico (1968), 'Il mostro dell'Opera', *Segnalazioni cinematografiche* 65, p. 315.
Centro Cattolico Cinematografico (1971), 'Nella stretta morsa del ragno', *Segnalazioni cinematografiche* 71, p. 198.
Centro Cattolico Cinematografico (1972a), '. . . Hanno cambiato faccia', *Segnalazioni cinematografiche* 72, p. 78.
Centro Cattolico Cinematografico (1972b), 'La notte dei diavoli', *Segnalazioni cinematografiche* 72, p. 239.
Centro Cattolico Cinematografico (1972c), 'La corta notte delle bambole di vetro', *Segnalazioni cinematografiche* 73, p. 14.
Centro Cattolico Cinematografico (1973a), 'La notte dei dannati', *Segnalazioni cinematografiche* 74, p. 166.
Centro Cattolico Cinematografico (1973b), 'Il plenilunio delle vergini', *Segnalazioni cinematografiche* 75, p. 185.
Centro Cattolico Cinematografico (1974), 'Il Conte Dracula', *Segnalazioni cinematografiche* 77, p. 255.
Centro Cattolico Cinematografico (1975a), 'L'uomo che uccideva a sangue freddo / Traitement de choc', *Segnalazioni cinematografiche* 78, p. 27.
Centro Cattolico Cinematografico (1975b), 'Le vergini cavalcano la morte', *Segnalazioni cinematografiche* 78, p. 557.
Centro Cattolico Cinematografico (1975c), 'Riti, magie nere e segrete orge nel Trecento', *Segnalazioni cinematografiche* 78, p. 560.
Centro Cattolico Cinematografico (1975d), 'Il cav. Costante Nicosia demoniaco, ovvero: Dracula in Brianza', *Segnalazioni cinematografiche* 79, p. 164.
Centro Cattolico Cinematografico (1975e), 'Dracula cerca sangue di vergine . . . e morì di sete!! / Blood for Dracula', *Segnalazioni cinematografiche* 79, pp. 204–5.
Centro Cattolico Cinematografico (1976), 'Il prato macchiato di rosso', *Segnalazioni cinematografiche* 80, p. 105.

Cereda, Giuseppe and Lopez, Giacomo (2005), 'Il cinema prodotto dalla TV e per la TV', in Vito Zagarrio (ed.), *Storia del cinema italiano. Volume XIII (1977–1985)*, Venice: Marsilio and Rome: Bianco e Nero, pp. 43–55.

Chatman, Seymour (1985), *Antonioni, or, The Surface of the World*, Berkeley: University of California Press.

Circi, Renato (1972), 'La scuola dei vampiri', *Cinesex* 56, February 1972, pp. 93–7.

Clarens, Carlos (1968), *Horror Movies: An Illustrated Survey*, London: Secker and Warburg.

Cohen, Jeffrey (1996), 'Monster Culture (Seven Theses)', in Jeffrey Cohen (ed.), *Monster Theory: Reading Culture*, Minneapolis: University of Minnesota Press, pp. 3–25.

Colombo, Maurizio and Tentori, Antonio (1990), *Lo schermo insanguinato: il cinema italiano del terrore 1957–1989*, Chieti: Solfanelli.

Conant, Michael (1985), 'The Paramount Decrees Reconsidered', in Tino Balio (ed.), *The American Film Industry*, revised edn, Madison: University of Wisconsin Press, pp. 537–73.

Comand, Mariapia (2010), *Commedia all'italiana*, Milan: Il Castoro.

Contaldo, Francesco and Fanelli, Franco (1979), *L'affare cinema: multinazionali, produttori e politici nella crisi del cinema italiano*, Milan: Feltrinelli.

Continenza, Alessandro and Tessari, Duccio (1961), 'Ercole contro i vampiri', Italian-language unpublished treatment.

Corsi, Barbara (2001), *Con qualche dollaro in meno. Storia economica del cinema italiano*, Rome: Editori riuniti.

Corsi, Barbara (2005), 'Alle origini della crisi. Industria e mercato', in Vito Zagarrio (ed.), *Storia del cinema italiano. Volume XIII (1977–1985)*, Venice: Marsilio and Rome: Bianco e Nero, pp. 329–46.

Cozzi, Luigi (1970), 'I maghi del terrore. Il vampiro in orbita. Intervista con Antonio Margheriti', *Horror* 6, May 1970, pp. 2–3.

Cozzi, Luigi (1970–1971), 'Operazione paura. Intervista a Mario Bava', *Horror* 13, December 1970–January 1971, pp. 24–6, 101.

Cozzi, Luigi (1971), 'I maghi del terrore. L'orribile segreto del dottor Hampton. Intervista a Riccardo Freda', *Horror* 15, April 1971, pp. 26–8.

Cozzi, Luigi (2007), 'Ancora Riccardo Freda', in Antonio Tentori and Luigi Cozzi (eds), *Guida al cinema gotico italiano: Horror Made in Italy*, revised edn, Rome: Profondo Rosso, pp. 321–6.

Cozzi, Luigi and Bissoli, Sergio (2012), *La storia dei Racconti di Dracula*, Rome: Profondo Rosso.

Cozzi, Luigi and Lombardi, Nicola (2013), *La storia dei KKK I classici dell'orrore – Incubi sul Tevere*, Rome: Profondo Rosso.

Craft, Christopher [1984] (1997), '"Kiss me with those red lips": Gender and Inversion in Bram Stoker's *Dracula*', in David J. Skal and Nina Auerbach (eds), *Dracula: Authoritative Text, Contexts, Reviews and Reactions, Dramatic and Film Variations, Criticism*, New York: W. W. Norton, pp. 444–59.

Crainz, Guido (1999), 'The Representation of Fascism and the Resistance in the Documentaries of Italian State Television', in R. J. B. Bosworth and Patrizia Dogliani

(eds), *Italian Fascism: History, Memory and Representation*, Basingstoke: Macmillan, pp. 124–40.
Crainz, Guido (2005a), *Storia del miracolo italiano. Culture, identità, trasformazioni fra anni Cinquanta e Sessanta*, Rome: Donzelli.
Crainz, Guido (2005b), *Il paese mancato. Dal miracolo economico agli anni Ottanta*, Rome: Donzelli.
Cranny-Francis, Anne (1988), 'Sexual Politics and Political Repression in Bram Stoker's *Dracula*', in Clive Bloom, Brian Docherty, Jane Gibb and Keith Shand (eds), *Nineteenth-Century Suspense: From Poe to Conan Doyle*, New York: St Martin's Press, pp. 64–79.
Creed, Barbara (1993), *The Monstrous-Feminine: Film, Feminism, Psychoanalysis*, London: Routledge.
Creed, Barbara (2005), *Phallic Panic: Film, Horror and the Primal Uncanny*, Carlton: Melbourne University Press.
Crofts, Stephen (1993), 'Reconceptualising National Cinema/s', *Quarterly Review of Film and Video* 14:3, pp. 49–67.
Curti, Roberto (2006), *Italia odia: il cinema poliziesco italiano*, Turin: Lindau.
Curti, Roberto (2011), *Fantasmi d'amore: il gotico italiano tra cinema, letteratura e TV*, Turin: Lindau.
Curti, Roberto (2013), *Italian Crime Filmography, 1968–1980*, Jefferson, NC: McFarland.
Curti, Roberto (2015), *Italian Gothic Horror Films, 1957–1969*, Jefferson, NC: McFarland.
Curti, Roberto (2017a), *Riccardo Freda: The Life and Works of a Born Filmmaker*, Jefferson, NC: McFarland.
Curti, Roberto (2017b), *Italian Gothic Horror Films, 1970–1979*, Jefferson, NC: McFarland.
Curti, Roberto (2018), *Mavericks of Italian Cinema: Eight Unorthodox Filmmakers, 1940s-2000s*, Jefferson, NC: McFarland.
Curti, Roberto (2019), *Italian Gothic Horror Films, 1980–1989*, Jefferson, NC: McFarland.
Curti, Roberto and Di Rocco, Alessio (2014), *Visioni proibite: i film vietati dalla censura italiana (1947–1968)*, Turin: Lindau.
D'Amico, Masolino (1985), *La commedia all'italiana: il cinema comico in Italia dal 1945 al 1975*, Milan: Mondadori.
Dadoun, Roger [1970] (1989), 'Fetishism in the Horror Film', in James Donald (ed.), *Fantasy and the Cinema*, London: BFI, pp. 39–61.
Davison, Carol (2004), *Anti-Semitism and British Gothic Literature*, Basingstoke: Palgrave.
De Berti, Raffaele (2000), *Dallo schermo alla carta: romanzi, fotoromanzi, rotocalchi cinematografici: il film e i suoi paratesti*, Milan: Vita e pensiero.
de Grazia, Victoria (1998), 'European Cinema and the Idea of Europe, 1925–1995', in Geoffrey Nowell-Smith and Steven Ricci (eds), *Hollywood and Europe: Economics, Culture, National Identity, 1945–1995*, London: BFI, pp. 19–33.
de Ossorio, Amando (1968), 'La nipote del vampiro (La sobrina de Dracula)', Italian-language unpublished screenplay.

De' Rossignoli, Emilio (1961), *Io credo nei vampiri*, Milan: Ferriani.

Della Casa, Stefano (1986), 'Una postilla sul cinema mitologico', in Enrico Magrelli (ed.), *Cinecittà 2. Sull'industria cinematografica italiana*, Venice: Marsilio, pp. 159–63.

Della Casa, Stefano (1989), 'Il mitologico-peplum', in Claver Salizzato (ed.), *Prima della rivoluzione. Schermi italiani 1960–1969*, Venice: Marsilio, pp. 89–93.

Della Casa, Stefano (1990), 'Memorie di un cinema tra l'utopia e il ghetto', *Cineforum* 299, November 1990, pp. 38–54.

Della Casa, Stefano (1993), 'Mille comparse o un attore? Intervista a Riccardo Freda', in Emanuela Martini and Stefano Della Casa (eds), *Riccardo Freda*, Bergamo: Bergamo Film Meeting, pp. 53–61.

Della Casa, Stefano (1995), 'Filmografia di Mario Bava', in Stefano Della Casa and Giulia D'Agnolo Vallan (eds), *Mario Bava: il cineasta che sapeva troppo*, Bellaria: Comune di Bellaria, pp. 25–47.

Della Casa, Stefano (2000), 'Cinema popolare italiano del dopoguerra', in Gian Piero Brunetta (ed.), *Storia del cinema mondiale. Volume 3.1*, Turin: Einaudi, pp. 779–823.

Della Casa, Stefano (2001a), 'I generi di profondità', in Giorgio De Vincenti (ed.), *Storia del cinema italiano. Volume X (1960–1964)*, Venice: Marsilio and Rome: Bianco e Nero, pp. 294–305.

Della Casa, Stefano (2001b), 'L'estetica povera del peplum', in Giorgio De Vincenti (ed.), *Storia del cinema italiano. Volume X (1960–1964)*, Venice: Marsilio and Rome: Bianco e Nero, pp. 306–18.

Della Casa, Stefano (2001c), 'L'horror', in Giorgio De Vincenti (ed.), *Storia del cinema italiano. Volume X (1960–1964)*, Venice: Marsilio and Rome: Bianco e Nero, pp. 319–30.

Della Casa, Stefano and Giusti, Marco (2013), *Il grande libro di Ercole: il cinema mitologico in Italia*, Rome: Sabinae.

Della Casa, Stefano and Giusti, Marco (2014), *Gotico italiano: il cinema orrorifico 1956–1979*, Rome: Centro Sperimentale di Cinematografia.

Demetrakopoulos, Stephanie (1977), 'Feminism, Sex Role Exchanges, and Other Subliminal Fantasies in Bram Stoker's *Dracula*', *Frontiers: A Journal of Women Studies* 2:3, pp. 104–13.

Di Chiara, Francesco (2009), *I tre volti della paura. Il cinema horror italiano (1957–1965)*, Ferrara: UNIFE Press.

Di Chiara, Francesco (2013), *Generi e industria cinematografica in Italia: il caso Titanus (1949–1964)*, Turin: Lindau.

Di Chiara, Francesco (2016a), *Peplum: il cinema italiano alle prese col mondo antico*, Rome: Donzelli.

Di Chiara, Francesco (2016b), 'Domestic Films Made for Export: Modes of Production of the 1960s Italian Horror Film', in Stefano Baschiera and Russ Hunter (eds), *Italian Horror Cinema*, Edinburgh: Edinburgh University Press, pp. 30–44.

Di Giammatteo, Fernaldo (1960), 'Prélude à Cottafavi', *Bianco e Nero* 10–11, October–November 1960, pp. 125–7.

Di Giulio, Gianni (1974), 'Sangue per il vampiro (Nosferatu story)', Italian-language unpublished screenplay.

Diak, Nicholas (2014), '"Permission to kill": Exploring Italy's 1960s Eurospy Phenomenon, Impact and Legacy', in Michele Brittany (ed.), *James Bond and Popular Culture: Essays on the Influence of the Fictional Superspy*, Jefferson, NC: McFarland, pp. 32–46.

Dimic, Milan (1984), 'Vampiromania in the Eighteenth Century: The Other Side of Enlightenment', in R. J. Merret (ed.), *Man and Nature: Conference Proceedings. Volume 3*, Edmonton: Canadian Society for Eighteenth-Century Studies, pp. 1–22.

Dingley, R. J. (1991), 'Count Dracula and the Martians', in Kath Filmer (ed.), *The Victorian Fantasists*, London: Macmillan, pp. 13–24.

Douglas, Drake (1967), *Horrors*, London: Baker.

Dyer, Richard (1997), *White*, London: Routledge.

Eco, Umberto (1964), 'Il nostro mostro quotidiano', in Umberto Eco, *Apocalittici e integrati: comunicazioni di massa e teorie della cultura di massa*, Milan: Bompiani, pp. 379–85.

Edwards, Justin and Höglund, Johan (eds) (2018), *B-Movie Gothic: International Perspectives*, Edinburgh: Edinburgh University Press.

Ehrenreich, Andreas (2017), 'Not Niche at All: The Distribution and Marketing of the "Giallo" Genre', *Bianco e Nero* 587, June 2017, pp. 113–26.

Eisenschitz, Bernard (2014), '*Days of Glory*, or Only Violence Helps Where Violence Rules', in Sergio Germani, Simone Starace and Roberto Turigliatto (eds), *Titanus. Cronaca familiare del cinema italiano*, Rome: Sabinae, pp. 155–9.

Eleftheriotis, Dimitris (2001), *Popular Cinemas of Europe: Studies of Texts, Contexts, and Frameworks*, New York: Continuum.

Eltis, Sos (2002), 'Corruption of the Blood and Degeneration of the Race: *Dracula* and Policing the Borders of Gender', in John Riquelme (ed.), *Dracula by Bram Stoker*, New York: St Martin's Press, pp. 450–65.

Eyles, Allan, Adkinson, Robert and Fry, Nicholas (1973), *House of Horror: The Story of Hammer Films*, London: Lorrimer.

Faldini, Franca and Fofi, Goffredo (eds) (1979), *L'avventurosa storia del cinema italiano raccontata dai suoi protagonisti: 1935–1959*, Milan: Feltrinelli.

Faldini, Franca and Fofi, Goffredo (eds) (1981), *L'avventurosa storia del cinema italiano raccontata dai suoi protagonisti: 1960–1969*, Milan: Feltrinelli.

Farina, Corrado (1968), 'Hanno cambiato faccia', Italian-language unpublished treatment.

Farina, Corrado (2016), *Attraverso lo schermo: film visti e film fatti*, Piombino: Il Foglio.

Farina, Massimo (1969), 'Omaggio al Signore delle Tenebre. Dracula vive ancora', *King Cinema* 5, September 1969, pp. 82–6.

Fassone, Riccardo and Nocturno editorial team (2009), 'La stagione delle streghe: guida al gotico italiano', *Nocturno Dossier* 80, March 2009.

Fazzini, Paolo (2004), *Gli artigiani dell'orrore: mezzo secolo di brivido dagli anni Cinquanta a oggi*, Rome: Un mondo a parte.

Ferraù, Alessandro (1958), 'Il pubblico ha risposto così', *Borsa Film* 48–49, December 1958, p. 1.

Fink, Guido (1960), 'Occhi senza volto', *Cinema nuovo* 147, September–October 1960, pp. 457–8.

Fink, Guido (1966), 'Nostalgia dei mostri', *Cinema nuovo* 180, March–April 1966, pp. 116–19.

Fisher, Austin (2011), *Radical Frontiers in the Spaghetti Western: Politics, Violence and Popular Italian Cinema*, London: I. B.Tauris.

Fisher, Austin (2019), *Blood in the Streets: Histories of Violence in Italian Crime Cinema*, Edinburgh: Edinburgh University Press.

Fisher, Austin and Walker, Johnny (2017), 'Italian Horror Cinema', *Journal of Italian Cinema and Media Studies* 5:2, pp. 153–7.

Flynn, John (1992), *Cinematic Vampires: The Living Dead on Film and Television, from 'The Devil's Castle' (1896) to 'Bram Stoker's Dracula' (1992)*, Jefferson, NC: McFarland.

Fofi, Goffredo (1963), 'Terreur en Italie', *Midi–Minuit Fantastique* 7, September 1963, pp. 81–3.

Foot, John (2009), *Italy's Divided Memory*, New York: Palgrave Macmillan.

Forgacs, David (1990), *Italian Culture in the Industrial Era, 1880–1980: Cultural Industries, Politics and the Public*, Manchester: Manchester University Press.

Forgacs, David (1999), 'Days of Sodom: The Fascism-Perversion Equation in Films of the 1960s and 1970s', in R. J. B. Bosworth and Patrizia Dogliani (eds), *Italian Fascism: History, Memory and Representation*, Basingstoke: Macmillan, pp. 216–36.

Fournier-Lanzoni, Rémi (2008), *Comedy Italian Style: The Golden Age of Italian Film Comedies*, New York: Continuum.

Frayling, Christopher (1991), 'Lord Byron to Count Dracula', in Christopher Frayling (ed.), *Vampyres. Lord Byron to Count Dracula*, revised edn, London: Faber and Faber, pp. 1–84.

Frayling, Christopher (1998), *Spaghetti Westerns: Cowboys and Europeans from Karl May to Sergio Leone*, revised edn, London: I. B. Tauris.

Frayling, Christopher (2011), 'Hammer's *Dracula*', in Darryl Jones, Elizabeth McCarthy and Bernice Murphy (eds), *It Came from the 1950s!: Popular Culture, Popular Anxieties*, Basingstoke: Palgrave Macmillan, pp. 108–35.

Freda, Riccardo, Fofi, Goffredo and Pistagnesi, Patrizia (1981), *Riccardo Freda. Divoratori di celluloide: 50 anni di memorie cinematografiche e non*, Milan: Emme.

Freud, Sigmund [1913] (1950), *Totem and Taboo: Some Points of Agreement between the Mental Lives of Savages and Neurotics*, trans. James Strachey, London: Routledge and Kegan Paul.

Freud, Sigmund [1919] (2003), 'The Uncanny', in Sigmund Freud, *The Uncanny*, trans. David McLintock, New York: Penguin, pp. 121–62.

Fruttero, Carlo (1960), 'Prefazione', in Carlo Fruttero and Franco Lucentini (eds), *Storie di fantasmi. Antologia di racconti anglosassoni del soprannaturale*, Turin: Einaudi, pp. v–xv.

Fulci, Lucio and Avati, Pupi (1975), 'Il cavaliere del lavoro Costante Bosisio demoniaco ovvero Dracula in Brianza', Italian-language unpublished screenplay.

Fullwood, Natalie (2015), *Cinema, Gender, and Everyday Space: Comedy, Italian Style*, New York: Palgrave Macmillan.

Garnett, Rhys (1990), '*Dracula* and *The Beetle*: Imperial and Sexual Guilt and Fear in Late Victorian Fantasy', in Rhys Garnett and R. J. Ellis (eds), *Science Fiction Roots and Branches*, New York: St Martin's Press, pp. 30–54.

Garofalo, Anna (1956), *L'italiana in Italia*, Bari: Laterza.
Gastaldi, Ernesto (1991), *Voglio entrare nel cinema: storia di uno che ce l'ha fatta*, Milan: Mondadori.
Gastaldi, Ernesto and Valerii, Tonino (1963), 'La maledizione dei Karnstein', Italian-language unpublished screenplay.
Gelder, Ken (1994), *Reading the Vampire*, London: Routledge.
Gelder, Ken (2012), *New Vampire Cinema*, London: BFI.
Ghelli, Nino (1959), 'Dracula il vampiro', *Rivista del cinematografo* 1, January 1959, pp. 31–2.
Ghigi, Giuseppe (1977), 'Come si spiegano le fortune dei "pepla" su cui sembra si torni a puntare', *Cineforum* 12, December 1977, pp. 733–46.
Ghione, Riccardo (1972), 'Vampiro 2000', Italian-language unpublished screenplay.
Giacci, Vittorio (1973), 'Il cinema "fantastico" in Italia', *Cineforum* 123, June 1973, pp. 399–415.
Giacovelli, Enrico (1995), *La commedia all'italiana*, Milan: Gremese.
Giacovelli, Enrico (1999), *Non ci resta che ridere: una storia del cinema comico italiano*, Turin: Lindau.
Gibson, Matthew (2006), *Dracula and the Eastern Question: British and French Vampire Narratives of the Nineteenth-Century Near East*, Basingstoke: Palgrave Macmillan.
Gifford, Denis (1969), *Movie Monsters*, London: Studio Vista.
Gili, Jean (ed.) (1980), *Arrivano i mostri: i volti della commedia italiana*, Bologna: Cappelli.
Gili, Jean (2010), 'Vittorio Cottafavi e la critica francese', in Adriano Aprà, Giulio Bursi and Simone Starace (eds), *Ai poeti non si spara: Vittorio Cottafavi tra cinema e televisione*, Bologna: Cineteca di Bologna, pp. 39–49.
Ginsborg, Paul (1990), *History of Contemporary Italy: Society and Politics 1943–1988*, London: Penguin.
Giovannini, Fabio (1997), *Il libro dei vampiri: dal mito di Dracula alla presenza quotidiana*, revised edn, Bari: Dedalo.
Giustiniani, M. (1971), 'Sesso nelle tenebre', *Cinesex* 37, April 1971, pp. 73–7.
Gomarasca, Manlio, Pulici, Davide and Nocturno editorial team (2004), 'Genealogia del delitto: il cinema di Mario e Lamberto Bava', *Nocturno Dossier* 24, July 2004.
Gomarasca, Manlio, Pulici, Davide, Stellino, Alex and Nocturno editorial team (2002), 'Vampiria', *Nocturno Dossier* 1, June 2002.
Griffin, Gail [1980] (1988), '"Your girls that you all love are mine": *Dracula* and the Victorian Male Sexual Imagination', in Margaret Carter (ed.), *Dracula: The Vampire and the Critics*, Ann Arbor, MI: UMI Research Press, pp. 137–48.
Grimaldi, Giovanni (1965), 'La vendetta di Lady Blackhouse', Italian-language unpublished screenplay.
Groom, Nick (2018), *The Vampire: A New History*, London: Yale University Press.
Guarneri, Michael (2019a), 'Interview with Corrado Farina (summer 2015)', *Cinepugno*, 12 May 2019, available at <https://cinepugno.home.blog/2019/05/12/interview-with-corrado-farina-summer-2015/> (last accessed 22 November 2019).

Guarneri, Michael (2019b), 'Interview with Ernesto Gastaldi (November 2018)', *Cinepugno*, 13 May 2019, available at <https://cinepugno.home.blog/2019/05/13/interview-with-ernesto-gastaldi-november-2018/> (last accessed 22 November 2019).
Guback, Thomas (1985), 'Hollywood's International Market', in Tino Balio (ed.), *The American Film Industry*, revised edn, Madison: University of Wisconsin Press, pp. 463–86.
Gundle, Stephen (2000), *Between Hollywood and Moscow: The Italian Communists and the Challenge of Mass Culture, 1943–1991*, Durham, NC: Duke University Press.
Günsberg, Maggie (2005), *Italian Cinema: Gender and Genre*, New York: Palgrave Macmillan.
Halberstam, Judith (1995), *Skin Shows: Gothic Horror and the Technology of Monsters*, Durham, NC: Duke University Press.
Hall, Stuart [1980] (2009), 'Encoding/Decoding', in Meenakshi Durham and Douglas Kellner (eds), *Media and Cultural Studies: Keyworks*, revised edn, Hoboken, NJ: Wiley, pp. 163–73.
Hatlen, Burton [1980] (1988), 'The Return of the Repressed/Oppressed in Bram Stoker's *Dracula*', in Margaret Carter (ed.), *Dracula: The Vampire and the Critics*, Ann Arbor, MI: UMI Research Press, pp. 117–35.
Heffernan, Kevin (2004), *Ghouls, Gimmicks, and Gold: Horror Films and the American Movie Business, 1953–1968*, Durham, NC: Duke University Press.
Hendershot, Cyndy (2001), *I Was a Cold War Monster: Horror Films, Eroticism, and the Cold War Imagination*, Bowling Green, OH: Bowling Green State University Popular Press.
Higson, Andrew (1989), 'The Concept of National Cinema', *Screen* 30:4, pp. 36–46.
Higson, Andrew (2000), 'The Limiting Imagination of National Cinema', in Mette Hjort and Scott MacKenzie (eds), *Cinema and Nation*, London: Routledge, pp. 57–68.
Housel, Rebecca and Wisnewski, J. J. (eds) (2009), *'Twilight' and Philosophy: Vampires, Vegetarians, and the Pursuit of Immortality*, Hoboken, NJ: Wiley.
Hudson, Dale (2017), *Vampires, Race, and Transnational Hollywoods*, Edinburgh: Edinburgh University Press.
Hunt, Leon [1992] (2000), 'A (Sadistic) Night at the *Opera*. Notes on the Italian Horror Film', in Ken Gelder (ed.), *The Horror Reader*, London: Routledge, pp. 324–35.
Hunt, Leon, Lockyer, Sharon and Williamson, Milly (eds) (2014), *Screening the Undead: Vampires and Zombies in Film and Television*, London: I. B. Tauris.
Hunter, Russ (2016), '*Preferisco l'Inferno*: Early Italian Horror Cinema', in Stefano Baschiera and Russ Hunter (eds), *Italian Horror Cinema*, Edinburgh: Edinburgh University Press, pp. 15–29.
Hunter, Russ (2017), '"I have a picture of the monster!": *Il mostro di Frankenstein* and the Search for Italian Horror Cinema', *Journal of Italian Cinema and Media Studies* 5:2, pp. 159–72.
Hutchings, Peter (2003), *Dracula*, London: I. B. Tauris.
Hutchings, Peter (2004), *The Horror Film*, Harlow: Longman.
Imbasciati, Antonio (1969), 'I personaggi femminili dei fumetti: Jodelle', *Quaderni di Ikon* 8, pp. 31–45.

Imbasciati, Antonio (1970a), 'Satanik', *Quaderni di Ikon* 12, pp. 73–99.
Imbasciati, Antonio (1970b), 'I fumetti neri', *Ikon* 20:75, October-December 1970, pp. 9–45.
Jameson, Fredric [1981] (2002), *The Political Unconscious: Narrative as a Socially Symbolic Act*, London: Routledge.
Jessua, Alain and Curel, Roger (1972), 'Terapia d'urto (Traitement de choc)', Italian-language unpublished screenplay.
Johnson, Alan (1984), '"Dual life": The Status of Women in Stoker's *Dracula*', in Don Cox (ed.), *Sexuality and Victorian Literature*, Knoxville: University of Tennessee Press, pp. 20–39.
Jones, Ernest (1931), *On the Nightmare*, London: Hogarth Press and the Institute of Psycho-analysis.
Kaes, Anton (2009), *Shell Shock Cinema: Weimar Culture and the Wounds of War*, Princeton, NJ: Princeton University Press.
Kannas, Alexia (2017), 'All the Colours of the Dark: Film Genre and the Italian Giallo', *Journal of Italian Cinema and Media Studies* 5:2, pp. 173–90.
Khair, Tabish and Höglund, Johan (eds) (2012), *Transnational and Postcolonial Vampires: Dark Blood*, New York: Palgrave Macmillan.
Kracauer, Siegfried [1947] (1971), *From Caligari to Hitler: A Psychological History of the German Film*, Princeton, NJ: Princeton University Press.
Krzywinska, Tanya (1995), 'La belle dame sans merci?', in Paul Burston and Colin Richardson (eds), *A Queer Romance: Lesbians, Gay Men and Popular Culture*, New York: Routledge, pp. 99–110.
Kuhn, Annette (1990), 'Introduction: Cultural Theory and Science Fiction Cinema', in Annette Kuhn (ed.), *Alien Zone: Cultural Theory and Contemporary Science Fiction Cinema*, London: Verso, pp. 1–18.
L. P. (1959), 'Dracula il vampiro', *La Stampa*, 15 January 1959, p. 4.
Lado, Aldo and von Spiehs, Ruediger (1971), 'La corta notte delle farfalle', Italian-language unpublished screenplay.
Lagny, Michèle (1992), 'Popular Taste. The Peplum', in Richard Dyer and Ginette Vincendeau (eds), *Popular European Cinema*, London: Routledge, pp. 163–80.
Lan. (1959), 'Dracula il vampiro', *Corriere della sera*, 2 January 1959, p. 6.
Lattarulo, Leonardo (1995), '"Antica storia narra così". Considerazioni sul fantastico italiano ottocentesco', in Monica Farnetti (ed.), *Geografia, storia e poetiche del fantastico*, Florence: Olschki, pp. 121–33.
Laura, Ernesto (1971), 'Nuove strade per l'incubo', *Horror* 16, May 1971, p. 1.
Laura, Ernesto (1981), *Comedy Italian Style*, Rome: ANICA.
Le Bris, Alain (1962a), 'Une constante fisherienne: le sang', *Midi–Minuit Fantastique* 1, May–June 1962, pp. 15–17.
Le Bris, Alain (1962b), 'Le thème du chateau dans l'oeuvre de Terence Fisher', *Midi–Minuit Fantastique* 1, May–June 1962, pp. 19–20.
Le Bris, Alain (1962c), 'Les temps sont durs pour les vampires', *Midi–Minuit Fantastique* 3, October–November 1962, p. 39.
Leutrat, Jean-Louis (1994), 'Le regard vampire', in Jean-Louis Leutrat (ed.), *Mario Bava*, Liège: Éditions du Cefal, pp. 41–8.

Levine, Elena and Parks, Lisa (eds) (2007), *Undead TV: Essays on 'Buffy the Vampire Slayer'*, Durham, NC: Duke University Press.

Lichtner, Giacomo (2013), *Fascism in Italian Cinema since 1945: The Politics and Aesthetics of Memory*, New York: Palgrave Macmillan.

Lippi, Giuseppe and Codelli, Lorenzo (1976), *Fant'Italia: 1957–1966 emergenza apoteosi e riflusso del fantastico nel cinema italiano*, Trieste: La Cappella Underground.

Lo Foco, Michele (1984), *Cinema: tutta la verità sul mondo del cinema*, Rome: Akropolis.

Longo, Luigi (1965), 'Prefazione', in Palmiro Togliatti, *L'emancipazione femminile. Discorsi alle donne*, Rome: Editori riuniti, pp. 7–19.

Lonzi, Carla [1970] (1991), 'Let's Spit on Hegel', in Paola Bono and Sandra Kemp (eds), *Italian Feminist Thought: A Reader*, Oxford: Blackwell, pp. 40–59.

Lotta Continua collective (1970), 'È il momento di fare i conti', *Lotta Continua* 1, 17 January 1970, pp. 1–2.

Lotta Continua collective (1971), 'Perché c'eravamo anche noi', *Lotta Continua* 19, 1 December 1971, p. 5.

Lotta Continua collective (1972a), 'Raccogliamo sangue per i compagni vietnamiti', *Lotta Continua* 30, 16 May 1972, p. 2.

Lotta Continua collective (1972b), 'Catania. Processo agli speculatori della banca del sangue', *Lotta Continua* 39, 26 May 1972, p. 3.

Lotta Continua collective (1972c), 'Mestre. Per un operaio ferito. Necessario del sangue', *Lotta Continua* 40, 27 May 1972, p. 4.

Lotta Continua collective (1972d), 'Montedison: una sanguisuga prodotto del fascismo (1)', *Lotta Continua* 148, 6 October 1972, p. 1.

Lotta Continua collective (1972e), 'Montedison: una sanguisuga prodotto del fascismo (2)', *Lotta Continua* 149, 7 October 1972, p. 4.

Lotta Continua collective (1974a), 'In un quartiere di Roma', *Lotta Continua* 207, 8 September 1974, p. 2.

Lotta Continua collective (1974b), 'La politica DC non cambia mai: è fatta col sangue degli operai', *Lotta Continua* 210, 12 September 1974, p. 2.

Lotta Continua collective (1976), 'Governo vampiro, vattene!', *Lotta Continua* 72, 27 March 1976, p. 3.

Lourcelles, Jacques and Mizrahi, Simon (1963), 'Entretien avec Riccardo Freda', *Présence du cinéma* 17, pp. 11–30.

Lucas, Tim (2007), *Mario Bava: All the Colors of the Dark*, Cincinnati: Video Watchdog.

Lucato, Claudio (1973), 'L'uomo che uccideva a sangue freddo', *Cineforum* 127, October-November 1973, pp. 828–31.

Lughi, Paolo [1991] (2008), 'Raccontarsi in "soggettiva". Intervista a Giacomo Gentilomo', in Luciano De Giusti (ed.), *Giacomo Gentilomo, cineasta popolare*, Turin: Kaplan, pp. 129–32.

MacGillivray, Royce (1972), '*Dracula*: Bram Stoker's Spoiled Masterpiece', *Queen's Quarterly* 79, pp. 518–27.

Magazù, Gino (1960), 'Musica leggera. Le canzoni del terrore', *Mascotte* 6, 30 February 1960, p. 18.

Magli, Adriano (1959), 'Psicologia e spettacolo. I vampiri minorenni', *Sipario* 163, November 1959, pp. 17–18.
Malchow, H. L. (1996), *Gothic Images of Race in Nineteenth-Century Britain*, Stanford, CA: Stanford University Press.
Mandarà, Lucio (1963), 'Di sexy si muore', *Giornale dello Spettacolo* 41, December 1963, p. 3.
Manzanos Brochero, Eduardo (1971), 'I diavoli sono tra noi', Italian-language unpublished treatment.
Manzoli, Giacomo (2012), *Da Ercole a Fantozzi. Cinema popolare e società italiana dal boom economico alla neotelevisione (1958–1976)*, Rome: Carocci.
Marchena, Oscar (2009), *Guida al cinema peplum: Ercole, Ursus, Sansone e Maciste alla conquista di Atlantide*, Rome: Profondo Rosso.
Marcus, Millicent (1986), *Italian Film in the Light of Neorealism*, Princeton, NJ: Princeton University Press.
Marcuse, Herbert [1964] (1968), *One-Dimensional Man*, London: Routledge and Kegan Paul.
Marcuse, Herbert [1958] (1969), *Soviet Marxism*, London: Routledge and Kegan Paul.
Marcuse, Herbert [1955] (2015), *Eros and Civilisation: A Philosophical Inquiry into Freud*, London: Routledge.
Marinucci, Vinicio (1957), 'I vampiri', *Momento Sera*, 31 May 1957, unnumbered page.
Martinelli, Vittorio (1991a), *Il cinema muto italiano: 1917*, Turin: Nuova ERI.
Martinelli, Vittorio (1991b), *Il cinema muto italiano: i film della Grande Guerra, 1918*, Turin: Nuova ERI.
Martinelli, Vittorio (1992a), *Il cinema muto italiano: i film della Grande Guerra, 1915. Parte prima*, Turin: Nuova ERI.
Martinelli, Vittorio (1992b), *Il cinema muto italiano: i film della Grande Guerra, 1915. Parte seconda*, Turin: Nuova ERI.
Martinelli, Vittorio (1992c), *Il cinema muto italiano: i film della Grande Guerra, 1916. Parte prima*, Turin: Nuova ERI.
Martinelli, Vittorio (1992d), *Il cinema muto italiano: i film della Grande Guerra, 1916. Parte seconda*, Turin: Nuova ERI.
Martinelli, Vittorio (1995a), *Il cinema muto italiano: i film del Dopoguerra, 1919*, Turin: Nuova ERI.
Martinelli, Vittorio (1995b), *Il cinema muto italiano: i film del Dopoguerra, 1920*, Turin: Nuova ERI; Rome: Centro Sperimentale di Cinematografia.
Martinelli, Vittorio (1996a), *Il cinema muto italiano: i film degli anni Venti, 1921*, Turin: Nuova ERI; Rome: Centro Sperimentale di Cinematografia.
Martinelli, Vittorio (1996b), *Il cinema muto italiano: i film degli anni Venti, 1922–1923*, Turin: Nuova ERI; Rome: Centro Sperimentale di Cinematografia.
Martinelli, Vittorio (1996c), *Il cinema muto italiano: i film degli anni Venti, 1924–1931*, Turin: Nuova ERI; Rome: Centro Sperimentale di Cinematografia.
Marx, Karl [1867] (1954), *Capital: A Critique of Political Economy. Volume 1*, trans. Samuel Moore and Edward Aveling, London: Lawrence and Wishart.

Mazzini Rizzo, Ercole (1961), 'Uno psichiatra dinanzi ai film dell'orrore', *Centrofilm* 27–28, November-December 1961, pp. 58–61.
McKee, Patricia (2002), 'Racialization, Capitalism, and Aesthetics in Stoker's *Dracula*', *Novel* 36:1, pp. 42–60.
Meikle, Denis (2009), *A History of Horrors: The Rise and Fall of the House of Hammer*, revised edn, Lanham, MD: Scarecrow Press.
Menarini, Roy (2001), *La parodia nel cinema italiano: intertestualità, parodia e comico nel cinema italiano*, Bologna: Hybris.
Menarini, Roy and Noto, Paolo (2005), 'Dall'economia di scala all'intertestualità di genere', in Giacomo Manzoli and Guglielmo Pescatore (eds), *L'arte del risparmio: stile e tecnologia*, Rome: Carocci, pp. 19–30.
Mendik, Xavier (2015), *Bodies of Desire and Bodies in Distress: The Golden Age of Italian Cult Cinema (1970–1985)*, Newcastle upon Tyne: Cambridge Scholars Publishing.
Menduni, Enrico (2005), 'La rivoluzione delle TV libere', in Vito Zagarrio (ed.), *Storia del cinema italiano. Volume XIII (1977–1985)*, Venice: Marsilio and Rome: Bianco e Nero, pp. 79–90.
Miotto, Antonio (1961), 'Il sottile fascino dell'orrore', *Centrofilm* 27–28, November–December 1961, pp. 62–5.
Mistrali, Franco (1869), *Il vampiro. Storia vera*, Bologna: Società tipografica dei compositori.
Monetti, Domenico (2008), 'Verso la crisi produttiva', in Flavio De Bernardinis (ed.), *Storia del cinema italiano. Volume XII (1970–1976)*, Venice: Marsilio and Rome: Bianco e Nero, pp. 496–502.
Monteleone, Franco (2005), 'Il cinema come genere televisivo', in Vito Zagarrio (ed.), *Storia del cinema italiano. Volume XIII (1977–1985)*, Venice: Marsilio and Rome: Bianco e Nero, pp. 56–66.
Mora, Teo (1978), *Storia del cinema dell'orrore (1957–1978). Volume 2.2*, Rome: Fanucci.
Mora, Teo (1986), 'Il cinema fantastico italiano: un fenomeno produttivo marginale', in Enrico Magrelli (ed.), *Cinecittà 2. Sull'industria cinematografica italiana*, Venice: Marsilio, pp. 193–9.
Morandini, Morando (1964), 'Al limite del proibito', *ABC* 51, December 1964, pp. 20–2, 49.
Moras, Silvia (2005), '*L'ultimo uomo della Terra / The Last Man on Earth*: alle origini della leggenda', *Cinergie* 10, September 2005, pp. 28–31.
Moretti, Franco [1983] (2005), 'The Dialectic of Fear', in Franco Moretti, *Signs Taken for Wonders: Essays in the Sociology of Literary Forms*, trans. Susan Fischer, David Forgacs and David Miller, London: Verso, pp. 83–108.
Morrissey, Paul (1974), 'Paul Morrissey Seminar', *Dialogue on Film* 2:2, pp. 20–32.
Moscon, Giorgio (1957), 'Una legge da rispettare', *Il ponte*, August-September 1957, pp. 1328–36.
Mulvey, Laura [1975] (1985), 'Visual Pleasure and Narrative Cinema', in Bill Nichols (ed.), *Movies and Methods: An Anthology. Volume 2*, Berkeley: University of California Press, pp. 303–15.

Mulvey-Roberts, Marie (1998), 'Dracula and the Doctors: Bad Blood, Menstrual Taboo and the New Woman', in William Hughes and Andrew Smith (eds), *Bram Stoker: History, Psychoanalysis and the Gothic*, Basingstoke: Macmillan, pp. 78–95.
Mulvey-Roberts, Marie (2016), *Dangerous Bodies: Historicising the Gothic Corporeal*, Manchester: Manchester University Press.
Murphy, Michael (1979), *The Celluloid Vampires: A History and Filmography (1897–1979)*, Ann Arbor, MI: Pierian Press.
Nakahara, Tamao (2004), 'Barred Nuns: Italian Nunsploitation Films', in Ernest Mathijs and Xavier Mendik (eds), *Alternative Europe: Eurotrash and Exploitation Cinema since 1945*, London: Wallflower, pp. 124–33.
Newman, Kim (1986a), 'Thirty Years in Another Town: The History of Italian Exploitation', *Monthly Film Bulletin* 624, January 1986, pp. 20–4.
Newman, Kim (1986b), 'Thirty Years in Another Town: The History of Italian Exploitation II', *Monthly Film Bulletin* 625, February 1986, pp. 51–5.
Newman, Kim (1986c), 'Thirty Years in Another Town: The History of Italian Exploitation III', *Monthly Film Bulletin* 626, March 1986, pp. 88–91.
Noto, Paolo (2011), *Dal bozzetto ai generi: il cinema italiano dei primi anni Cinquanta*, Turin: Kaplan.
Noto, Paolo (2016), 'Italian Horror Cinema and Italian Film Journals of the 1970s', in Stefano Baschiera and Russ Hunter (eds), *Italian Horror Cinema*, Edinburgh: Edinburgh University Press, pp. 207–21.
Nowell-Smith, Geoffrey, Hay, James and Volpi, Gianni (1996), *The Companion to Italian Cinema*, London: BFI.
Nullaosta 4783 (1948), *La casa degli orrori*, public-screening permission.
Nullaosta 7425 (1950), *Dies Irae*, public-screening permission.
Nullaosta 23894 (1957), *I vampiri*, public-screening permission.
Nullaosta 25288 (1957), *La maschera di Frankenstein*, public-screening permission.
Nullaosta 28085 (1958), *Dracula il vampiro*, public-screening permission.
Nullaosta 28463 (1959), *Il sangue del vampiro*, public-screening permission.
Nullaosta 29018 (1959), *Il bacio dello spettro*, public-screening permission.
Nullaosta 30310 (1959), *Tempi duri per i vampiri*, public-screening permission.
Nullaosta 31205 (1960), *L'uomo senza corpo*, public-screening permission.
Nullaosta 31701 (1960), *L'amante del vampiro*, public-screening permission.
Nullaosta 32584 (1960), *La maschera del demonio*, public-screening permission.
Nullaosta 32613 (1960), *Il mulino delle donne di pietra*, public-screening permission.
Nullaosta 33224 (1960), *Le spose di Dracula*, public-screening permission.
Nullaosta 33364 (1960), *L'ultima preda del vampiro*, public-screening permission.
Nullaosta 33435 (1960), *Il sangue e la rosa*, public-screening permission.
Nullaosta 35277 (1961), *Maciste contro il vampiro*, public-screening permission.
Nullaosta 35906 (1961), *Ercole al centro della Terra*, public-screening permission.
Nullaosta 36600 (1962), *La strage dei vampiri*, public-screening permission.
Nullaosta 37710 (1962), *L'orribile segreto del Dr. Hichcock*, public-screening permission.
Nullaosta 40624 (1963), *Danza macabra*, public-screening permission.
Nullaosta 40988 (1963), *I tre volti della paura*, public-screening permission.
Nullaosta 41880 (1963), *Ercole contro Moloch*, public-screening permission.

Nullaosta 42091 (1964), *Roma contro Roma*, public-screening permission.
Nullaosta 42808 (1964), *La cripta e l'incubo*, public-screening permission.
Nullaosta 43135 (1964), *Il mostro dell'Opera*, public-screening permission.
Nullaosta 43266 (1964), *Maciste e la regina di Samar*, public-screening permission.
Nullaosta 45399 (1965), *Amanti d'oltretomba*, public-screening permission.
Nullaosta 45744 (1965), *La vendetta di Lady Morgan*, public-screening permission.
Nullaosta 46568 (1966), *Dracula, Principe delle Tenebre*, public-screening permission.
Nullaosta 54087 (1969), *Malenka, la nipote del vampiro*, public-screening permission.
Nullaosta 57934 (1971), *. . . Hanno cambiato faccia*, public-screening permission.
Nullaosta 58702 (1971), *La notte dei dannati*, public-screening permission.
Nullaosta 58787 (1971), *Nella stretta morsa del ragno*, public-screening permission.
Nullaosta 58956 (1971), *La corta notte delle bambole di vetro*, public-screening permission.
Nullaosta 60050 (1972), *La notte dei diavoli*, public-screening permission.
Nullaosta 60795 (1972), *Riti, magie nere e segrete orge nel Trecento . . .* , public-screening permission.
Nullaosta 61372 (1972), *Il prato macchiato di rosso*, public-screening permission.
Nullaosta 61865 (1973), *L'uomo che uccideva a sangue freddo*, public-screening permission.
Nullaosta 62028 (1973), *Il plenilunio delle vergini*, public-screening permission.
Nullaosta 62852 (1973), *Le vergini cavalcano la morte*, public-screening permission.
Nullaosta 62939 (1973), *Il Conte Dracula*, public-screening permission.
Nullaosta 64499 (1974), *Dracula cerca sangue di vergine . . . e morì di sete!!!*, public-screening permission.
Nullaosta 67018 (1975), *Il cav. Costante Nicosia demoniaco, ovvero: Dracula in Brianza*, public-screening permission.
O'Brien, Daniel (2013), 'Hercules versus Hercules: Variation and Continuation in Two Generations of Heroic Masculinity', in Louis Bayman and Sergio Rigoletto (eds), *Popular Italian Cinema*, Basingstoke: Palgrave, pp. 183–99.
O'Brien, Daniel (2014), *Classical Masculinity and the Spectacular Body on Film: The Mighty Sons of Hercules*, Basingstoke: Palgrave Macmillan.
O'Leary, Alan (2011), *Tragedia all'italiana: Italian Cinema and Italian Terrorisms, 1970–2010*, New York: Peter Lang.
O'Leary, Alan and O'Rawe, Catherine (2011), 'Against Realism: On a "Certain Tendency" in Italian Film Criticism', *Journal of Modern Italian Studies* 16:1, pp. 107–28.
O'Rawe, Catherine (2008), '"I padri e i maestri": Genre, Auteurs and Absences in Italian Film Studies', *Italian Studies* 63:2, pp. 173–94.
Olney, Ian (2012), '*The Whip and the Body*: Sex, Violence and Performative Spectatorship in Euro-Horror S&M Cinema', in Karen Ritzenhoff and Karen Randell (eds), *Screening the Dark Side of Love: From Euro-Horror to American Cinema*, New York: Palgrave Macmillan, pp. 1–17.
P. (1959), 'Un celebre mostro ritorna sullo schermo', *Stampa sera*, 16 January 1959, p. 8.
Packard, Vance [1957] (2007), *The Hidden Persuaders*, New York: Ig Publishing.

Palmerini, Luca and Mistretta, Gaetano (1996), *Spaghetti Nightmares: Italian Fantasy-Horrors as Seen through the Eyes of Their Protagonists*, Key West, FL: Fantasma Books.
Paolella, Domenico (1965), 'La psychanalyse du pauvre', *Midi–Minuit Fantastique* 12, May 1965, pp. 1–8.
Parca, Gabriella [1959] (1966), *Le italiane si confessano*, Milan: Feltrinelli.
Parca, Gabriella [1965] (1977), *I sultani: mentalità e comportamento del maschio italiano*, Milan: Rizzoli.
Parke, Maggie and Wilson, Natalie (eds) (2011), *Theorizing 'Twilight': Critical Essays on What's at Stake in a Post-Vampire World*, Jefferson, NC: McFarland.
Pasolini, Pier Paolo [1968] (1979), 'Il perché di questa rubrica', in Pier Paolo Pasolini, *Il caos*, Rome: Editori riuniti, pp. 36–40.
Pautasso, Guido (1998), 'Il vampiro nella letteratura italiana', in AA. VV., *Vampiri: miti, leggende, letteratura, cinema, fumetti, multimedialità*, Milan: Editrice Nord, pp. 56–63.
Peirse, Alison (2013), *After Dracula: the 1930s Horror Film*, London: I. B. Tauris.
Penati, Cecilia (2015), 'The Hearth of Our Times: RAI and the Domestication of Italian Television in the 1950s', *Comunicazioni sociali* 1, pp. 36–45.
Peruzzi, Giuseppe (1972), '. . .Hanno cambiato faccia', *Cinema nuovo* 217, May–June 1972, pp. 216–18.
Pesce, Sara (2008), *Memoria e immaginario: la Seconda Guerra Mondiale nel cinema italiano*, Recco: Le Mani.
Pettarin, Francesco (1980), 'Considerazioni sui pochi dati reperibili', in Laura Barbiani and Alberto Abruzzese (eds), *Pornograffiti: da Jacula a Oltretomba, da Cappuccetto Rotto a Mercenari. Trame e figure del fumetto italiano per adulti*, Rome: Napoleone, pp. 99–106.
Pezzotta, Alberto (1997), 'Doppi di noi stessi', *Segnocinema* 85, May-June 1997, pp. 25–31.
Pezzotta, Alberto (2008), 'L'allegra parabola del western italiano', in Flavio De Bernardinis (ed.), *Storia del cinema italiano. Volume XII (1970–1976)*, Venice: Marsilio and Rome: Bianco e Nero, pp. 55–66.
Pezzotta, Alberto (2013), *Mario Bava*, revised edn, Milan: Il Castoro.
Pezzotta, Alberto (2014), 'Il boom? È gotico (e anche un po' sadico)', *Bianco e Nero* 579, April–July 2014, pp. 34–48.
Phillips, Kendall (2005), *Projected Fears: Horror Films and American Culture*, Westport, CT: Praeger.
Pirie, David (1977), *The Vampire Cinema*, London: Hamlyn.
Pirie, David (2008), *A New Heritage of Horror: The English Gothic Cinema*, London: I. B. Tauris.
Pironi, Gualtiero (1977), 'Cinema italiano '77: una stagnazione che non è solo economica', *Cineforum* 12, December 1977, pp. 723–31.
Pirro, Ugo (1965), 'Da "Caltiki" a "Un pugno di dollari"', *I problemi di Ulisse* 9:56, October 1965, pp. 38–44.
Piselli, Stefano and Guidotti, Roberto (1989), *Diva Cinema, 1951–1965*, Florence: Glittering Images.

Piselli, Stefano, Morrocchi, Riccardo and Bruschini, Antonio (1996), *Horror all'italiana, 1957–1979*, Florence: Glittering Images.
Pisoni, Roberto and Ferrarese, Michele [1999] (2007), 'Il padre del mostro. Intervista a Riccardo Freda', in Gabriele Acerbo and Roberto Pisoni (eds), *Kill Baby Kill! Il cinema di Mario Bava*, Rome: Un mondo a parte, pp. 43–4.
Pitassio, Francesco (2005), 'L'orribile segreto dell'horror italiano', in Giacomo Manzoli and Guglielmo Pescatore (eds), *L'arte del risparmio: stile e tecnologia*, Rome: Carocci, pp. 31–41.
Pizzagalli, Angelo Maria (1936), 'Prefazione', in Somadeva Bhatta and Mary Tibaldi Chiesa, *Gli enigmi del vampiro*, Milan: Mondadori, pp. 15–25.
Platts, Todd (2017), 'A Comparative Analysis of the Factors Driving Film Cycles: Italian and American Zombie Film Production, 1978–1982', *Journal of Italian Cinema and Media Studies* 5:2, pp. 191–210.
Prawer, Siegbert (1980), *Caligari's Children: The Film as Tale of Terror*, Oxford: Oxford University Press.
Prono, Luca (2001), 'Città aperta o cultura chiusa?: The Homosexualisation of Fascism in the Perverted Cultural Memory of the Italian Left', *International Journal of Sexuality and Gender Studies* 6:4, pp. 333–51.
Punter, David (1996a), *The Literature of Terror. A History of Gothic Fictions from 1765 to Present Day. Volume 1: The Gothic Tradition*, revised edn, New York: Longman.
Punter, David (1996b), *The Literature of Terror. A History of Gothic Fictions from 1765 to Present Day. Volume 2: The Modern Gothic*, revised edn, New York: Longman.
Quaglietti, Lorenzo (1980), *Storia economico-politica del cinema italiano 1945–1980*, Rome: Editori riuniti.
Quarantotto, Claudio (1960), 'Non calpestate il cinema', *Il Borghese* 32, 11 August 1960, p. 239.
Quarantotto, Claudio (1965), 'Orrore all'italiana', *Il Borghese* 32, 12 August 1965, p. 768.
Quarantotto, Claudio (1969), 'Orrore all'italiana cercasi', *Il Borghese* 40, 28 September 1969, pp. 282–3.
RAI (1977), *TV titoli: opere liriche, operette e commedie musicali, drammi e commedie, originali televisivi, riduzione di opere letterarie, films, telefilms trasmessi in televisione dal 1954 al 1975*, Turin: ERI.
Reich, Jacqueline (2004), *Beyond the Latin Lover: Marcello Mastroianni, Masculinity, and Italian Cinema*, Bloomington: Indiana University Press.
Renga, Dana (2011), 'Pastapocalypse! End Times in Italian Trash Cinema', *The Italianist* 31:2, pp. 243–57.
Rey, Isabella (1971), 'Voglio la vampira che mi piace tanto', *Cinesex* 36, April 1971, pp. 1–11.
Richardson, Maurice (1959), 'The Psychoanalysis of Ghost Stories', *The Twentieth Century* 166, July–December 1959, pp. 419–31.
Rigby, Jonathan (2016), *Euro Gothic: Classics of Continental Horror Cinema*, Cambridge: Signum Books.

Righi, Andrea (2011), *Biopolitics and Social Change in Italy: from Gramsci to Pasolini to Negri*, New York: Palgrave Macmillan.

Rigoletto, Sergio (2014), *Masculinity and Italian Cinema. Sexual Politics, Social Conflict and Male Crisis in the 1970s*, Edinburgh: Edinburgh University Press.

Risé, Claudio (1964), 'I documentari "sexy"', in Vittorio Spinazzola (ed.), *Film 1964. Film di massa e cinema d'avanguardia*, Milan: Feltrinelli, pp. 86–101.

Rivolta Femminile [1970] (1991), 'Manifesto', in Paola Bono and Sandra Kemp (eds), *Italian Feminist Thought: A Reader*, Oxford: Blackwell, pp. 37–40.

Rohdie, Sam (1990), *Antonioni*, London: BFI.

Romanelli, Claudia (2016), 'French and Italian Co-productions and the Limits of Transnational Cinema', *Journal of Italian Cinema and Media Studies* 4:1, pp. 25–50.

Rondi, Gian Luigi (1961a), 'I film e la critica', *Giornale dello spettacolo* 6, February 1961, p. 3.

Rondi, Gian Luigi (1961b), 'I film e la critica', *Giornale dello spettacolo* 15, April 1961, p. 3.

Rondolino, Gianni (ed.) (1975), *Catalogo Bolaffi del cinema italiano: 1966–1975*, Turin: Bolaffi.

Rondolino, Gianni (ed.) (1976), *Catalogo Bolaffi del cinema italiano, n. 3: tutti i film della stagione 1975–1976*, Turin: Bolaffi.

Rondolino, Gianni (ed.) (1977), *Catalogo Bolaffi del cinema italiano, n. 4: tutti i film della stagione 1976–1977*, Turin: Bolaffi.

Rondolino, Gianni and Levi, Ornella (eds) (1967), *Catalogo Bolaffi del cinema italiano. Tutti i film del dopoguerra (1945–1965)*, Turin: Bolaffi.

Rosen, Philip (1984), 'History, Textuality, Nation. Kracauer, Burch and Some Problems in the Study of National Cinemas', *Iris* 2:2, pp. 69–84.

Rossi-Osmida, Gabriele (1978), *Uomini o vampiri*, Milan: Curcio.

Roszak, Theodore (1969), *The Making of a Counter Culture: Reflections on the Technocratic Society and Its Youthful Opposition*, London: Faber and Faber.

Rotellar, Manuel (1952), 'Terrore sugli schermi', *Cinema* 99–100, December 1952, pp. 296–306.

Roth, Lane (1979), 'Dracula Meets the Zeitgeist: *Nosferatu* (1922) as Film Adaptation', *Literature/Film Quarterly* 7:3, pp. 309–13.

Roth, Lane [1984] (2004), 'Film, Society, and Ideas: *Nosferatu* and *Horror of Dracula*', in Barry Grant and Christopher Sharrett (eds), *Planks of Reason: Essays on the Horror Film*, revised edn, Lanham, MD: Scarecrow Press, pp. 255–64.

Roth, Phyllis [1977] (1997), 'Suddenly Sexual Women in Bram Stoker's *Dracula*', in David J. Skal and Nina Auerbach (eds), *Dracula: Authoritative Text, Contexts, Reviews and Reactions, Dramatic and Film Variations, Criticism*, New York: W. W. Norton, pp. 411–21.

Salotti, Marco (1986), '1957–1964: l'industria cinematografica italiana gonfia i muscoli. Il film mitico-muscolare', in Enrico Magrelli (ed.), *Cinecittà 2. Sull'industria cinematografica italiana*, Venice: Marsilio, pp. 145–58.

Santevril, Tazio (1972), 'Da vamp ... a vampira', *Cinesex Attualità* 13, November 1972, pp. 6–11.

Scaglioni, Massimo (2015), 'Television as a Project: The Relation between Public Service Broadcasting and Italian Historical Cultures (1954–1994)', *Comunicazioni sociali* 1, pp. 7–21.
Schneider, Steven (ed.) (2003), *Fear without Frontiers: Horror Cinema across the Globe*, Godalming: FAB Press.
Segre, Stefano (1982), 'Introduzione', in Stefano Segre (ed.), *L'antimaschio*, Milan: Gammalibri, pp. 13–46.
Senf, Carol (1982), 'Stoker's Response to New Woman', *Victorian Studies* 26:1, pp. 33–49.
Senf, Carol (1988), *The Vampire in Nineteenth-Century English Literature*, Bowling Green, OH: Bowling Green State University Popular Press.
Senf, Carol [1979] (1997), 'Dracula: The Unseen Face in the Mirror', in David J. Skal and Nina Auerbach (eds), *Dracula: Authoritative Text, Contexts, Reviews and Reactions, Dramatic and Film Variations, Criticism*, New York: W. W. Norton, pp. 421–31.
Servadio, Emilio (1959), 'Il vampiro e i film dell'orrore. Vaneggiamenti primordiali nel mondo di oggi', *La Stampa*, 2 June 1959, p. 3.
Simonelli, Giorgio [1971] (2002), 'Il cinema presentato dalla TV', in Gianni Canova (ed.), *Storia del cinema italiano. Volume XI (1965–1969)*, Venice: Marsilio and Rome: Bianco e Nero, pp. 526–34.
Sorlin, Pierre (1996), *Italian National Cinema 1896–1996*, London: Routledge.
Spagnol, Mario and Santi, Giovenale (eds) (1966), *Guida all'Italia leggendaria, misteriosa, insolita, fantastica. Volume 1: Nord*, Milan: Sugar.
Spagnol, Mario and Santi, Giovenale (eds) (1967), *Guida all'Italia leggendaria, misteriosa, insolita, fantastica. Volume 2: Centro-Sud e Isole*, Milan: Sugar.
Spear, Jeffrey (1993), 'Gender and Sexual Dis-ease in *Dracula*', in Lloyd Davis (ed.), *Virginal Sexuality and Textuality in Victorian Literature*, Albany: State University of New York Press, pp. 179–92.
Spinazzola, Vittorio (1962), 'La Resistenza dall'epica al romanzo storico', in Vittorio Spinazzola (ed.), *Film 1962. Cinema del miracolo: Italia, Francia, Stati Uniti*, Milan: Feltrinelli, pp. 43–76.
Spinazzola, Vittorio (1963), 'Ercole alla conquista degli schermi', in Vittorio Spinazzola (ed.), *Film 1963. Il cinema è diventato maggiorenne*, Milan: Feltrinelli, pp. 75–111.
Spinazzola, Vittorio (1964), 'Cinema italiano 1963', in Vittorio Spinazzola (ed.), *Film 1964. Film di massa e cinema d'avanguardia*, Milan: Feltrinelli, pp. 11–54.
Spinazzola, Vittorio (1965a), 'Significato e problemi del film storico-mitologico', *Cinema nuovo* 176, July–August 1965, pp. 270–9.
Spinazzola, Vittorio (1965b), 'Successo di pubblico e critica inadeguata', *Cinema nuovo* 178, November–December 1965, pp. 418–21.
Spinazzola, Vittorio (1985), *Cinema e pubblico: lo spettacolo filmico in Italia, 1945–1965*, revised edn, Rome: Bulzoni.
Stoker, Bram [1897] (1980), *Dracula*, London: Hutchinson.
Stott, Rebecca (1992), *The Fabrication of the Late-Victorian Femme Fatale: The Kiss of Death*, Basingstoke: Macmillan.
Subini, Tomaso (2015), 'I cattolici e l'osceno: tra censura amministrativa e revisione cinematografica', *Arabeschi* 6, July–December 2015, pp. 64–72.

Sullerot, Evelyne [1970] (1977), 'I fotoromanzi', in Noel Arnaud, Francis Lacassin and Jean Tortel (eds), *La paraletteratura: il melodramma, il romanzo popolare, il fotoromanzo, il romanzo poliziesco, il fumetto*, trans. Marina Pisaturo, Naples: Liguori, pp. 100–14.

Švábenický, Jan (2014), *Aldo Lado ed Ernesto Gastaldi: due cineasti, due interviste. Esperienze di cinema italiano raccontate da due protagonisti*, Piombino: Il Foglio.

Tagliabue, Carlo (2005), 'Fuga dal cinema. La crisi dell'esercizio', in Vito Zagarrio (ed.), *Storia del cinema italiano. Volume XIII (1977–1985)*, Venice: Marsilio and Rome: Bianco e Nero, pp. 347–56.

Tambor, Molly (2014), *The Lost Wave: Women and Democracy in Postwar Italy*, Oxford: Oxford University Press.

Tardiola, Giuseppe (1991), *Il vampiro nella letteratura italiana*, Anzio: De Rubeis.

Tasca, Laura (2004), 'The "Average Housewife" in Post-World-War-II Italy', *Journal of Women's History* 16:2, pp. 92–115.

Tassone, Aldo, Pieri, Françoise, Roquier, Michèle, Bourguignon, Thomas, Rouyer, Philippe, Branca, Fabrice, Tranchant, Marie-Noëlle, Delli Colli, Laura and Giaccone, Ilaria (1995), '98 protagonisti si raccontano', in Jean Gili and Aldo Tassone (eds), *Parigi-Roma: 50 anni di coproduzioni italo–francesi, 1945–1995*, Florence: Il Castoro, pp. 37–223.

Tavernier, Bertrand (1963), 'Entretien avec Terence Fisher', *Midi–Minuit Fantastique* 7, September 1963, pp. 9–12.

Togliatti, Palmiro [1945] (1965a), 'L'emancipazione della donna: un problema centrale del rinnovamento dello Stato italiano e della società', in Palmiro Togliatti, *L'emancipazione femminile. Discorsi alle donne*, Rome: Editori riuniti, pp. 21–48.

Togliatti, Palmiro [1953] (1965b), 'È stato giusto dare il voto alle donne?', in Palmiro Togliatti, *L'emancipazione femminile. Discorsi alle donne*, Rome: Editori riuniti, pp. 73–89.

Togliatti, Palmiro [1954] (1965c), 'La questione della posizione fatta alle donne nella società, che è in sostanza la questione dei rapporti generali che si stabiliscono fra le donne e gli uomini, non può venire ridotta al solo aspetto economico', in Palmiro Togliatti, *L'emancipazione femminile. Discorsi alle donne*, Rome: Editori riuniti, pp. 91–105.

Togliatti, Palmiro [1959] (1965d), 'La chiave per la soluzione del problema dell'emancipazione sta nel fatto che le donne accedano a quella che è, nei rapporti sociali, la sostanza della persona umana, cioè il lavoro', in Palmiro Togliatti, *L'emancipazione femminile. Discorsi alle donne*, Rome: Editori riuniti, pp. 137–49.

Treveri Gennari, Daniela (2009), *Post-War Italian Cinema: American Intervention, Vatican Interests*, Hoboken, NJ: Taylor & Francis.

Troiano, Francesco (1985), 'Un po' di Italian Horror', *Cinemasessanta* 165, September–October 1985, pp. 35–40.

Troiano, Francesco (1989), 'L'horror', in Claver Salizzato (ed.), *Prima della rivoluzione. Schermi italiani 1960–1969*, Venice: Marsilio, pp. 95–101.

Tudor, Andrew (1974), *Image and Influence: Studies in the Sociology of Film*, London: George Allen and Unwin.

Twitchell, James (1981), *The Living Dead: A Study of the Vampire in Romantic Literature*, Durham, NC: Duke University Press.
Twitchell, James (1985), *Dreadful Pleasures: An Anatomy of Modern Horror*, Oxford: Oxford University Press.
Ulin, Julieann (2015), 'Sheridan Le Fanu's Vampires and Ireland's Invited Invasion', in Sam George and Bill Hughes (eds), *Open Graves, Open Minds: Representations of Vampires and the Undead from the Enlightenment to the Present Day*, Manchester: Manchester University Press, pp. 39–55.
Unknown (1959), 'Il mulino delle donne di pietra', Italian-language unpublished treatment.
Unknown (1959–1960), 'Il Vij', Italian-language unpublished treatment.
Unknown (1960), 'La maschera del diavolo', English-language unpublished shooting script.
Unknown (1963), 'La conquista di Micene', Italian-language unpublished screenplay.
Unknown (1971), 'E venne l'alba . . . ma tinta di rosso', Italian-language unpublished screenplay.
Unknown (1973), 'Sangue per Dracula', Italian-language unpublished screenplay.
Ursini, James and Silver, Alain (1975), *The Vampire Film*, London: Tantivy Press.
Valdez Moses, Michael (1997), 'The Irish Vampire: *Dracula*, Parnell, and the Troubled Dreams of Nationhood', *Journal X* 2:1, pp. 66–111.
Valente, Joseph (2002), *Dracula's Crypt: Bram Stoker, Irishness and the Question of Blood*, Urbana: University of Illinois Press.
Valli, Bernardo (1999), *Il film ideale: i cattolici, il cinema e le comunicazioni sociali*, Milan: Angeli.
Veeder, William (1980), 'Carmilla: The Arts of Repression', *Texas Studies in Literature and Language* 22:2, pp. 197–223.
Ventavoli, Bruno (1999), *Al diavolo la celebrità: Steno dal Marc'Aurelio alla televisione: 50 anni di cinema e spettacolo in Italia*, Turin: Lindau.
Ventavoli, Luciano (1992), *Pochi, maledetti e subito: Giorgio Venturini alla FERT (1952–1957)*, Turin: Museo Nazionale del Cinema.
Venturini, Simone (2001), *Galatea SPA (1952–1965): storia di una casa di produzione cinematografica*, Rome: Associazione italiana per le ricerche di storia del cinema.
Venturini, Simone (2014), *Horror italiano*, Rome: Donzelli.
Venturini, Simone (2019), 'La produzione modulare: vampiri, cinemobili e whammo charts', *Schermi* 5, pp. 47–63.
Verdone, Mario (1960), 'Gara ingloriosa fra i produttori. Il cinema peggiora per fronteggiare la TV', *Il quotidiano*, 28 April 1960, p. 3.
Viazzi, Glauco (1940), 'Vampyr', *Bianco e Nero* 10, October 1940, pp. 92–5.
Vice (1959), 'Dracula il vampiro', *Corriere d'informazione*, 2–3 January 1959, p. 9.
Vitali, Valentina (2016), *Capital and Popular Cinema. The Dollars are Coming!*, Manchester: Manchester University Press.
von Krafft-Ebing, Richard [1886] (1991), 'Psychopatia Sexualis', in Christopher Frayling (ed.), *Vampyres. Lord Byron to Count Dracula*, revised edn, London: Faber and Faber, pp. 390–7.

Wagstaff, Christopher (1992), 'A Forkful of Westerns: Industry, Audiences and the Italian Western', in Richard Dyer and Ginette Vincendeau (eds), *Popular European Cinema*, London: Routledge, pp. 245–61.

Wagstaff, Christopher (1998), 'Italian Genre Films in the World Market', in Geoffrey Nowell-Smith and Steven Ricci (eds), *Hollywood and Europe: Economics, Culture, National Identity, 1945-1995*, London: BFI, pp. 74–85.

Wagstaff, Christopher (1999), 'Il nuovo mercato del cinema', in Gian Piero Brunetta (ed.), *Storia del cinema mondiale. Volume 1*, Turin: Einaudi, pp. 847–903.

Wagstaff, Christopher (2013), 'Italian Cinema, Popular?', in Louis Bayman and Sergio Rigoletto (eds), *Popular Italian Cinema*, Basingstoke: Palgrave, pp. 29–51.

Waller, Gregory (1985), *The Living and the Undead: from Stoker's 'Dracula' to Romero's 'Dawn of the Dead'*, Urbana: University of Illinois Press.

Warren, Louis (2002), 'Buffalo Bill Meets Dracula: William F. Cody, Bram Stoker, and the Frontiers of Racial Decay', *The American Historical Review* 107:4, pp. 1124–57.

Weinstock, Jeffrey (2012), *The Vampire Film: Undead Cinema*, London: Wallflower.

West, Rebecca (2006), '"What" as Ideal and "Who" as Real: Portraits of Wives and Mothers in Italian Postwar Domestic Manuals, Fiction and Film', in Penelope Morris (ed.), *Women in Italy, 1945–1960: An Interdisciplinary Study*, Basingstoke: Palgrave, pp. 21–34.

Wilcox, Rhonda and Lavery, David (eds) (2002), *Fighting the Forces: What's at Stake in 'Buffy the Vampire Slayer'*, Lanham, MD: Rowman and Littlefield.

Willemen, Paul (2006), 'The National Revisited', in Paul Willemen and Valentina Vitali (eds), *Theorising National Cinema*, London: BFI, pp. 29–43.

Williams, Linda (1984), 'When the Woman Looks', in Mary Ann Doane, Patricia Mellencamp and Linda Williams (eds), *Re-vision: Essays in Feminist Film Criticism*, Frederick, MD: University Publications of America, pp. 83–99.

Williamson, Milly (2005), *The Lure of the Vampire: Gender, Fiction and Fandom from Bram Stoker to Buffy*, London: Wallflower.

Willson, Perry (2010), *Women in Twentieth-Century Italy*, Basingstoke: Macmillan.

Wilson, Katharina (1985), 'The History of the Word "Vampire"', *Journal of the History of Ideas* 46:4, pp. 577–83.

Wood, Mary (2005), *Italian Cinema*, Oxford: Berg.

Wood, Robin (1979a), 'Der Erlkönig: The Ambiguities of Horror', in Robin Wood and Richard Lippe (eds), *American Nightmare: Essays on the Horror Film*, Toronto: Festival of Festivals, pp. 29–32.

Wood, Robin [1970] (1979b), 'The Dark Mirror: Murnau's *Nosferatu*', in Robin Wood and Richard Lippe (eds), *American Nightmare: Essays on the Horror Film*, Toronto: Festival of Festivals, pp. 43–9.

Wood, Robin [1979] (1985), 'An Introduction to the American Horror Film', in Bill Nichols (ed.), *Movies and Methods: An Anthology. Volume 2*, Berkeley: University of California Press, pp. 195–220.

Wood, Robin [1983] (1996), 'Burying the Undead: The Use and Obsolescence of Count Dracula', in Barry Grant (ed.), *The Dread of Difference: Gender and the Horror Film*, Austin: University of Texas Press, pp. 364–78.

Worland, Rick (2014), 'The Gothic Revival (1957–1974)', in Harry Benshoff (ed.), *A Companion to the Horror Film*, Hoboken, NJ: Wiley, pp. 273–91.

Yacowar, Maurice (1993), *The Films of Paul Morrissey*, Cambridge: Cambridge University Press.

Yavneh, Naomi (2001), 'Dante's "dolce serena" and the Monstrosity of the Female Body', in Keale Jewell (ed.), *Monsters in the Italian Literary Imagination*, Detroit, MI: Wayne State University Press, pp. 109–36.

Zagarrio, Vito (2008), 'La televisione produttrice di cinema', in Flavio De Bernardinis (ed.), *Storia del cinema italiano. Volume XII (1970–1976)*, Venice: Marsilio and Rome: Bianco e Nero, pp. 363–77.

Zanger, Jules (1991), 'A Sympathetic Vibration: Dracula and the Jews', *English Literature in Transition 1880–1920* 34:1, pp. 33–44.

Zanotto, Piero (1961), 'Il film terrorifico e galattico', *Centrofilm* 27–28, November–December 1961, pp. 3–57.

Zimmerman, Bonnie [1981] (2004), 'Daughters of Darkness: The Lesbian Vampire on Film', in Barry Grant and Christopher Sharrett (eds), *Planks of Reason: Essays on the Horror Film*, revised edn, Lanham, MD: Scarecrow Press, pp. 72–81.

INDEX

5 tombe per un medium, 63
40 gradi all'ombra del lenzuolo, 6, 121

A cena col vampiro, 7
A cuore freddo, 162
A Fistful of Dollars see *Per un pugno di dollari*
Abbott and Costello Meet Frankenstein, 16
Abruzzese, Alberto, 7
Accattone, 138
Addessi, Giovanni, 51–2, 61
Adelli, L., 20n
adultery, 88, 94, 104n, 122n
Albertazzi, Giorgio, 73n
Alessi, Ottavio, 121
Alighieri, Dante, 78–9, 83
Always on Sunday see *Una domenica d'estate*
Amendola, Mario, 6, 108, 147n
American International Pictures, 41, 59–60, 66, 83, 148n
. . . And God Created Woman see *Et Dieu . . . créa la femme*

And God Said to Cain see *E Dio disse a Caino . . .*
Andreotti, Giulio, 23, 25–6, 28, 31, 35, 58
Anemia, 7
Anselmetti, Ferdinando, 58
Antonioni, Michelangelo, 4, 31, 110, 161
apocalypticism, 18, 138, 141, 155, 158, 163
Argento, Dario, 6, 7, 12, 67, 73n, 160, 176
Arnaud, Fede, 104n
Arrivederci Roma, 24
Assignment Terror see *Los monstruos del terror*
Atom Age Vampire see *Seddok, l'erede di Satana*
austerity, 4, 127, 149, 155, 165, 168
autunno caldo, 150, 155, 168
Avanti a lui tremava tutta Roma, 143
Avventura a Capri, 71n

Bacchini, Romolo, 6
Baffico, Mario, 20n

INDEX

Baker, Roy Ward, 66, 68
Balderston, John L., 1
Balpêtré, Antoine, 40n
Bandini, Giorgio, 7
Barboni, Enzo, 34
Barros, Esmeralda, 175
Barton, Charles T., 16
Báthory, Erzsébet, 7, 66, 78, 97
Batzella, Luigi, 11, 62, 63, 99, 174
Bava, Lamberto, 7
Bava, Mario, 8, 9, 24, 32, 36, 37, 50–1, 59, 66, 69, 79, 105n, 119, 146, 157
Beach Casanova see *I Don Giovanni della Costa Azzurra*
Beatrice Cenci (1854 novel), 13
Before Him All Rome Trembled see *Avanti a lui tremava tutta Roma*
Belle ma povere, 24
Bellezze a Capri, 71n
Bene, Carmelo, 6
Berenice, 83
Bertolini, Francesco, 20n
Bertolucci, Bernardo, 63
Bianchi, Adelchi, 71n
Bianchi, Andrea, 62
Bianchi, Giorgio, 71n
Bianchi, Pietro, 14
Bicycle Thieves see *Ladri di biciclette*
Big Deal on Madonna Street see *I soliti ignoti*
Bigari, Walter, 49, 50, 63, 174
Bitter Rice see *Riso amaro*
Black Sabbath see *I tre volti della paura*
Black Sunday see *La maschera del demonio*
Blasetti, Alessandro, 31, 32–3, 34, 108
Blatty, William Peter, 63
Blood and Roses see *Il sangue e la rosa*
Blood and Sand (1941 film), 48

Blood for Dracula see *Dracula cerca sangue di vergine . . . e morì di sete!!!*
Blood of the Vampire, 71n
Bloody Pit of Horror see *Il boia scarlatto*
Boese, Carl, 15
Bolognesi, Bruno, 49
Bolognini, Mauro, 110
Boni, Enrico, 13
Bonnard, Mario, 20n
Borghesio, Carlo, 110
Borsato, Umberto, 50
Bosé, Lucia, 63, 97
Braddon, Mary Elizabeth, 20n
Bragaglia, Carlo Ludovico, 24
Bram Stoker's Dracula, 1
Bramieri, Gino, 45, 109
Brazzi, Oscar, 6
Brazzi, Rossano, 63
Brevi amori a Palma di Majorca, 71n
Brice, Pierre, 63
Bride of Frankenstein, 14
Brocani, Franco, 6
Brofferio, Angelo, 13, 48
Brooks, Mel, 67
Browning, Tod, 1, 15, 16, 20n, 140
Buffy the Vampire Slayer (TV series), 2
Buñuel, Juan Luis, 6
Burial Ground see *Le notti del terrore*
Buzzanca, Lando, 62, 115, 121, 165, 171n

C'è un fantasma nel castello, 48
Cabiria, 118, 144
Caiano, Carlo, 53, 71n
Caiano, Mario, 9, 52, 53, 62, 71n
Calandra, Edoardo, 13
Caltiki il mostro immortale, 6, 15, 51, 69, 177
Caltiki, the Immortal Monster see *Caltiki il mostro immortale*
Camerini, Mario, 32, 71n

210

Caminito, Augusto, 7
Canale, Gianna Maria, 24, 25, 103n
Capuana, Luigi, 13
Cardinali, Katia, 175
Cardone, Alberto, 173
Carmilla (1871 novella), 1, 13, 46, 50, 52, 70, 80, 104n
Carpentieri, Luigi, 23–8, 52
Carsten, Peter, 61
case chiuse, 86–7, 89
Cass, Henry, 71n
Castelnuovo, Nino, 63
Castle of Blood see *Danza macabra*
Catalano, Elisabetta, 99
Catene, 90
Celi, Adolfo, 157
Chains see *Catene*
Chiari, Walter, 48
Christian Democracy, 7, 16, 19, 25, 26, 28, 29, 31, 43, 44, 84, 86, 87, 89, 90, 108, 114, 127, 128, 129, 132, 137, 138, 145, 146, 149, 152, 153, 168
Cicero, Nando, 123n
Cifra, 13
City of Women see *La città delle donne*
Civita, Cesare, 20n
Cold Blooded Beast see *La bestia uccide a sangue freddo*
Cold War, 68, 145, 149, 169
Come Have Coffee with Us see *Venga a prendere il caffè . . . da noi*
Come persi la guerra, 110
Comencini, Luigi, 71n, 144
compromesso storico, 169
Conan the Barbarian (1982 film), 35
congiuntura, 133, 141, 152, 153, 154, 155
Conte, Richard, 175
Conquest of Mycene see *Ercole contro Moloch*
Coppola, Francis Ford, 2, 39

Corman, Roger, 41
Corona, Achille, 26, 36, 149
Costa Azzurra, 71n
Cottafavi, Vittorio, 141
Count Dracula see *Il Conte Dracula*
Countess Dracula, 73n
Crawford, Francis Marion, 19n, 20n
Croce, Benedetto, 12, 14, 68, 143
Crypt of the Vampire see *La cripta e l'incubo*
cultural instrumentality, 4, 18, 19n, 23, 141, 144
Curse of the Undead, 71n
Curtiz, Michael, 15, 50, 66

D'Amico, Luigi Filippo, 123
D'Annunzio, Gabriele, 13, 121
Damon, Mark, 51, 63
Dance of the Vampires, 67, 97, 121, 170n
Danger: Diabolik see *Diabolik* (1967 film)
Danza macabra, 9, 51–2, 54, 57, 59, 61, 63, 66, 73n, 83, 90, 94, 97, 104n, 105n, 112, 115, 140–1, 177
Das Cabinet des Dr. Caligari, 15
Das Wachsfigurenkabinett, 15
Daughters of Darkness see *Les lèvres rouges*
Day of Wrath see *Vredens dag*
de Concini, Ennio, 91
de Feo, Giuseppe, 13
De Gasparini, A., 13
De Laurentiis, Dino, 32, 53, 56
de Liguoro, Giuseppe, 20n
de Ossorio, Amando, 6, 62, 67
De Santis, Giuseppe, 30, 143, 161
De Sica, Vittorio, 4, 109–10, 144
De Simone, Ugo, 14
De Toth, André, 15, 50, 66
Deane, Hamilton, 1
Dein, Edward, 47, 71n
del Colle, Ubaldo Maria, 20n
Demicheli, Tulio, 7

Der Golem, wie er in die Welt kam, 15
Der Student von Prag (1913 film), 15
Der Student von Prag (1926 film), 15
di Giulio, Gianni, 175–6
di Leo, Fernando, 74n
Diabolik (1967 film), 157
Dialogo di Federico Ruysch e delle sue mummie, 13
Diciottenni al sole, 71n
Dinner with a Vampire see *A cena col vampiro*
divorce, 50, 88, 101, 122n
Doctor Blood's Coffin, 71n
Domenica d'agosto, 71n
Don Giovanni in Sicilia, 165
Don Juan in Sicily see *Don Giovanni in Sicilia*
Donati, Ermanno, 23–8, 52
Donner, Clive, 67
Doria, Enzo, 60, 160
Douglas, Kirk, 32
Dr. Jekyll and Mr. Hyde (1920 film), 15
Dr. Jekyll and Mr. Hyde (1931 film), 15
Dr. Jekyll and Mr. Hyde (1941 film), 15, 47
Dracula (1897 novel), 1, 13–14, 20n, 45, 81, 118, 135–6, 156
Dracula (1931 film), 1, 3, 15
Dracula (1958 film), 1, 3, 12, 17, 30, 34, 41–4, 46, 47, 48, 49, 50, 53, 54, 58, 59, 66, 69, 70, 72n, 77, 78, 108, 115, 116, 117, 120, 122n, 134, 136, 139, 146, 156, 169n
Dracula 3D, 6, 7
Dracula ai bagni, 139
Dracula and Son see *Dracula père et fils*
Dracula cerca sangue di vergine . . . e morì di sete!!!, 11, 18, 60, 61, 62, 65, 66–7, 96, 97, 104n, 113, 114, 121, 150, 163–5, 178

Dracula Has Risen from the Grave, 66, 156
Dracula in the Provinces see *Il cav. Costante Nicosia demoniaco, ovvero: Dracula in Brianza*
Dracula père et fils, 67
Dracula: Prince of Darkness, 45, 59, 66, 71n, 91, 156
Dracula's Daughter, 16
Dracula's Guest, 63
Dracula terrore d'oltre tomba, 174–5, 178
Dreyer, Carl Theodor, 15, 20n, 50, 91, 104n

E Dio disse a Caino . . . , 61
'E scugnizze, 20n
economic miracle, 4, 18, 84, 88, 108, 110, 127–32, 133, 134, 137, 138, 139, 151, 152, 168
Eger, Raymond, 50
Eighteen in the Sun see *Diciottenni al sole*
El ataúd del vampiro, 41
El vampiro, 41, 71n
Embassy Pictures, 32, 71n, 148n
Emmer, Luciano, 71n, 73n
Ercole al centro della Terra, 8, 53, 56, 73n, 113, 114, 118, 141, 142, 143, 144, 146, 147, 177
Ercole contro Moloch, 9, 53–4, 56, 113, 114, 118, 141, 142, 144, 146, 147, 177
Erika, 62
Estate violenta, 144
Et Dieu . . . créa la femme, 50
Europa di notte, 31, 34, 108
European Nights see *Europa di notte*
Everybody Go Home! see *Tutti a casa*
Eyes without a Face see *Les yeux sans visage*

Fabiola, 32
Fangs of the Living Dead see *Malenka, la nipote del vampiro*

Farina, Corrado, 7, 10, 62, 155–60, 162, 164, 169n, 170n
Fascism, 14, 16, 18, 26, 40n, 84, 86, 87, 108, 109, 110, 128, 131, 141–7, 151, 162, 170n
Faust (1914 film), 20n
Faust (1926 film) see *Faust: Eine deutsche Volkssage*
Faust: Eine deutsche Volkssage, 15
Fellini, Federico, 4, 110, 113
Fellini's Casanova see *Il Casanova di Federico Fellini*
feminism, 2, 3, 17, 81, 83, 84, 89, 90, 95, 100–2, 119, 158
  autocoscienza, 100, 101, 102
  gender struggle, 3, 18, 84–90, 101, 108–9
  gynophobia, 81–3
  gynosociality, 81, 89, 101
  heteronormativity, 80–1, 86, 94, 121, 122n, 167
  housewife, 78, 85, 88–9, 95, 108–9, 120
  Italian feminist groups, 89, 100–3
  Lost Wave, 84, 85, 89, 101
  machismo, 112, 113, 115, 118, 121
  marriage, 18, 80, 87, 94, 95, 119, 137, 138, 151, 164, 165
  masculinity, 3, 18, 80–1, 87, 103, 107–21, 122n
  matriarchy, 83, 84, 89–90, 95
  misogyny, 3, 18, 81, 85, 89, 90–1, 102–3, 107, 117, 119
  monogamy, 18, 94, 95, 114–15, 138
  motherhood, 80, 85–6, 87, 89, 101
  patriarchy, 3, 18, 80–4, 86–90, 93–5, 100, 102, 108, 119–21, 145
  virility, 18, 85, 109, 110, 113
Fenech, Edwige, 121
Ferragosto in bikini, 71n
Ferrer, Mel, 50
Ferreri, Marco, 110, 161
Ferroni, Giorgio, 8, 9, 10, 50, 60, 63
Festa Campanile, Pasquale, 123n, 165
fetishism, 82–3
Fifa e arena, 48
Fisher, Terence, 1, 41–4, 45, 46, 59, 66, 71n, 108, 116, 122n, 140, 169n
Fleming, Victor, 15
Flemyng, Robert, 52
Flesh for Frankenstein see *Il mostro è in tavola . . . barone Frankenstein*
Football Crazy see *L'arbitro*
For the Blood Is the Life, 20n
Fracchia contro Dracula, 7
Franchi, Franco, 48, 171n
Franciolini, Gianni, 71n
Francis, Freddie, 66, 67
Francisci, Pietro, 32, 41, 146
Franco, Jesús, 10, 60, 67, 96
Franju, Georges, 50
Frankenstein (1931 film), 15
Frankenstein and Company, 46
Frateili, Arnaldo, 20n
Fratter, Roger A., 7
Freda, Riccardo, 6, 7, 8, 9, 15, 16, 17, 23–9, 33, 40n, 41, 48, 51, 52, 66, 69, 78, 91, 103n, 110, 139, 140, 146
Freund, Karl, 15
Friedkin, William, 12, 67
Frusta, Arrigo, 20n
Fulci, Lucio, 11, 62, 67, 69, 165–6, 169, 171n
Furie, Sidney J., 71n

Gabel, Scilla, 104n
Galatea, 32, 51, 54, 59, 60, 73n, 148n
Galeen, Henrik, 15
Gallone, Carmine, 20n, 143
Gassman, Vittorio, 139
Gastaldi, Ernesto, 49, 52
Gebissen wird nur nachts, 67
Geminus, 73n

INDEX

Gender stereotypes
  damsel in distress, 78, 80, 82, 94, 96, 104n, 112
  dashing hero, 78, 81, 94
  dominatrix, 83–4, 94, 102, 120, 121, 167
  femme fatale, 80, 93, 107
  gallo, 18, 110, 113–19, 122n
  Madonna, 81, 86–7, 93, 105n
  Magdalen, 81, 87, 93
  pater familias, 18, 120
  strega, 78–9, 82, 91, 96, 98–9, 101–3, 105n, 108
General Della Rovere see *Il generale Della Rovere*
Genina, Augusto, 20n
Gentilomo, Giacomo, 8, 9, 148n
Ghione, Riccardo, 11, 62, 161–2, 164, 170n
Gibson, Alan, 120
Giorni di gloria, 143–4
Giovanna d'Arco al rogo, 91
Girolami, Marino, 49, 71n
Gli enigmi del vampiro, 14
Gogol, Nikolaj, 50–1
Golgi, Maria Antonietta, 111
Goliath and the Vampires see *Maciste contro il vampiro*
Good Lady Ducayne, 20n
Granata, Graziella, 104n
Grau, Jorge, 11, 60
Grimaldi, Alberto, 71n
Grimaldi, Giovanni, 123n, 141, 165
Grunstein, Pierre, 67
Guazzoni, Enrico, 20n
Guerrazzi, Francesco Domenico, 13
Guerrini, Mino, 6
Guest, Val, 51
Guidi Cingolani, Angela Maria, 84, 108

Hackett, Pat, 104n
Hammer, 1, 3, 12, 17, 30, 31, 34, 41–3, 45, 47, 48, 49, 50, 53, 58, 59, 60, 66, 67, 68, 69, 70, 72n, 73n, 77, 78, 91, 96, 105n, 108, 112, 114, 115, 116, 117, 118, 120, 134, 136, 139, 146, 156
... *Hanno cambiato faccia*, 10, 18, 62, 63, 64, 67, 97, 102, 150, 155–9, 160, 161, 169n, 170n, 178
Hardwicke, Catherine, 3
Hargitay, Mickey, 63, 110
Hercules (1958 film) see *Le fatiche di Ercole*
Hercules against the Moon Men see *Maciste e la regina di Samar*
Hercules in the Haunted World see *Ercole al centro della Terra*
Hillyer, Lambert, 16
Hitchcock, Alfred, 52
Hoepli, Gianni, 20n
Holiday Island see *Vacanze a Ischia*
Hollywood, 15, 25–6, 30–2, 35, 38–9, 40n, 41, 42, 45, 47, 50, 66, 81, 109
  Columbia, 41
  dumping, 25, 30, 40n
  MGM, 30, 31
  Motion Picture Association of America, 31
  Paramount, 12, 30, 31, 33, 50, 55, 70
  runaway productions, 7, 31–2
  Universal, 1, 12, 41, 42, 44, 45, 66, 77, 83, 92
  Warner Bros., 30, 31, 41, 42, 52, 56
Homo eroticus, 123n, 165
homosexuality
  gay male vampires, 67, 115, 122n
  lesbian vampires, 68, 78, 80–1, 84, 90, 94, 98–9, 102–3, 104n, 105n, 122n
Homunculus, 15
honour killing, 88, 109
Horror (magazine), 66, 73n
House of Dracula, 16, 71n
House of Wax (1953 film), 15, 50, 66

I Am Legend (1954 novel), 24
I Don Giovanni della Costa Azzurra, 71n
I figli di nessuno, 90
I'll Never Forget What's'isname, 156
I mostri, 147n
I racconti di Canterbury, 35
I racconti di Dracula, 46–7, 60, 117
I rettili umani, 20n
I soliti ignoti, 110
I tartassati, 148n
I tre volti della paura, 9, 51–2, 56, 59, 66, 72n, 73n, 82–3, 94, 97, 102, 105n, 110, 111–12, 113, 115, 119–20, 140, 177
I vampiri, 6, 7, 8, 15, 16, 17, 20n, 23–30, 32, 40n, 41, 42, 48, 49, 50, 55, 58, 59, 66, 68, 71n, 78, 80, 91, 92, 94, 97, 103n, 112, 139, 140, 161, 177
I vampiri. Romanzo umoristico, 13
I vampiri tra noi: 37 storie vampiriche, 45, 73n
I vitelloni, 110
I Wurdalak see *I tre volti della paura*
Il bell'Antonio, 110
Il boia scarlatto, 63, 110
Il cappello da prete, 20n
Il carro armato dell'8 settembre, 144
Il Casanova di Federico Fellini, 113
Il caso Valdemar, 20n
Il cav. Costante Nicosia demoniaco, ovvero: Dracula in Brianza, 11, 18, 62, 65, 66–7, 108, 113, 114, 115, 118, 121, 150, 165–9, 171n, 178
Il Conte Dracula, 10, 60, 64, 66, 96, 97, 113, 114, 115, 116, 120–1, 178
Il cuore rivelatore, 20n
Il Decameron (1971 film), 34–5
Il diavolo zoppo, 20n
Il dottor Nero, 13
Il fantasma, 20n
Il federale, 144
Il figlio di Dracula, 7, 169n
Il gatto di Brooklyn aspirante detective, 6
Il gatto mammone, 123n
Il Gattopardo (1958 novel), 134, 140
Il generale Della Rovere, 144
Il gobbo, 144
Il Grande Persuasore, 156
Il grido, 110
Il ladro di Bagdad, 53
Il magnate, 165, 171n
Il merlo maschio, 123n
Il mio amico Jekyll, 49
Il mondo di notte, 34
Il mostro dell'Opera, 9, 52, 53, 57, 58, 63, 104n, 113, 114, 116, 119, 140, 177
Il mostro di Frankenstein, 20n
Il mostro è in tavola . . . barone Frankenstein, 62, 178
Il mulino delle donne di pietra, 8, 30, 50, 51, 54, 55, 59, 63, 78, 80, 91, 92–5, 104n, 107, 112, 161, 177
Il plenilunio delle vergini, 11, 62, 63, 65, 67–8, 73n, 74n, 96, 97, 98–9, 102–3, 121, 174, 178
Il prato macchiato di rosso, 11, 18, 62–3, 65, 67, 73n, 102, 150, 159, 161–3, 170n, 178
Il sangue e la rosa, 8, 30, 46, 50, 51, 55, 70, 72n, 90, 94, 97,104n, 105n, 140, 173, 177
Il seduttore, 110
Il sindacalista, 165, 171n
Il suicida n. 359, 14
Il teschio del vampiro, 173, 177
Il trionfo della morte, 13
Il vampiro (1801 opera seria), 13
Il vampiro (1827 comedy), 13, 48
Il vampiro (1902 short story), 13
Il vampiro (1908 short story), 13
Il vampiro (1914 film), 6, 19n
Il vampiro (1917 short story), 13

INDEX

Il vampiro (1921 short story), 13
Il vampiro (1940 short story), 13
Il vampiro (1964 monograph), 46
Il vampiro della foresta, 13
Il vampiro della strada, 7
Il vampiro. Storia vera, 13
Il vichingo venuto dal sud, 123n
Incanto di mezzanotte, 20n
Ingrassia, Ciccio, 48, 67, 171n
Interview with the Vampire (1994 film), 2
Io credo nei vampiri, 46
Io e lui, 123n
It Happened in 1943 see *La lunga notte del '43*
Italian Communist Party, 19, 85, 86, 87, 100, 128, 132, 145, 146, 148n, 154, 169
Italian Constitution, 85, 128, 131, 135
Italian film industry
  cinema attendance, 38
  European co-productions, 7, 25, 31, 33, 35–7, 40n, 50, 51, 52, 54, 58, 60–1, 70, 71n, 72n, 73n, 160, 162
  Italian Film Censorship Office, 4, 5–6, 7, 8–11, 15, 16, 17, 19n, 20n, 28, 42–4, 47–8, 54, 55–7, 58, 64–5, 67–8, 70, 71n, 79, 97, 103, 104n, 122n, 127, 137, 141, 147, 147n
  Italian Show Business Bureau, 4, 5, 7, 24, 26, 28, 39n, 49, 51, 52, 53, 54, 60, 61, 62, 71n, 72n, 73n, 93, 104n, 127, 137, 141, 147n, 149, 173, 174, 177
  joint participations, 35, 40n, 70, 73n
  law 1213 of 4 November 1965, 26, 36
  law 161 of 21 April 1962, 54, 128
  law 448 of 26 July 1949, 26, 27
  law 897 of 31 July 1956, 26
  law 958 of 29 December 1949, 26, 28
  minimo garantito, 23, 27, 28, 30, 32, 33, 34, 35, 38, 49, 50, 51, 52, 53, 54, 58, 61, 62, 173
  preventive censorship, 28, 39n, 40n, 54, 69, 72n, 105n, 173, 175
  prima, *seconda* and *terza visione* theatres, 32, 33, 34, 39, 40n, 44, 49, 58, 63
  productive crisis, 7, 17, 25, 31, 36–9, 54
  'special norm' of 1951, 31–2, 40n
  state credit, 24, 26–7, 28, 29, 30, 32, 34, 48, 51, 53, 54, 58
  Vatican censorship, 16, 44, 55–7, 58, 64–5, 68, 122n
Italian genre cinema, 19, 32, 39, 96, 110, 138, 141, 146, 159
  commedia all'italiana, 110, 113, 139, 144
  decamerotico, 34–5, 36, 121
  erotic-exotic doc/mock/shockumentaries, 34, 108, 117
  fagioli western, 34, 36, 40n
  filone, 17, 30, 34–7, 39, 48, 49, 58, 59–60, 66, 67, 71n, 77, 80, 82, 83, 89, 95, 96, 99, 101, 107, 110, 112, 113, 117, 139, 141, 144, 159
  giallo, 20n, 35, 36, 67, 74n, 159, 176
  horror, 5, 7–12, 15, 16, 18, 23–5, 28, 30, 34, 36, 41, 49–70, 77–84, 89, 90–103, 107–8, 110–14, 116–21, 139–41, 149, 155–65, 170n, 173–6
  melodrama, 5, 90–3, 95
  parody, 18, 30, 34, 48–9, 54, 67, 133, 139, 141, 149, 165, 168, 169n
  peplum, 17, 30, 32–6, 41, 51, 52, 53–4, 58, 59, 83, 89, 91, 103n, 108, 110, 114, 118, 141–7, 148n, 149
  spaghetti western, 34, 36, 40n, 59, 60, 61

Italian private TV networks, 38, 40n, 72n
Italian Republic, 26, 80, 85, 87, 109, 146, 152
Italian Socialist Party, 127, 128, 132, 146, 149, 153, 154
Italian State Radio, 45, 86, 89, 146
Italian State TV, 38, 40n, 45, 52, 58, 72n, 73n, 86, 89, 108, 109, 146, 156

Jacula (comic book), 67, 99–100, 121, 122n
Jekyll, 73n
Jessua, Alain, 11, 60, 162, 164
Joan of Arc at the Stake see Giovanna d'Arco al rogo
Jordan, Neil, 2
Journey to the Center of the Earth (1959 film), 53
Julian, Rupert, 15
Juliette, 13
Jus primae noctis, 165

Kalida'a la storia di una mummia, 20n
Karloff, Boris, 51
Kenton, Erle C., 16, 71n
Kinski, Klaus, 61
KKK, 46, 60, 117
Körkarlen, 15
Koscina, Sylva, 49, 63, 175
Kümel, Harry, 67, 96

L'altro io, 20n
L'amante del demonio, 6
L'amante del vampiro, 8, 30, 49, 54, 55, 58, 59, 63, 71n, 80, 83, 94, 95, 104n, 113, 114, 116–17, 119–20, 139, 140
L'arbitro, 123n
L'arte di arrangiarsi, 110
L'esorciccio, 67
L'imperatore di Capri, 71n
L'inafferrabile invincibile Mr. Invisibile, 61
L'Inferno (1911 film), 20n
L'ispettore Bramiè: La fine del vampiro, 58
L'orribile segreto del Dr. Hichcock, 9, 52, 56, 58, 59, 72n, 80, 94, 95, 110–12, 119, 140, 161, 177
L'uccello dalle piume di cristallo, 12, 67, 68
L'uccello migratore, 165
L'ultima preda del vampiro, 8, 30, 49–50, 54, 55, 58, 59, 63, 72n, 83, 112, 113, 114, 116, 119, 140, 177
L'ultimo uomo della Terra, 7
L'uomo che dormì 130 anni, 20n
L'uomo che uccideva a sangue freddo, 11, 18, 60, 61, 65, 66, 67, 73n, 150, 159, 161–3, 178
L'uomo dall'orecchio mozzato, 20n
La ballata della strega, 20n
La bara di vetro, 20n
La bestia uccide a sangue freddo, 74n
La carezza del vampiro, 6, 19n
La cavallona see 40 gradi all'ombra del lenzuolo
La ciociara, 144
La città delle donne, 110
La classe operaia va in paradiso, 158
La corta notte delle bambole di vetro, 10, 18, 60–1, 64, 67, 73n, 150, 159–61
La cripta e l'incubo, 9, 52, 57, 59, 63, 72n, 80–1, 90–1, 94, 95, 98, 104n, 105n, 140, 177
La dama bianca, 20n
La dolce vita, 110
La famille du Vourdalak, 51–2, 73n, 102, 105n
La frusta e il corpo, 119
La giovinezza del diavolo, 20n
La lunga notte del '43, 144
La madre e la morte, 20n
La maschera del demonio, 8, 30, 37, 50–1, 52, 53, 55, 59, 69, 72n, 78–80, 82, 90–2, 94–5, 98, 103n, 104n, 105n, 110–12, 115, 140, 177

INDEX

La morte negli occhi del gatto, 6
La notte dei dannati, 10, 62–3, 64, 67–8, 73n, 74n, 96, 97, 98, 99, 102–3, 178
La notte dei diavoli, 10, 60, 61–2, 63, 64, 66, 73n, 96, 97, 102, 115, 178
La paura fa 90, 20n
La prima notte del Dottor Danieli, industriale, col complesso del . . . giocattolo, 123n
La rivoluzione sessuale, 162
La sposa dei secoli, 20n
La strage dei vampiri, 8, 52, 53, 56, 59, 63, 80, 83, 94, 104n, 112, 113, 114, 116, 119, 140, 177
La strega di Siviglia, 20n
La terrificante visione, 14
La torre dei vampiri, 6, 19n
La vampira indiana, 6, 19n
La vendetta di Lady Morgan, 10, 52, 53, 57, 70, 72n, 112, 115, 140–1, 178
Lado, Aldo, 10, 60, 159–61, 164
Ladri di biciclette, 109
Ladrón de cadáveres, 41
Lady Frankenstein, 62
Landis, James, 71n
Landres, Paul, 71n
Las alegres vampiras de Vögel, 67
Last Tango in Paris see *Ultimo tango a Parigi*
Lattuada, Alberto, 20n, 97, 165
Laurenti, Mariano, 121
Lazzarella, 24
Le Fanu, Sheridan, 1, 13, 81, 140
Le fatiche di Ercole, 32–4, 41, 49, 51, 146
Le frisson des vampires, 98
Le notti del terrore, 62
Le vergini cavalcano la morte, 11, 60, 61, 65, 66, 73n, 96, 97, 102, 178
LeBorg, Reginald, 71n
Lee, Christopher, 43, 45, 49, 52, 53, 59, 60, 68, 114, 115, 118, 175

Leni, Paul, 15
Lenzi, Umberto, 74n
Leone, Sergio, 34, 59
Leoni, Guido, 48
Leonor, 6
Leopardi, Giacomo, 12, 13, 14, 68
Leroux, Gaston, 53
LeRoy, Mervyn, 31
Les lèvres rouges, 67, 96, 98
Les sorcières de Salem, 91
Les yeux sans visage, 50
Levin, Henry, 53
Lipartiti, Giuseppe, 71n
Lizzani, Carlo, 144, 161
Lo chiamavano Trinità . . ., 34, 40n
Lo sceicco bianco, 110
Lo spettro (1907 film), 20n
Lo spettro (1963 film), 110
Lombardo, Paolo, 6
London after Midnight, 16
Longo, Tiziano, 50
Los monstruos del terror, 7
Love on the Riviera see *Racconti d'estate*
Lubin, Arthur, 15, 53
Lugosi, Bela, 20n, 116
Lulu the Tool see *La classe operaia va in paradiso*
Lust of the Vampire see *I vampiri*
Lux, 32, 33, 51

Macario, Erminio, 110
Maciste all'Inferno (1962 film), 91
Maciste contro il vampiro, 8, 53–4, 56, 113, 114, 118, 141, 142, 143, 144, 146, 147, 148n, 177
Maciste e la regina di Samar, 9, 53, 54, 57, 83, 89, 90, 141, 142, 143, 144, 146, 147, 148n, 177
Maggi, Luigi, 20n
Magnaghi, Ubaldo, 20n
Majano, Anton Giulio, 6
Maldera, Roberto, 61
Malenka, la nipote del vampiro, 6, 19n, 62, 67

Malìa (magazine), 47, 60, 71n, 72n, 117, 173
Malicious see *Malizia*
Malizia, 63
Malombra (1917 film), 20n
Malombra (1942 film), 20n
Mamma Roma, 138
Mamoulian, Rouben, 15, 48
Manetti, Antonio, 7
Manetti, Marco, 7
Mangano, Silvana, 32
Manichaeism, 78, 90, 118, 142, 144, 146, 159, 161
Manzanos Brochero, Eduardo, 61
Manzoni, Alessandro, 12, 14, 68
Marcuse, Herbert, 149, 152, 156–8
Margheriti, Antonio, 6, 9, 10, 11, 51, 60, 61, 62, 63, 66, 69, 73n
Mark of the Vampire, 16, 20n
Marrama, Daniele Oberto, 13
Martella, Vittorio, 13
Martinelli, Elsa, 50
Martino, Sergio, 6, 121
Marxism, 2–3, 17, 18, 80, 83, 100, 127, 132, 138, 139, 141, 149, 151, 154, 163–5, 169, 170n
   aristocracy, 1, 19n, 20n, 48, 92, 114, 116, 118, 120, 128, 131, 134–41, 147n, 159, 163–5, 167, 168
   bourgeoisie, 2, 3, 34, 67, 93, 112, 127, 130–41, 148n, 149, 154, 155, 158, 161–3, 165–9
   class struggle, 2, 18, 127, 133–41, 149–69
   consumer capitalism, 18, 80, 89, 108–9, 129–32, 137, 149, 151, 156, 159, 170n
   feudalism, 131, 133, 135, 137–8, 139, 165
   imperialism, 2, 38, 127, 151, 162
   serfdom, 134, 136, 137–41, 163, 164, 166
   working class, 33, 88–9, 128–32, 137, 152–9, 162–9

Masi, Marco, 173
Mastriani, Francesco, 13
Mastrocinque, Camillo, 9, 20n, 52, 71n
Matarazzo, Raffaello, 90, 92
Matheson, Richard, 24, 40n
Mattoli, Mario, 48, 71n
Mauri, Roberto, 8, 52
Mazzolotti, Pier Angelo, 20n
Mendez, Fernando, 41, 71n
Meyer, Stephenie, 1
Milius, John, 35
Mill of the Stone Women see *Il mulino delle donne di pietra*
Miller, Arthur, 91, 105n
Minnelli, Vincente, 45
Mistrali, Franco, 13, 15
Mistress of the Devil see *Leonor*
Mitchell, Gordon, 175
Molinaro, Édouard, 67
Mondadori, Alberto, 20n
Mondaini, Sandra, 45
Monicelli, Mario, 20n, 110
Montesi, Wilma, 20n
Montresor, Beni, 24
Morando, Francesco Ernesto, 13
Morrissey, Paul, 11, 60, 62, 163–4
Movimento Sociale Italiano, 145–6
Mr. Superinvisible see *L'inafferrabile invincibile Mr. Invisibile*
Murnau, F. W., 3, 15, 20n, 127
My Friend, Dr. Jekyll see *Il mio amico Jekyll*
Mystery of the Wax Museum, 15, 50, 66

Nazism, 18, 84, 102, 141–4, 146, 148n, 162, 170n
necrophilia, 52, 72n, 78, 110
Necropolis, 6
Nella città vampira, 7
Nella stretta morsa del ragno, 10, 60, 61, 63, 64, 66, 68, 73n, 97, 105n, 115, 178
neorealism, 30, 68, 141–2
Neri, Rosalba, 98–9, 175

INDEX

Night of the Damned see *La notte dei dannati*
Night of the Devils see *La notte dei diavoli*
Night of the Living Dead (1968 film), 12, 66, 68, 73n
Nightmare Castle see *Amanti d'oltretomba*
No One Will Notice You are Naked see *Il vichingo venuto dal sud*
Nobody's Children see *I figli di nessuno*
Nonostante le apparenze . . . e purché la nazione non lo sappia . . . all'Onorevole piacciono le donne, 165, 171n
Norman, Leslie, 51
Nosferatu: A Symphony of Horror see *Nosferatu, eine Symphonie des Grauens*
Nosferatu a Venezia, 7
Nosferatu, eine Symphonie des Grauens, 3, 15, 20n, 127
Nota, Maria, 104n
Notari, Elvira, 20n
Notte romantica di Dolly, ovvero: Angoscia di Dolly, 20n
Nyby, Christian, 15

Old Dracula, 67
Orlacs Hände, 15
Oxilia, Nino, 20n

Padovan, Adolfo, 20n
Paganini, Luciano, 7
Pagliero, Marcello, 143
Palomba, Giuseppe, 13, 48
Paluzzi, Luciana, 175
Parenti, Neri, 7
Park, Reg, 53
Pasolini, Pier Paolo, 4, 34–5, 138, 149, 154
Pastrone, Giovanni, 118
Peccati d'estate, 71n
Per un pugno di dollari, 34, 59

Pérez Tabernero, Julio, 67
Pesola, Gianni, 175
Petri, Elio, 158
Petroni, Giulio, 71n
Pisanti, Achille, 7
Pius XII, 79, 86, 89
Poe, Edgar Allan, 12, 41, 46, 59, 60, 83
Poggioli, Ferdinando Maria, 20n
Polanski, Roman, 12, 67, 97, 121, 175
Polidori, John, 1, 13, 45
Polselli, Renato, 8, 9, 10, 49, 50, 52, 62, 63, 69
Ponti, Carlo, 32, 62
Prest, Thomas Peckett, 19n
Psycho (1960 film), 52
psychoanalysis, 2–3, 17, 80, 82–4, 100, 158
  castration anxiety, 80, 82, 83
  incest, 102, 105n, 107, 162
  sexual repression, 2, 3, 80–1, 170n
  vagina dentata, 2, 83
Puccini, Gianni, 144
Pupillo, Massimo, 10, 52, 63, 110
Purgatorio, 78–9

Quel fantasma di mio marito, 20n
Quel gran pezzo della Ubalda tutta nuda e tutta calda, 121
Quo Vadis (1951 film), 31–2

Racconti d'estate, 71n
Radcliffe, Ann, 19n
Ragona, Ubaldo, 7
Rapsodia satanica, 20n
Rascel, Renato, 45, 48, 50, 58, 114, 138
Rascel marine, 48
Rascel-fifi, 48
Ratti, Filippo Walter, 10, 62
reconstruction, 18, 84, 89, 127, 128, 143
Regnoli, Piero, 8, 49–50, 52
Reich, Wilhelm, 162

Rémy, Hélène, 49
Requiem for a Vampire see *Requiem pour un vampire*
Rice, Anne, 1
Rippert, Otto, 15
Risi, Dino, 24, 147n
Riso amaro, 30, 32
Riti, magie nere e segrete orge nel Trecento . . ., 10, 62, 63, 65, 67–8, 74n, 96–7, 113, 114, 116, 178
Riuscirà l'avvocato Franco Benenato a sconfiggere il suo acerrimo nemico il pretore Ciccio De Ingras?, 6
Rivière, Georges, 51
Roberti, Roberto, 6, 14, 20n
Robertson, John S., 15
Rocco and his Brothers see *Rocco e i suoi fratelli*
Rocco e i suoi fratelli, 138
Rolando, Maria Luisa, 104n
Rollin, Jean, 67, 96, 98, 99
Roma città aperta, 30, 143
Roma contro Roma, 9, 53, 54, 56, 58, 59, 73n, 83, 89, 90, 111, 141, 142, 143, 144, 146, 147, 148n, 177
Rome, Open City see *Roma città aperta*
Romero, George, 12, 66, 73n
Rosemary's Baby (1968 film), 12, 67, 68
Rosenfeld, Arturo, 20n
Rossellini, Roberto, 4, 30, 91, 143, 144
Rossi, Franco, 110
Rossi Pianelli, Vittorio, 6
Requiem pour un vampire, 99
Rouleau, Raymond, 91
Rowland, Roy, 24
Rye, Stellan, 15
Rymer, James Malcolm, 19n

sadism, 44, 68, 82, 83, 93, 117
sadomasochism, 119, 121

Sala, Vittorio, 71n
Salazar, Abel, 41
Salce, Luciano, 123n, 144, 165
Salgari, Emilio, 13
Salkow, Sidney, 7
Salomé (1972 film), 6
Samperi, Salvatore, 60, 63
Sangue per il vampiro (Nosferatu story), 175–6
Sasdy, Peter, 66, 73n
Satana, 20n
Satanik (comic book), 80
Scandali al mare, 71n
Scars of Dracula, 66, 156
Scott, Gordon, 53–4
Second World War, 18, 25, 30, 84, 85, 108, 110, 113, 141, 142, 145, 168
  1943 armistice, 141, 142, 143, 144
  Liberation, 40n, 141
  Repubblica Sociale Italiana, 141, 142–3, 144, 145
  Resistance, 84, 143, 144, 145–6
Seddok, l'erede di Satana, 6
Serandrei, Mario, 143
Sessantotto, 151–2, 154, 156, 159
Sete da vampira, 7
Sette orchidee macchiate di rosso, 74n
Seven Blood-Stained Orchids see *Sette orchidee macchiate di rosso*
Seven Dead in the Cat's Eye see *La morte negli occhi del gatto*
Seven Hills of Rome see *Arrivederci Roma*
Sex with a Smile see *40 gradi all'ombra del lenzuolo*
Sexy proibitissimo, 6, 108, 117, 147n
Sherman, Vincent, 16
Shock Treatment see *L'uomo che uccideva a sangue freddo*
Short Night of Glass Dolls see *La corta notte delle bambole di vetro*
Simonelli, Giorgio, 20n, 48
Siodmak, Robert, 16

Sjöström, Victor, 15
Slaughter of the Vampires see *La strage dei vampiri*
sociology
   conspicuous consumption, 131–2, 166
   economic capital, 131, 134, 164, 166
   social capital, 134, 164, 166
   social distinction, 131–2, 134, 167
   social promotion, 131–2, 137, 139–40, 165
   symbolic capital, 131, 166, 167
Soldati, Mario, 20n
Son of Dracula, 16
Sordi, Alberto, 110, 139
Spartaco (1953 film), 103n
Steele, Barbara, 51, 52, 53, 59, 99
Steiner, John, 115
Steno, 8, 45, 48, 123n, 138–9, 148n, 165, 168, 171n
Stevenson, Robert Louis, 14, 46
Stoker, Bram, 1, 13–14, 20n, 45, 60, 63, 81, 118, 135, 136, 140, 156, 157, 160
Strano, Dino, 175
strategia della tensione, 155, 159
student movement, 100–1, 150, 152, 154, 155

Tambroni, Fernando, 145, 149, 151, 152, 154
Taste the Blood of Dracula, 66, 156
Tempi duri per i vampiri, 8, 18, 30, 45, 48–9, 50, 53, 54, 55, 58, 71n, 73n, 108, 113, 114–15, 118, 122n, 133–9, 140, 141, 147n, 148n, 149, 168, 177
Tender Dracula see *Tendre Dracula*
Tendre Dracula, 67
Teodora, imperatrice di Bisanzio, 33
Teodora, Slave Empress see *Teodora, imperatrice di Bisanzio*
Terror-Creatures from the Grave see *5 tombe per un medium*

Testa, Eugenio, 20n
The Art of Getting Along see *L'arte di arrangiarsi*
The Bird with the Crystal Plumage see *L'uccello dalle piume di cristallo*
The Black Sleep, 71n
The Blob (1958 film), 51
The Body Snatcher (1957 film) see *Ladrón de cadáveres*
The Brides of Dracula, 71n, 122n, 156
The Cabinet of Dr. Caligari see *Das Cabinet des Dr. Caligari*
The Canterbury Tales (1972 film) see *I racconti di Canterbury*
The Castle of Otranto, 19n
The Crucible (1953 play), 91, 105n
The Crucible (1957 film) see *Les sorcières de Salem*
The Curse of Frankenstein, 41, 42, 50
The Decameron see *Il Decameron* (1971 film)
The Devil's Lover see *L'amante del demonio*
The Devil's Wedding Night see *Il plenilunio delle vergini*
The Eroticist see *Nonostante le apparenze . . . e purché la nazione non lo sappia . . . all'Onorevole piacciono le donne*
The Exorcist (1971 novel), 63
The Exorcist (1973 film), 12, 67, 68
The Exorcist: Italian Style see *L'esorciccio*
The Fall of the House of Usher (1960 film), 41
The Fascist see *Il federale*
The Ghost see *Lo spettro* (1963 film)
The Godfather (1972 film), 39
The Golem see *Der Golem, wie er in die Welt kam*
The Gorgon, 71n
The Hands of Orlac see *Orlacs Hände*
The Hunchback see *Il gobbo*

The Invisible Man (1933 film), 15
The Italian, or the Confessional of the Black Penitents, 19n
The Last Man on Earth see *L'ultimo uomo della Terra*
The Leech Woman, 47
The Legend of Blood Castle see *Le vergini cavalcano la morte*
The Legend of the 7 Golden Vampires, 68
The Lovemarkers see *La prima notte del Dottor Danieli, industriale, col complesso del . . . giocattolo*
The Most Prohibited Sex see *Sexy proibitissimo*
The Mummy (1932 film), 15, 92
The Mummy (1959 film), 71n
The Naked Cello see *Il merlo maschio*
The Overtaxed see *I tartassati*
The Phantom Carriage see *Körkarlen*
The Phantom of the Opera (1909–1910 novel), 53
The Phantom of the Opera (1925 film), 15
The Phantom of the Opera (1943 film), 15
The Playgirls and the Vampire see *L'ultima preda del vampiro*
The Quatermass Xperiment, 51
The Reincarnation of Isabel see *Riti, magie nere e segrete orge nel Trecento . . .*
The Return of Doctor X, 16
The Return of Dracula, 71n
The Revenge of Frankenstein, 71n
The Sadist, 71n
The Satanic Rites of Dracula, 120
The Shiver of the Vampires see *Le frisson des vampires*
The Student of Prague (1913 film) see *Der Student von Prag* (1913 film)
The Student of Prague (1926 film) see *Der Student von Prag* (1926 film)
The Suicide Club, 14
The Terror of Dr. Hichcock see *L'orribile segreto del Dr. Hichcock*
The Thief of Baghdad (1961 film) see *Il ladro di Bagdad*
The Thing from Another World, 15
The Vampire (1957 film), 71n
The Vampire and the Ballerina see *L'amante del vampiro*
The Vampire Happening see *Gebissen wird nur nachts*
The Vampyre, 1, 13, 45
The Vij (1835 short story), 50
The Whip and the Body see *La frusta e il corpo*
The White Sheik see *Lo sceicco bianco*
The Witch's Curse see *Maciste all'Inferno*
They Call Me Trinity see *Lo chiamavano Trinità . . .*
Thunderball, 157
Tipi da spiaggia, 71n
Titanus, 23–5, 27, 29, 33, 51, 55, 62, 63, 65, 143
Tognazzi, Ugo, 45, 48, 49, 139
Tolstoy, Aleksey, 51, 66, 73n, 102, 105n
Tomasi di Lampedusa, Giuseppe, 134
Tonsi, Giuseppe, 13
Top sensation, 121
Torelli, Lucia, 104n
Tormento, 90
Totò, 48, 148n
Totò nella Luna, 48
trasformismo, 159, 163, 169
Trash, 62
Turini, Gino, 49, 175
Tutti a casa, 144
Twilight (2008 film), 3
Two Weeks in Another Town, 45
Two Women see *La ciociara*

Ulisse, 32
Ultimo tango a Parigi, 63
Ulysses see *Ulisse*
Un caso di coscienza, 123n

INDEX

Un eroe dei nostri tempi, 110
Un juke-box per Dracula, 45
Un vampiro, 13
Una domenica d'estate, 71n
Uncle was a Vampire see *Tempi duri per i vampiri*
US film market, 25, 30–1, 32, 33, 42
  drive-in circuit, 33, 59
  Paramount Decree, 30, 31, 33, 70
  syndicated TV, 33, 41, 59

Vacanze a Ischia, 71n
Vadim, Roger, 8, 45–6, 50, 105n, 173
Vailati, Bruno, 53
vampire fiction
  Anglophone vampires, 1–3
  definition of vampire movie, 6
  feminist readings *see* feminism
  Marxist readings *see* Marxism
  non-Anglophone vampires, 3–5
  psychoanalytic readings *see* psychoanalysis
Vampire in Venice see *Nosferatu a Venezia*
Vampiri, 13, 48
Vampiro innocente, 13
Vampyr, 15, 20n, 50
Vampyr, ou l'étrange aventure de David Gray see *Vampyr*
Vampyros Lesbos, 67, 96, 98
Vancini, Florestano, 144
Vanzi, Luigi, 34
Vari, Giuseppe, 9
Varney the Vampire; or, the Feast of Blood, 19n
Velle, Gaston, 20n
Venga a prendere il caffè . . . da noi, 97

Vianello, Raimondo, 45, 48, 49
Vicario, Marco, 46, 123n, 165
Vidali, Enrico, 20n
Violent Summer see *Estate violenta*
Visconti, Luchino, 4, 31, 105n, 138, 143, 161
Vivere in pace, 143
voyeurism, 82–3, 104n
Vredens dag, 91
Vukotic, Milena, 97–8

Walpole, Horace, 19n
War of the Zombies see *Roma contro Roma*
Waxworks see *Das Wachsfigurenkabinett*
Web of the Spider see *Nella stretta morsa del ragno*
Wegener, Paul, 15
Welles, Mel, 62
Whale, James, 14, 15
Wiene, Robert, 15
Winner, Michael, 156
World by Night see *Il mondo di notte*

X the Unknown, 51

Yeaworth Jr., Irvin S., 51
Young, Terence, 157
Young Frankenstein, 67

Zaccaria, Gino, 6
Zampa, Luigi, 110, 143
Zora la vampira (2000 film), 7
Zora la vampira (comic book), 67, 99, 117, 121
Zucker, Ralph, 63, 174–5
Zurlini, Valerio, 144

EU representative:
Easy Access System Europe
Mustamäe tee 50, 10621 Tallinn, Estonia
Gpsr.requests@easproject.com

www.ingramcontent.com/pod-product-compliance
Lightning Source LLC
Chambersburg PA
CBHW071839230426
43671CB00012B/2010